FIELD GUIDE
TO THE BIRDS OF
THE KRUGER NATIONAL PARK

To Robert, Elaine, Raymond and Vivienne
Ian Sinclair

To Bill and Mollie Whyte, Merle, Lorna and Neil
Ian Whyte

IAN SINCLAIR AND IAN WHYTE

FIELD GUIDE
TO THE BIRDS OF
THE KRUGER NATIONAL PARK

Dear Kieth,

Many thanks for your contribution
to our elephant policy review. I hope
we may continue to do "birding" and
elephanting in other parts of Africa in
future.

With best wishes,

Ian.

STRUIK

11 February, 1996

This book has been produced by Struik Publishers, Cape Town, in collaboration with the
National Parks Board, Pretoria

Cover photographs: (top left) Southern Yellowbilled Hornbill (J.J. Brooks);
(top right) Lilacbreasted Roller (D. Balfour);
(bottom left) Lappetfaced and Whitebacked vultures (D. Balfour);
(bottom right) Bateleur (J.J. Brooks)

Struik Publishers
(a member of the Struik Group (Pty) Ltd)
Struik House
Oswald Pirow Street
Foreshore
Cape Town
8001

Reg. No.: 63/00203/07

First published in 1991

Designed by Petal Palmer, Cape Town
Edited by Philippa Parker, Cape Town
DTP conversion by Bellset, Cape Town
Reproduction by Fotoplate (Pty) Ltd, Cape Town
Printed and bound by National Book Printers, Goodwood

ISBN 1 86825 107 1

CONTENTS

ACKNOWLEDGEMENTS

Alan and Meg Kemp introduced me to the Kruger National Park in 1970, and in a matter of days revealed over 150 'lifers' and instilled in me a broader interest in birds. Rodney Cassidy first showed me the 'exotic north' of the Park where we encountered many new and exciting birds, and Flip Nel took the time to show me his Dickinson's Kestrels. Jackie, my wife, had the arduous task of working on the manuscript of this book, and to her I extend my thanks for her patience.
IAN SINCLAIR

For the assistance I received from Don English, Flip Nel and Scott Ronaldson, rangers from the Kruger National Park whose wide knowledge of the area's birds and interest in this project have made a considerable difference to the contents of this book, I express my sincere gratitude.
IAN WHYTE

INTRODUCTION

That the Kruger National Park is one of Africa's most select game parks is borne out by the fact that more than 650 000 people visit it each year. While it has traditionally been a place to which people go to view game, over the past decade there has been a growing interest in the birds of the Park and now a fair percentage of the visitors comprises those whose main interest is birds.

The casual birder will be rewarded with a startling variety of birds, many of them confiding and approachable, both in the restcamps and on the long stretches of road between the camps. The more serious birding enthusiast will discover many species that are more readily found in the Park than elsewhere in South Africa, and even those which are not known to occur anywhere else in the Republic.

Although not intended to replace illustrated field guides, where distinctions between sexes and age groups can be more accurately portrayed, this photographic field guide aims to facilitate the task of identifying the more than 475 bird species found in the Kruger National Park. The photographs selected were those that show most clearly the diagnostic field characters of the different species.

Species chosen for inclusion are those that have been positively recorded within the Park's boundaries. Several 'doubtful' species have been omitted because their presence in the Park has not yet been proven, but the present list will undoubtedly increase as the occurrence of further species in the Park is confirmed and so added to the list.

The species accounts provide the information necessary to distinguish a particular species from other similar-looking birds, and taxonomic grouping has in some cases been re-ordered to allow for direct comparison between like species. The vernacular or common names used for birds in the book comply with those listed by the Southern African Ornithological Society (SAOS), apart from a few minor changes. The scientific names are those used by the List Committee of the SAOS.

HOW TO USE THIS BOOK

Perhaps one of the best ways to use this and other similar field guides is to familiarize yourself with as many of the colour plates as possible before you actually venture out into the field. Any spare moments would be well spent browsing through the book, concentrating on the arrangement of plates, which is based on family groupings, and making mental notes of family characteristics and distinguishing features. Being able to establish to which family a bird belongs – be it crows, warblers, ducks, sunbirds, etc. – will take you a long way towards the identification of a particular species merely by eliminating a large number of other possibilities. Once you have done this you can then turn to the relevant section of the book and through a simple process of elimination should be able to identify the bird. The status entries and distribution maps will also prove useful by indicating whether or not the bird occurs in a particular part of the Park and its associated habitat. Even though a species may be rare within the Park, the map may show a widespread distribution, indicating that the bird could occur throughout.

Although by far the most effective way of using the book in the field, the task of identification will not be as straightforward as it may seem in all instances. Many species have very variable plumage, some differing considerably between the male and female and immature bird. In such instances you will have to rely on a bird's specific field marks, details of size and shape and on call in order to determine identity.

The idea of learning the relevant field marks of all the different species may at first seem daunting and impossible. However, many field marks are obvious and very memorable, such as the lilac breast on the brightly coloured Lilacbreasted Roller and the white head and breast of the African Fish Eagle. The more subtle field characters are learned over time and with experience, and some will seem hardly noticeable except to the trained eye, such as the different coloured flanks of the Greater Blue-eared and Glossy starlings. The text will guide you as to which field marks to look out for.

As time is of essence in the field, there will be little opportunity to page through the book, and few birds will pose conveniently while you do so. Therefore, it is a good idea to take rough but accurate field notes and sketches of the bird, noting features such as length of the bill, tail and legs, any striking coloration or patterns and where they occur, and general size and shape. Study the sketches of bird topography which appear on page 231 as these will help you when taking down a description.

By assessing the size of the bird and knowing, for example, that a cisticola is sparrow-sized and a francolin bantam-sized, you will be able to rule out many possibilities. Length measurements are provided for all species in the individual species entries. These are taken from the tip of the bill to the tip of the tail of an outstretched bird, but where a bird has an exceptionally long bill or tail, these features are not included in the overall measurement.

Second to field marks in identifying a bird is the voice, which in some instances is the only way to correctly identify a species. There is no easy way of learning calls except by perseverance and by listening to as many tapes of bird calls as possible. You can purchase commercial tapes, but by far the best way is to locate a call or song that you hear in field and to identify the bird vocalizing. Many birds remain hidden when singing and it may take hours or days to track down a particular call. One way of speeding up the process is to carry a small tape-recorder and a directional microphone. On hearing an unusual and unfamiliar call, record it by holding the microphone towards the source, and then immediately play back the recording. Invariably the bird which made the call will venture forth to see who is answering its call. From here you can go about ascertaining its identity.

Apart from a notebook and pencil, and possibly a tape-recorder, a pair of binoculars is an essential item of field equipment when bird-watching. Be selective when making this purchase and avoid buying those with very high magnifications as they tend to be unwieldy and, if used for prolonged periods, can lead to eye-strain. In fact, a good rule is never to buy binoculars with a magnification of below X7 or above X10. The diameter of the lens is equally important: the object lens should be not below 30 mm on magnification 7 and 8 and not below 40 mm on X9 or X10. If the diameter of the lens is below 30 mm on any of the above magnifications then the field of view will be very narrow and the amount of light entering the lens will be reduced with the result that the image will be very dark. Among the best binoculars (and most costly) are the Zeiss and Leitz ranges, but there are more moderately priced Japanese makes which will serve you well, provided you select from the magnifications and object lens diameters suggested above.

IAN SINCLAIR

BIRDING IN THE KRUGER NATIONAL PARK

The Kruger National Park comprises an area of two million hectares in the eastern Transvaal Lowveld. This represents only a fraction of the total area of southern Africa but, within its boundaries, in the order of 500 bird species have been recorded – about 56 % of the 900 on the current checklist for the region. This diversity includes a number of vulnerable or otherwise rare species, and of the 167 bird species designated by Kemp in 1980 as 'vulnerable or warranting conservation attention', 102 are reported to occur or likely to occur in the Kruger National Park. This highlights the importance of the area for the conservation of birds. It is usually these rarer species which are of greatest interest to serious birdwatchers and which make the Park such a worthwhile place to see birds.

Motoring is the usual way to visit and experience the Park. This means that the visitor is confined to the restcamps, a picnic spot or a car, and places some limitations on the number and variety of birds which may be seen. There is another way to see birds, however – on one of the six Wilderness Trails which operate in the Park. These trails accommodate groups of eight tourists who, under the guidance of two rangers, set out on foot from isolated basecamps each day to experience the bird- and wildlife at closer quarters. These trails are:

1.   Nyalaland Trail   – in the Punda Maria/Pafuri area.

2.	Olifants Trail	– on the Olifants River.
3.	Sweni Trail	– on the Sweni Spruit between Satara and Nwanetsi.
4.	Metsi-metsi Trail	– in the Tshokwane area.
5.	Wolhuter Trail	– in the Malelane hills.
6.	Bushman's Trail	– in the Malelane hills.

MAJOR BIRD HABITATS OF THE PARK

The diversity in the Park's avifauna can be attributed to the diversity of habitats found in its area. This in turn is due to the underlying geology of the region, which consists basically of granitic soils in the western half and basaltic soils in the east, separated in the middle by a belt of sandy Karoo sediments. All of these soils give rise mainly to deciduous woodlands or savannas. Also contributing to the diversity in birdlife is the fact that the Park stretches northwards into the tropical lowlands of the Limpopo Basin where many tropical bird species – some found nowhere else in South Africa – occur.

From a botanical point of view the Park has been classified into 35 different 'landscape' types. A landscape can be defined as an area with a recurrent pattern of plant communities with their associated fauna and abiotic habitat. This classification is too fine for highly mobile creatures like birds and can be simplified into one more appropriate for birds (see habitat map, p. 20). This system condenses the 35 botanical landscapes into 13 habitat types, as follows:

1. Aquatic habitats

Rivers

The Park is drained by five major river systems: the Limpopo/Luvuvhu, Shingwedzi, Olifants/Letaba, Sabie and the Crocodile. Of these, only the Olifants and Sabie are considered to be perennial as all the others have been known to cease flowing during winters or droughts. These others however, still have many permanent pools, as do some of their larger tributaries, and are of obvious importance to the waterbirds of the area. Their importance is not restricted to the water they provide but also to the dense riparian or riverine bush and tall trees which they support. The riverine thickets constitute forest 'corridors' which are used by some of the forest species of the escarpment to the west; these birds undertake 'altitudinal migrations' down to the Lowveld along the corridors to escape the severe escarpment winters. They also provide the only habitats for many of the more secretive species, while the taller trees provide nesting sites for other species, particularly raptors.

Dams

Before dams were built in the Park, waterbirds were relatively scarce, many species seldom, if ever, being recorded. The dams have had an obvious influence on the ecology of the waterbirds in this part of the subcontinent, and many of these birds once considered 'rarities' have become more and more common. Nor is the process complete, as dams are dynamic in nature, undergoing gradual changes as they get older: silting provides more and larger mudflats and the invertebrate fish and frog communities – which are the food resource for many birds – take many years to achieve their full potential. The presence of permanent water also affects the riparian zone, some trees dying as their roots become immersed and others becoming established on the new waterline. Beds of reeds and bulrushes also gradually develop due to the presence of more permanent water. It can therefore be expected that many interesting and exciting sightings will be made as these dams become more firmly established as part of the general ecology of waterbirds in the Lowveld.

Of the Park's dams, 45 are accessible to the general public and, for the bird enthusiast, are always worth a visit. Some have been built in the permanent rivers and are always full, while others have been constructed in the dry tributaries to catch run-off, and tend to have fluctuating water levels. The latter can be very good for waders as levels drop to expose mud-flats. Generally, the dams in the western half of the Park on granitic soils tend to be less interesting birding localities than those on the basalts in the east. This is due to the more sandy and less

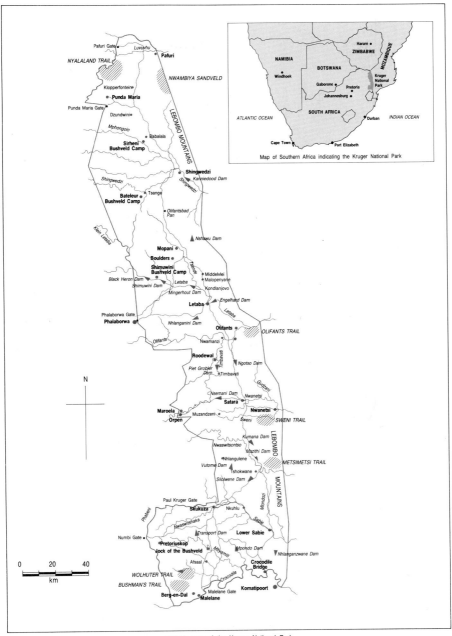

Visitor's map of the Kruger National Park

Map of Southern Africa indicating the Kruger National Park

11

productive nature of the granitic soils and to the undulating character of the terrain, which results in steeper shorelines, giving only limited access to waders.

Pans
Most pans in the Park are small and hold their water for insufficient time to develop a food source which may attract waterbirds in any number. There are some exceptions, Leeupan, Nkayapan and Olifantsbadpan, for instance, which in wetter years can prove fruitful for birdwatching.

2. Baobab rugged veld
This habitat contains the majority of the Park's baobabs and thus many of the hole-nesting species associated with these trees, particularly the Spinetails. It is an arid area, the grass cover usually sparse and, apart from baobabs, the dominant tree is the mopane. The baobab rugged veld can be reached by the tarred road running north from Shingwedzi and Punda Maria to Pafuri. It is the only habitat in South Africa in which the Threebanded Courser has been recorded.

3. Punda Maria sandveld
Two types of sandveld occur in this area: the western part, which is reached by travelling on the Mahogany Loop, is an undulating sandveld and is botanically very diverse; the eastern part consists of an extensive series of sandstone koppies, but is accessible only to tourists on the Nyalaland Trail. Although in general not an area of particular ornithological interest, it has produced a few rarities, and in the heavily wooded kloofs Bluespotted Dove and Mashona Hyliota have been recorded.

4. Nwambiya sandveld
In the far north-east, there is a small area of sandveld (also known as the 'Nyandu Bush') which forms part of a much larger area mostly in Mozambique. Due to its remoteness and proximity to a potentially hostile neighbour, it is not accessible to tourists. It is a very flat habitat of dense and homogeneous shrubveld on bright red sandy soils. The few pans in the area do not hold their water for any length of time, making it a mostly unrewarding area for the bird enthusiast, although Pinkthroated Twinspot have been recorded here.

5. Mopane forest
Although mopane occurs abundantly in the northern areas of the Park, it forms tall forests in only a very restricted part of this range. These forests are very homogeneous but nonetheless full of atmosphere and well worth a visit for their own sake. They are also the only habitat in the Park for Arnot's Chat.

6. Mixed mopane woodlands on undulating granitic soils
Through most of this area mopane is the dominant tree, though in large parts it occurs in mixed communities with other trees such as knob-thorn and rooibos. It is one of the poorer habitats in the Park from a birding point of view, though it has proved to be the habitat of choice of the Yellowbilled Oxpecker.

7. Broadleaved woodlands on undulating granitic soils
This is similar in character to the previous habitat type, except for the absence of mopane. It is similar also from an ornithological point of view and although it supports a broad spectrum of species, it is another of the poorer habitats for birds. Taller trees along the drainage lines offer excellent nesting sites, especially for raptors such as Wahlberg's Eagle and the Bateleur.

8. Open savannas on flat basaltic soils
These are the plains habitats of the Park and are usually characterized by shrub knob-thorn and/or mopane, interspersed with larger trees such as marula. They also have a well-developed

grass layer and therefore are ideal localities for grassland species such as bustards, francolins and quails. In summer, with luck, the migrant harriers (Pallid and Montagu's) can be seen. Flat-topped umbrella thorn trees on the plains provide nesting sites for the Lappetfaced Vulture and Secretarybird, and shrub knob-thorns are favoured by the colonial nesters – the queleas and Wattled Starling.

9. Acacia thickets on Karoo sediments
This very dense habitat consists mainly of thornveld with a fairly sparse grass layer. It is a good area for the small leaf-gleaners, and any bird party should be closely examined for eremomelas, apalises, etc. This habitat separates the habitats occurring on granite in the west from those on basalts in the east. Leeupan, near Tshokwane, is situated in this habitat type.

10. Sabie River thickets
This habitat is characterized by a dense woody vegetation and comprises mainly thorny thickets. Birds are present in some number but the bird communities rarely contain species of great interest. Many records of Violeteared Waxbill have been made here and it is also good for the small leaf-gleaners and bird parties.

11. Pretoriuskop Middleveld
Although similar in character to the broadleaved woodland habitat, this has a much taller grass layer and is higher in altitude. It is the only place in the Park where some of the 'Middleveld' birds can be encountered, including the Redthroated Wryneck (only recorded at Numbi Gate), Black Sunbird, Broadtailed Warbler and Yellowfronted Tinker Barbet.

12. Hilly south-west
A very undulating, even mountainous, terrain where the highest altitudes in the Park occur. The higher ground comprises either open grassland or prominent rocky koppies which are separated by deep, densely wooded gullies. In these gullies, the Narina Trogon and Gorgeous Bush Shrike have been recorded, while the rocky slopes and koppies are home to the Redwinged Starling and Mocking Chat. The best way to experience this habitat and its grand landscapes is to participate on the Bushman's Wilderness Trail.

13. The Lebombo Mountains
The Lebombo Mountains are not as well developed in the Park as they are further south in Swaziland and northern Natal, and the habitats they support are in many ways similar to the broadleaved woodlands found further west. There are two habitat types in these mountains which are very different from those to the west. These are the Lebombo Ironwood forests and the gorges which the major rivers have cut through this range. The forests are very dense with homogeneous stands of Lebombo ironwood trees interspersed with euphorbias, a vegetation which does not allow for a wide diversity of bird species, although a few interesting species do occur there. Yellowspotted Nicator is quite common as is the Yellowbellied Bulbul. A record of the Spotted Creeper in this area requires confirmation. The riverine gorges provide nesting sites for some of the rarer waterbirds such as the Goliath Heron and for cliff-nesters, such as the Black Stork.

WHERE TO WATCH BIRDS IN THE PARK
Perhaps the simplest way of dealing with the subject of where to watch birds in the Park is to use the various restcamps as the base or starting point from which the surrounding areas can be examined, and specific routes leading to good birding localities can be discussed. In fact, the restcamps themselves have well-developed gardens full of indigenous plants, and these are well worth spending some time in as many species have become quite tame and can be recorded at leisure. It is worth remembering that in January the restcamps' gates open at 04h30, giving the visitor the opportunity of seeing some of the nocturnal birds (and mammals) which would not ordinarily be seen during the day.

The restcamps are dealt with below in alphabetic order. When reading about one particular restcamp it would be wise to read the sections dealing with neighbouring camps, as in many instances these are within easy reach. Many of the place names and serial numbers applying to roads, and quoted in the text, are based on those used in the Park's tourist map. This is readily available at all shops in the Park and should be used in conjunction with this book.

Berg-en-dal

Berg-en-dal is situated in the most mountainous part of the Park and the terrain is such that little access to the hills and their associated deep wooded kloofs can be obtained. It is possible, however, to travel through part of this terrain by using the loop roads. These are worth exploring for the Gorgeous Bush Shrike, Mocking Chat, Redwinged Starling and, with luck, Narina Trogon.

Crocodile Bridge

This area has produced records for some of the Park's rarer species as it is the northern limit for some of these birds in South Africa. The Purplebanded Sunbird has been seen a few times in the area, although has been recorded more often just outside the Park. It may be more common in the Park than suspected and all dark sunbirds should be carefully examined. The Goldenrumped Tinker Barbet can often be seen in the restcamp itself and along the river roads in the vicinity of the camp, and the Blackbellied Starling occurs in small numbers along the Crocodile River.

The hippo pool just to the west of the camp is often home to waterbirds such as the Goliath and Greenbacked herons and the Little Egret. The vlei area to the west of the S28 gravel road leading north to Lower Sabie has produced a few sightings of Black Coucal, and further north along this road, the Nhlanganzwane Dam is a good spot for waders and storks. The new S130 gravel road gives access to a few pans which are of interest when full. (See also the section on Lower Sabie.)

The plains to the north-east of Crocodile Bridge along the S28 present a good opportunity for seeing Ostrich, Kori Bustard and Swainson's Francolin, and in wetter years quails and buttonquails occur in fair numbers. The tarred road to Lower Sabie (H4-2) cuts through the dense 'Gomondwane Bush' which is good for the small leaf-gleaners, and bird parties may yield Burntnecked Eremomela, Yellowbreasted Apalis and Stierling's Barred Warbler among others.

Letaba

Letaba is well situated for a number of rewarding birding localities. It gives easy access to both the Letaba and Olifants rivers and also to a few very good dams. The mopane is the dominant tree and shrub however, and this is not a very productive bird habitat.

The camp itself provides some interesting birding opportunities: African Fish Eagles are easily viewed as there is a pair that has become very tame and perches in the trees on the riverfront virtually inside the camp; Redwinged Starlings have colonized the camp as have Mourning Doves, and Natal Robins are resident here and can often be seen in the shrubbery between the 'A' circle of huts and the staff quarters. At sunset, a large number of Redbilled Oxpeckers comes in to roost in the tall lala palms at the entrance to the camp's restaurant – an event worth witnessing – and at sunrise and sunset, hundreds of guineafowls congregate on the sandbanks in front of the camp to drink.

There is good access to the Letaba and Olifants rivers by means of loop roads. Whitecrowned Plovers are common on the sandbanks of the Olifants River, yet paradoxically are absent from the entire length of the Letaba River in the Park. Goliath and other herons are common on both rivers, however. Carefully examine any swallows and swifts along these rivers as they may be Greyrumped Swallow, Brownthroated Martin or Horus Swift.

Both the Mingerhout and Engelhard dams are worth a visit. The Engelhard, in particular, is an excellent spot for birding and is conveniently close to the restcamp with access roads on both of its banks. Redwinged Pratincoles have bred right next to the road, along the southern bank of the dam in early summer for the past few years, and can easily be seen. Pelicans and flamingoes appear regularly but usually do not stay for long. The sand- and mudbanks provide for a wide variety of waterbirds: Openbilled Storks are nearly always present as are Spoonbills and nearly all of the larger herons. With careful scanning, something of interest can nearly always be found.

On the route north to the Nshawu Dam (S50 gravel road), the Kondlanjovo plain (about 12 km north of Letaba) and the Malopenyane and Middelvlei windmills are worth a little time. Secretarybirds and Kori Bustards are often seen here and Rufousnaped, Redcapped and Sabota larks can also be ticked. In wetter summers when there is a good grass cover, Montagu's and Pallid harriers may be seen.

The high-water bridge over the Letaba River shelters hundreds of Little Swifts. In summer, bats roost under the bridge in vast numbers and at sunrise and sunset a Bat Hawk may be seen here. Occasionally some of the other small raptors such as the Gabar Goshawk, European Hobby and even Wahlberg's Eagle can be seen hunting bats and swifts here.

The koppie at the Masorini open-air museum near Phalaborwa is a good spot for the Mocking and Familiar chats, and Black Eagles have been seen here periodically, though these are probably from the more extensive series of koppies further north.

Lower Sabie

Geographically, Lower Sabie is situated relatively close to the Mozambique coast and from time to time some of the species associated with this coastal strip move up the Sabie River as far as the camp. This makes the camp itself a good place to spend a bit of time birding. Interesting sightings have been made here, including the Wattle-eyed Flycatcher. When in bloom, the aloes in the camp's gardens attract a host of sunbirds, starlings, bulbuls and Blackheaded Orioles.

There are two dams in the immediate vicinity of the camp. The first, in the Sabie River right in front of the camp, is relatively new so has not had time to develop a riverine fringe and is not a particularly good birding site. However, the overflow from the dam is a good spot for some of the fish-eating species, in particular the Goliath and Greenbacked herons. The second dam, just half a kilometre to the west of the camp gate, is an excellent spot. Many of the storks can be seen there, including the Black, Woollynecked, Openbilled, Yellowbilled and Marabou. About 20 km to the south-east of this dam, the Nhlanganzwane Dam can also be very good for waterbirds.

To the west of the camp at the Nwatimhiri causeway (on the S79), Whitecrowned Plovers are regularly recorded – the only place south of the Olifants River where they can be seen.

The plains areas to the north-east and south-east of Lower Sabie may yield Kori Bustard, Redcrested and Blackbellied korhaans, Ostrich and, particularly if the veld has been burned or overgrazed, Lesser Blackwinged Plover and Temminck's Courser. Swainson's Francolin is common on these plains as are the quails – Harlequin and Common, and also the Kurrichane Buttonquail, though it does not readily emerge from the long grass.

Mopani

This new restcamp is situated on the edge of the Pioneer Dam which has proved to be a good locality for waterbirds. Whitebreasted Cormorants breed in the dead trees standing in the water, and Reed Cormorants and Darters are also common here.

The Nshawu Dam (on the S50 gravel road to Shingwedzi) nearly always provides something of interest. Redwinged Pratincoles nest here in early summer and Kittlitz's Plovers are common, the only place in the Park that this is so, while Caspian Plovers can also be ticked with luck. Blackbacked Cisticolas occur below the dam wall in the reedbeds, though any dam in the north and east of the Park should be scrutinized for these birds. The reedbeds below the Nshawu Dam wall also provide the only realistic chance of seeing the African Marsh Harrier in the Park. Quail finches are common in the area and may be seen coming to drink at the dam.

A few large buffalo herds occur in the area of the restcamp and if seen, should be carefully scanned for Yellowbilled Oxpeckers. This species is sure to be greatly outnumbered by Redbilled Oxpeckers which occur in hundreds on some of the larger herds.

Generally, the area in the vicinity of the camp is not one of the best for birds. The grassy flats to the east and mopaneveld to the west are relatively homogeneous habitats, not allowing for a wide diversity in bird species, and dams will undoubtedly provide the most interesting opportunities. The flats could offer Secretarybirds, Ostriches and Kori Bustards and, with luck, perhaps Pallid and Montagu's harriers in the summer.

Olifants
Most of the localities discussed under Letaba are relevant to the Olifants area due to its close proximity. The camp itself has well-developed gardens and trees and it is worth spending a few hours birding here. Yellowbellied Bulbuls and Redwinged Starlings are easily seen among many other more common species. The verandah in front of the restaurant provides an excellent lookout over the riverbed where many birds gather. Saddlebilled Storks nest below the camp and Black Storks nest on the cliffs a few kilometres downstream and can often be seen flying to and from these cliffs. In summer, Yellowbilled Kites perform spectacular flight displays around the lookout, and in fact have become a slight nuisance as they have learned to pinch meat off plates around braaivleis fires when backs are turned. At sunset in summer, bats are common around the camp and these attract a variety of raptors, including the Gabar Goshawk, European Hobby and occasionally a Bat Hawk.

Pafuri
The area around Pafuri is a unique habitat within the Park as it has a very well-developed riverine forest which, even without its birdlife, has a character and atmosphere all its own. Nyala and bushbuck are common and it is without doubt the best and most exciting birding locality in the Park. Pafuri is within easy reach of both the Shingwedzi and Punda Maria restcamps, and a bird enthusiast would do well to budget a full day to spend here. Many of the more tropical species reach their southern limit at Pafuri and it is only here that there is any real chance of seeing some of them in the Republic. Pafuri has an excellent picnic spot situated right on the Luvuvhu River among tall riverine trees; this in itself is a very good place to see many different species, especially Narina Trogon, Wattle-eyed Flycatcher and Yellow White-eye. Whitecrowned Plovers can be seen on the sandbanks in front of the picnic spot.

Motoring can reveal some exciting birds, the Tropical Boubou and Gorgeous Bush Shrike being common along the river, though more easily heard than seen. Other interesting species seen south of the Luvuvhu River on the eastern boundary are the Longtailed Starling and Crested Guineafowl. The characteristic screeching of Cape Parrots makes these birds easy to locate, while the Trumpeter Hornbill and Bleating Warbler are both very common and their respective calls form part of the characteristic sounds of the area.

In the arid bushveld to the north of the river, Threebanded Coursers have been seen on a few occasions, once even with young, and the only records of Crimsonbreasted Shrike in the Park have also been made here. Both of these species are probably resident in the area. In summer the Mottled Spinetail can easily be seen at nesting sites in baobabs, although both this and the Böhm's Spinetail can be seen at any time of year by a bit of patient 'skywatching'. Summer is also the time to see the Lemonbreasted Canary, Bluecheeked Bee-eater and Broadbilled Roller. The Crowned Hornbill, Racket-tailed Roller and Yellowspotted Nicator (if you get to know this bird's call it can be quite easy to locate) are resident in the area, and the Terrestrial and Yellowbellied bulbuls are not uncommon.

The Nyalaland Trail is based very close to the Luvuvhu River and is probably the best way to experience the Pafuri area and its birds. On foot and in the company of a knowledgeable ranger, it is possible to see birds such as Pel's Fishing Owl, the Crowned Eagle (which nests close by), Peregrine Falcon and the African Finfoot, while the large baobab in the Trails camp itself is a breeding and roosting site for Mottled Spinetails. A Black Eagle pair nest on a rock ledge within sight of the camp and in the breeding season, can be watched at leisure. A wide variety of owls occurs in the immediate vicinity of the camp.

Phalaborwa
Phalaborwa is situated in the middle of the mopaneveld and therefore is not a particularly interesting locality for birds. It does give access to the Letaba and Olifants restcamps and

surrounding areas however, which are more rewarding birding localities (see the respective sections).

Pretoriuskop

Pretoriuskop is located in the higher-lying parts and is the only place in the Park where some of the 'Middleveld' birds can be encountered. These include the Redthroated Wryneck (only recorded at Numbi Gate), Black Sunbird, Broadtailed Warbler and Yellowfronted Tinker Barbet, while Greyhooded Kingfishers have been known to nest at Numbi Gate in summer.

In the thick bush of Shabeni koppie, the Gorgeous Bush Shrike is a resident species, as is the Freckled Nightjar (also on other rocky koppies of the area), and might be seen on a very early outing in summer along the loop roads around these koppies. Such an early morning drive may also be rewarded with a sighting of the Pennantwinged Nightjar which has often been recorded in the area.

The 'River road' (S3) to Skukuza gives good exposure to the Sabie River's riverine bush and in winter some of the forest species from the escarpment to the west move down the river to escape the severe conditions prevailing in the higher altitudes. These include the Bluemantled Flycatcher and Grey Cuckooshrike. The African Finfoot may be seen at the hippo pool along this road, or elsewhere along the river, parts of which are visible from the road. Oddities such as the Rufousbellied and Squacco herons have been recorded at the Mestel Dam.

Punda Maria

Punda Maria is situated in a botanically very diverse area of the Park which, in conjunction with its proximity to the almost tropical habitats of the Limpopo and Luvuvhu rivers and the forests of the Soutpansberg, has resulted in many unusual bird records. Some of the more interesting records include the Mashona Hyliota and the Bluespotted Dove, the latter having been seen in the restcamp itself. A short walking trail has been laid out in the camp and species which may encountered are the Bearded and Whitethroated robins, African Goshawk, flycatchers such as the Black, Bluegrey, Fantailed and the Paradise Flycatcher (after which the trail is named), and the Yellowbellied and Terrestrial bulbuls, which are easily located by their calls.

The Mahogany Loop (S99) is well worth taking, particularly if you also have an interest in trees, as this road passes through the Punda Maria sandveld habitat type. A very early morning drive on this loop may be rewarded with a sighting of the Pennantwinged Nightjar which is quite common here in summer, and by the Barred, Barn and Spotted Eagle owls.

Punda Maria is the obvious base from which to visit Pafuri (see above). Both the S60 and the H13-1 lead to Pafuri and both take the tourist through areas of tall, well-developed mopane forest. This is the only habitat type in the Park in which Arnot's Chat can be seen. The S60 also passes the only known nesting site of Yellowbilled Oxpeckers in the Park. By continuing along this road you will come to Klopperfontein which, when filled with water, has produced African Rail, and both Moorhen and Lesser Moorhen. There are many buffalo in the area which should be carefully scanned for Yellowbilled Oxpeckers. Once on the H1-8, which passes through parts of the flat grassy plains, Dickinson's Kestrel can be seen and any bird perched in a dead tree is worth identifying.

Satara

Satara, positioned well away from any of the Park's major rivers, supports those birds associated with savanna, where the diversity of species is relatively low. However, this habitat does have its own community of species which are of interest. Ostriches, Kori Bustards and Secretarybirds all stalk the plains while in the more grassy areas, Swainson's Francolin and quails such as the Harlequin and Kurrichane Buttonquail can be seen. In summer after the rains, Monotonous Larks occur in abundance and their continuous calling adds to the atmosphere of the area. In the less well-grassed or overgrazed parts, Sabota Lark, Grassveld Pipit and Chestnutbacked Finchlark are common. Hornbills are well represented, the Redbilled, Southern Yellowbilled and Ground hornbills all being easily seen. The Longtailed Shrike and the two bushveld tchagras – Threestreaked and Blackcrowned – are also common. The dwarf knob-thorn veld which covers much of the area to the north and east of Satara is the habitat favoured by both the Wattled Starling and Redbilled Quelea for breeding, and in summer these birds nest in colonies of many thousands or, in the case of the queleas, even millions. These colonies are of absorbing interest with thousands of birds coming and going and many raptors being in attendance.

Satara is in the heart of the Park's predator country and vultures are therefore often seen, the four common species, Lappetfaced, Whiteheaded, Whitebacked and Hooded, invariably being present at a kill. With luck the less common Cape Vulture may also be seen.

Seven kilometres west of Satara on the H7, the Nsemani Dam is worth visiting for the waterbirds: Whitebacked Duck, Hottentot Teal and Fulvous Duck. Just west of this dam, the thornveld habitat on sedimentary soils is a good spot for many of the small leaf-gleaners. Burntnecked Eremomela, Yellowbreasted Apalis and Longbilled Crombec are not uncommon, while Puffback, Chinspot Batis and Whitebrowed Robin are also easy to record. The Satara camp itself is inhabited by many birds, mostly the more common species. Burchell's Starling and the Redbilled Buffalo Weaver are the characteristic birds of this camp. The large pond near the entrance gate has been colonized by Black Crakes which even breed there, giving excellent opportunities for close observation and photography.

Shingwedzi

This is one of the best camps for the keen birder to visit for a few days. Not only is it within easy reach of Pafuri, but it has the Kanniedood Dam on its doorstep and offers many drives along the Shingwedzi River and its larger tributaries. The Kanniedood Dam is an excellent spot and as the water level recedes during winter and early summer, the exposed mudflats are very well utilized by waders and other waterbirds. In summer, Greenshank, Ruff, Little Stint, Threebanded Plover and Wood, Common and Curlew sandpipers are all common and easy to see, while Whitefronted Plovers are usually present in small numbers. Blackwinged Stilts are nearly always found in the upper reaches of the dam and the storks are well represented. Openbilled, Yellowbilled, Marabou and Saddlebilled storks should all be recorded, though the Spoonbills, Woollynecked and Black storks are less common. A wide variety of herons, including Goliath, Purple, Great White Egret and, with luck, the Whitebacked Night Heron also add to the wealth of birdlife at this dam. In summer, a few pairs of Broadbilled Rollers breed between the high-water bridge and the Kanniedood Dam's wall and are quite easily seen.

Shingwedzi is frequented by hundreds of starlings and it provides a good opportunity to sort out the differences between the Greater Blue-eared and the Glossy starlings as they can be examined at close range. Other characteristic birds of this camp are the Mourning Dove, Redheaded Weaver, Bennett's Woodpecker and the Cut-throat Finch. In summer this finch uses the abandoned nests of Redheaded Weavers to breed in, but during the rest of the year, can be seen at sunset entering these characteristic nests to roost.

The high-water bridge over the Shingwedzi River is a good site to spend half an hour at sunset or sunrise. Little Swifts roost and breed under the bridge in their hundreds and give an interesting display as they come and go. Böhm's Spinetails also roost and possibly breed here, but careful searching is required to distinguish them among the hundreds of swifts. Bats also roost in hundreds under the bridge and at sunrise and sunset may attract a Gabar Goshawk, European Hobby and occasionally a Bat Hawk.

Skukuza

Skukuza is a camp that has no particular localities which serve as an attraction for the bird enthusiast. It does, however, have a wide variety of birds but a bit of effort is needed to find them. The camp itself has many large trees and well-established lawns, and time spent birding here will be rewarded with any of the birds found in the Lowveld riparian forest. There is a good chance of seeing the Purplecrested Lourie. The camp offers an excellent view of the Sabie River where the African Black Duck and Halfcollared Kingfisher can be seen. In summer, the large sycamore fig tree in front of the restaurant is used for nesting by large numbers of weavers, both Spottedbacked and Lesser Masked, and their frantic nesting activities are both interesting and entertaining. When this tree is bearing fruit, Green Pigeons are attracted to it.

Bats roost in the camp and Staff Village at Skukuza and when they emerge in the evenings attract a variety of hopeful raptors. In summer, European Hobbies can easily be seen; up to six at a time have been recorded chasing bats at sunset. Bat Hawks have also often been recorded, but it is easy to confuse these two species when engaged in this activity. The Skukuza section of the Sabie River is also one of the few places in the Park where the African Goshawk occurs, and these birds are often seen in their early morning display. African Goshawks also hunt bats at Skukuza.

Palm Swifts used to nest in some numbers in exotic palm trees in the Staff Village, but possibly since the removal of these trees (exotic plants are not encouraged in National Parks) have taken to nesting on many of the houses and other buildings in the camp.

The nursery at Skukuza attracts many birds: Scarletchested, Marico, Whitebellied and Collared sunbirds are all to be seen, and the Greyheaded Bush Shrike has become very tame here. On the access road to the nursery is a large dam which serves as an emergency water supply for the camp and is pumped full. Water levels do not fluctuate, and waders are scarce but Whitebreasted and Reed cormorants are nearly always present as are Darters. Red Bishops and Thickbilled Weavers nest in some numbers in the bulrushes which fringe this dam and can be seen from the lookout point. The dam has also been a favoured locality for Osprey, which in summer may be sighted by carefully scanning trees in the vicinity.

The low-level bridge over the Sabie River is a good spot to look for the Halfcollared Kingfisher, which is known to have nested here. The African Finfoot has also been seen from the bridge but, being secretive, does not appear for long, particularly if there is traffic about. With luck however, it may be seen on any of the other pools in this river.

References

Kemp, A.C. 1980. 'The distribution and status of the birds of the Kruger National Park.' *Koedoe* Monograph No.2. Pretoria: National Parks Board.

Kemp, A.C. 1980. 'The importance of the Kruger National Park for bird conservation in the Republic of South Africa.' *Koedoe* 23:99-122.

Newman, K.B. 1987. *Birds of the Kruger National Park.* Johannesburg: Southern Book Publishers.

Tarboton, W.R., Kemp, M.I. and Kemp, A.C. 1987. *Birds of the Transvaal.* Pretoria: Transvaal Museum.

IAN WHYTE

Abbreviations and symbols

The following abbreviations and symbols have been used in this book:

ad. (ads.) = adult(s)
imm. (imms.) = immature(s)
cm = centimetre(s)
br. = breeding
non-br. = non-breeding
♂ = male
♀ = female
o = (on maps) one record only

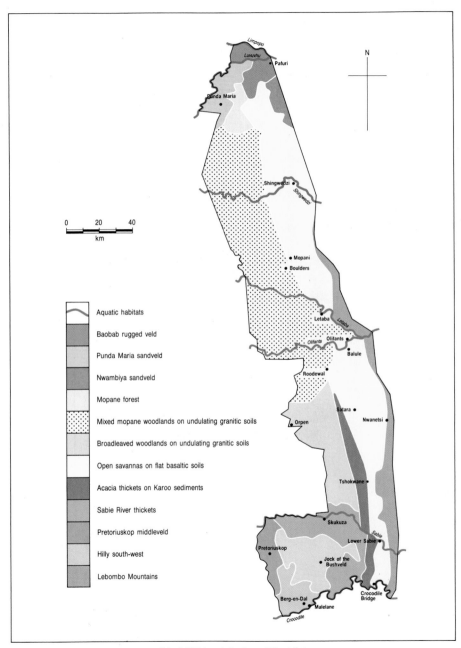

N

Aquatic habitats

Baobab rugged veld

Punda Maria sandveld

Nwambiya sandveld

Mopane forest

Mixed mopane woodlands on undulating granitic soils

Broadleaved woodlands on undulating granitic soils

Open savannas on flat basaltic soils

Acacia thickets on Karoo sediments

Sabie River thickets

Pretoriuskop middleveld

Hilly south-west

Lebombo Mountains

Major habitat types in the Kruger National Park

FIELD GUIDE
TO THE BIRDS OF
THE KRUGER NATIONAL PARK

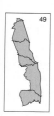

White Pelican *Pelecanus onocrotalus* (49) 180 cm
Noticeably larger than Pinkbacked Pelican and with white, not greyish colouring which at close range shows a definite pinkish hue, especially when breeding. The bill pouch is yellow and not greyish-pink as in Pinkbacked Pelican. In flight the contrasting black and white pattern between the flight feathers and wing coverts is evident. *Status.* Not resident in the Park but occasionally may be seen on the rivers or dams. *Call.* Usually silent except when breeding. *Afrikaans.* Witpelikaan.

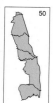

Pinkbacked Pelican *Pelecanus rufescens* (50) 140 cm
A small pelican which is greyish when compared to the startling white of the White Pelican. In flight the wings appear uniform greyish in colour with only a slight contrast between the flight feathers and wing coverts. The bill pouch is greyish-pink and not bright yellow as in White Pelican. *Status.* Not resident in the Park but occasionally may be seen on the rivers or dams. *Call.* Usually silent except when breeding. *Afrikaans.* Kleinpelikaan.

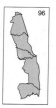

Greater Flamingo *Phoenicopterus ruber* (96) 127 cm
Of the two flamingo species this one is paler with red coloration restricted to the wings. Size disparity between the two is most apparent when birds are together and this species is seen to almost dwarf the Lesser Flamingo. Diagnostic in all plumages is the dark-tipped bill which is more bulbous than the Lesser Flamingo's, and pink rather than deep red. *Status.* Not resident in the Park but occasionally may be seen on the rivers or dams. *Call.* A goose-like honking. *Afrikaans.* Grootflamink.

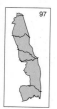

Lesser Flamingo *Phoenicopterus minor* (97) 100 cm
Noticeably smaller than Greater Flamingo and almost always much pinker, the whole neck, head and body being suffused with a deep reddish-pink. The bill is smaller, less curved and is deep red in colour but at a distance appears black, and therefore is quite distinct from the pink and black bill of Greater Flamingo. *Status.* Not resident in the Park but occasionally may be seen on the rivers or dams. *Call.* A goose-like honking. *Afrikaans.* Kleinflamink.

White Pelican (ad.)

White Pelican (imm.)

Pinkbacked Pelican (imm. left, ad. right)

Greater Flamingo

Lesser Flamingo

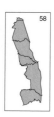

Reed Cormorant *Phalacrocorax africanus* (58) 52 cm
Of the two cormorants that occur in the Park this is the smaller and more slender. Ad. is overall oily black with pale barring on the back, and when breeding has an orange or yellow face patch and a small crest. Imm. is dark brown with white underparts and might be confused with imm. Whitebreasted Cormorant but is very much smaller and has a longer, thinner tail.
Status. A common breeding resident, seen on the major rivers and water bodies. *Call.* Silent except when breeding. *Afrikaans.* Rietduiker.

Whitebreasted Cormorant *Phalacrocorax carbo* (55) 90 cm
Larger than Reed Cormorant and ad. is easily recognized by its white throat and breast which contrast with its otherwise black coloration. For a short time during breeding season both sexes show a white patch on the thigh. Imm. has completely white underparts and might be mistaken for imm. Reed Cormorant but is very much larger, more robust and has a proportionately shorter tail.
Status. An uncommon resident which may be seen on any of the rivers and dams. Breeds in small numbers on some of the dams. Sometimes enters the Park in large numbers up the major rivers (particularly Olifants River) from the large dams in Mozambique. *Call.* Usually silent except in breeding season when grunts and squeaks are given. *Afrikaans.* Witborsduiker.

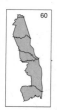

Darter *Anhinga melanogaster* (60) 80 cm
Closely resembles a cormorant but differs by having a very small head, a pointed, not hooked bill and a very long, thin neck. The head is held in a kinked position both at rest and in flight, and the tail is very long, graduated, and often fanned in flight. Unlike cormorants frequently flies high in thermals when its long tail is particularly noticeable. When swimming it often keeps its body low or entirely submerged, leaving only the long, thin neck and head showing, as it scythes through the water with serpentine movements.
Status. A common breeding resident, seen on all rivers and dams.
Call. Normally silent. *Afrikaans.* Slanghalsvoël.

Reed Cormorant (ad.)   Reed Cormorant (imm.)

Whitebreasted Cormorant (ad.)   Whitebreasted Cormorant (imm.)

Darter (ad.)   Darter (imm.)

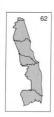

✓Grey Heron *Ardea cinerea* (62) 100 cm
May be confused with the similarly sized and coloured Blackheaded Heron but is distinguished by its yellow bill, black eye-stripe which extends to the nape, its white rather than black crown, and black streaking down the front of its neck. In flight the underwing appears a uniform dark grey, whereas the Blackheaded Heron has a black and white underwing. *Status.* A common breeding resident. May be seen on any of the rivers and dams. *Call.* A harsh, booming 'kraaunk' given in flight. *Afrikaans.* Bloureier.

Goliath Heron *Ardea goliath* (64) 140 cm
The large size of this species should rule out confusion with all other herons. At long range when size comparison is more difficult, it may be identified by its bright rufous head and neck. The flight is very slow and ponderous, and the wings are uniform grey both above and below. *Status.* Uncommon generally but common and conspicuous on the larger rivers. *Call.* A loud, low-pitched 'kwaark'. *Afrikaans.* Reuse Reier.

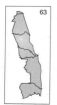

Blackheaded Heron *Ardea melanocephala* (63) 96 cm
Slightly smaller than the similar Grey Heron and immediately identified by the black crown which extends down the back of the neck and contrasts with the white throat. In flight the black and white patterned underwing distinguishes it from Grey Heron. Imm. has a grey, not black crown and hind neck.
Status. Uncommon and probably not resident; occasionally breeds in the Park. Usually seen in marshy headwaters of the larger dams. *Call.* A loud 'aaaark' and various hoarse cackles; also bill clappering at nest.
Afrikaans. Swartkopreier.

Purple Heron *Ardea purpurea* (65) 91 cm
Although much shyer and more secretive than other herons, this species will feed in the open in twilight and it is often seen flying over reedbeds. Might be confused with the very much larger Goliath Heron because they both show a chestnut neck, but the great disparity in size should rule out confusion. Imm. is drabber than the ad. with less streaking and it lacks the dark cap, grey nape and mantle. *Status.* Secretive but not uncommon. A breeding resident which can be seen on any of the larger water bodies in the Park, particularly where beds of reeds and rushes occur. *Call.* A typical heron-like 'kraaak'.
Afrikaans. Rooireier.

Grey Heron

Goliath Heron

Blackheaded Heron (ad.)

Blackheaded Heron (imm.)

Purple Heron

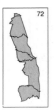

Squacco Heron *Ardeola ralloides* (72) 42 cm
At rest the all-white wings are covered by the back and breast feathers which in breeding plumage are buff and brown and less streaked than in non-breeding bird. However in flight, the contrast between the brown-streaked head and body and the white wings can be clearly seen. Skulks more often than other 'white' herons. *Status.* Rare but widespread on rivers and dams. Might be located by carefully scanning floating vegetation. *Call.* A low-pitched, rattling 'kek-kek-kek'. *Afrikaans.* Ralreier.

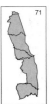

Cattle Egret *Bubulcus ibis* (71) 54 cm
Breeding bird might be confused with the smaller Squacco Heron but the buff coloration is confined to the crown, breast and back, and is never as dark as in Squacco Heron. Non-breeding bird is all-white with a yellow bill and dark legs. Feathering from bill to throat often appears shaggy and imparts a distinctly jowled appearance. The only white egret to freely associate with cattle and game. Often seen flying in formation to and from roosts. *Status.* A not uncommon bird of open veld and the waterside. Often seen feeding in association with larger herbivores such as buffalo. Conspicuous in the evenings along the rivers and at dams when flying to roosting sites. *Call.* Typical heron-like 'aaark' or 'pok-pok'. *Afrikaans.* Bosluisvoël.

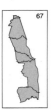

Little Egret *Egretta garzetta* (67) 65 cm
When seen, the yellow toes are diagnostic, and distinguish this species from any other 'white' egret or heron. The bill is slender, pointed and black. When breeding, elongated plumes are evident on the back and breast. Very active when feeding, using its feet to stir up the shallows and dashing to and fro in pursuit of prey. *Status.* A fairly common resident along the larger rivers and dams. *Call.* Similar to that of other egrets, a harsh 'waaark'. *Afrikaans.* Kleinwitreier.

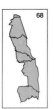

Yellowbilled Egret *Egretta intermedia* (68) 66 cm
Most likely to be confused with Great White Egret but is smaller and has a shorter neck which is not as obviously kinked in an 'S' shape. More subtle differences are the greenish-yellow garters at the tops of the legs, and the gape, which does not extend behind the eye but ends just below it. Does not feed over open water like Great White Egret but prefers flooded veld and damp, grassy areas. Differs from Cattle Egret by being larger, having a longer neck and being more slender in appearance. *Status.* A rare visitor to the Park, seen on the larger rivers and dams. *Call.* Typical heron-like 'waaark'. *Afrikaans.* Geelbekwitreier.

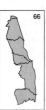

Great White Egret *Egretta alba* (66) 95 cm
Much larger than any other 'white' heron or egret and has a very long, thin neck which is often held in an exaggerated 'S' shape. The bill is long, dagger-shaped and yellow except when breeding when it turns black. *Status.* A widespread and common breeding resident. May be seen on any of the Park's rivers and dams. *Call.* A low, heron-like 'waaaark'. *Afrikaans.* Grootwitreier.

Squacco Heron (br.)

Squacco Heron (non-br.)

Cattle Egret

Little Egret

Yellowbilled Egret

Great White Egret (non-br.)

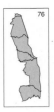

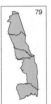

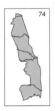

Blackcrowned Night Heron *Nycticorax nycticorax* (76) 56 cm
The black crown and back of this small, dumpy heron contrast with its grey body. In breeding plumage it shows a long, wispy, white nape plume. Imm. differs from ad. in being brown above, freckled with white spots, and paler below with dark streaking. A nocturnal species, it hides in thick vegetation and trees during the day. *Status.* Difficult to observe because of its nocturnal habits. Not common but occasionally seen on the quieter ponds and dams surrounded by trees and dense vegetation. *Call.* A harsh, low 'kwok-kwok' when flushed from cover. *Afrikaans.* Gewone Nagreier.

Dwarf Bittern *Ixobrychus sturmii* (79) 25 cm
A very small, almost rail-like heron. It is dark slate above with creamy underparts which are heavily streaked with black from the throat to the belly. Imm. is also very dark but has a buff-streaked head and neck; distinguished from imm. Little Bittern by being generally darker and by having more heavily streaked underparts. *Status.* Very rare and secretive. A floodplain species recorded at only a few scattered points in the Park. *Call.* Soft, frog-like croaks. *Afrikaans.* Dwergrietreier.

Greenbacked Heron *Butorides striatus* (74) 40 cm
A small, chunky heron with yellowish legs and a dark greenish cast to the back. The black crown is sometimes erected to show a wispy crest. Imm. is dark brown above with paler brown-streaked underparts and has orange legs. *Status.* Common on all rivers and dams. Breeds in the Park. *Call.* A loud 'baaek' when alarmed. *Afrikaans.* Groenrugreier.

30

Blackcrowned Night Heron (ad.)

Blackcrowned Night Heron (imm.)

Dwarf Bittern

Greenbacked Heron

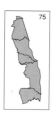

Rufousbellied Heron *Ardeola rufiventris* (75) 58 cm
At rest might be confused with Black Egret but is smaller and more compact and shows a dark rufous belly and yellow legs. In flight the rufous belly and wing coverts are more noticeable and the yellow legs project beyond the end of the tail. Female is duller than male, and imm. has a buff-streaked head and neck. *Status.* A very rare visitor to the Park, recorded only during extremely wet years. Utilizes emergent vegetation on the edges of the quieter stretches of the Park's dams. Usually only seen when flushed. *Call.* Typical heron-like 'waaaark' and low grunts. *Afrikaans.* Rooipensreier.

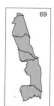

Black Egret *Egretta ardesiaca* (69) 66 cm
A small, slate black egret with a hunched appearance. Like Little Egret it has black legs and yellow toes and is distinguished from Rufousbellied Heron by its lack of the rufous belly and shoulders. When feeding it creates a canopy with its wings, holding them outstretched over its lowered head, quite unlike any other bird. *Status.* Rare in the Park, but occasionally seen in the quiet shallows of dams and rivers. *Call.* Normally silent. *Afrikaans.* Swartreier.

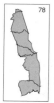

✓**Little Bittern** *Ixobrychus minutus* (78) 36 cm
An unmistakable, small, reed-dwelling bird, mostly seen flying over reeds, showing buff underparts and pale, buffy wing coverts which contrast with the black flight feathers. Female is browner than male; imm. resembles female but has more heavily striped underparts, and differs from imm. Greenbacked Heron by being paler and having green, not orange legs. *Status.* A rare visitor, mostly associated with reedbeds and thus difficult to see in the Park. *Call.* A soft, frog-like cheeping. *Afrikaans.* Woudapie.

Whitebacked Night Heron *Gorsachius leuconotus* (77) 53 cm
The most secretive of all the herons and very rarely seen. The dark head with large, pale eye-area, cinnamon neck and breast, and dark back and wings render the bird unmistakable. In flight a small amount of white is visible on the lower back. *Status.* Rare but widespread on the dams and rivers of the Park. A nest with chicks has been recorded, suggesting that it is resident. The secretive, nocturnal habits make it a very difficult bird to see. *Call.* Normally silent but will give a sharp 'kaaark' when startled. *Afrikaans.* Witrugnagreier.

Rufousbellied Heron

Black Egret

Little Bittern ♂

Little Bittern ♀

Whitebacked Night Heron

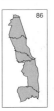

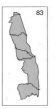

Openbilled Stork *Anastomus lamelligerus* (87) 94 cm
A large stork with an iridescent, all-black plumage and a noticeably pale bill which has a diagnostic 'nutcracker-like' opening between the mandibles. This unusual feature is not easily seen unless the bird is silhouetted or seen at close range. Imm. is duller than ad. and lacks the gap in the bill. *Status*. A fairly common and conspicuous bird occurring along rivers and dams, and particularly on water bodies with exposed mudflats where its chief food item, mussels, occurs. Occasionally breeds in the extreme north on the Limpopo floodplain. *Call*. Mostly silent. *Afrikaans*. Oopbekooievaar.

Yellowbilled Stork *Mycteria ibis* (90) 95 cm
Might be confused with White Stork but the long, slightly decurved, yellow bill and red face distinguish it. When breeding, a pinkish flush is noticeable on the wings and back. In flight, if the bill is not discernible then the black tail should distinguish this species from White Stork. Imm. is similar to ad. but lacks pinkish tinge on wings and has a greyish, not white head. *Status*. An uncommon stork occurring throughout the Park. Occasional nesting has been recorded in late winter. May be seen at pans, rivers or dams. *Call*. Squeaks and hisses at the nest. *Afrikaans*. Nimmersat.

Woollynecked Stork *Ciconia episcopus* (86) 85 cm
An easily recognized stork and the only one to show the combination of a white neck, and a white belly and undertail. The neck and partly white head have a fluffy appearance and the black plumage is iridescent. The bill and legs are a dull red, and in flight the legs project well beyond the slightly forked tail. Imm. is duller than ad. and its black forehead is streaked with white. *Status*. A rare resident stork which may be seen on any of the Park's rivers, dams or pans. Breeding has been reported. *Call*. Silent unless breeding.
Afrikaans. Wolnekooievaar.

White Stork *Ciconia ciconia* (83) 102 cm
Distinguished from the similar Yellowbilled Stork by its red legs and shorter, straight, red bill. Also, it lacks the pink flush on wings and has a white, not black tail. The red legs are often discoloured white or grey as the bird deliberately excretes down them to help it cool down. Imm. is tinged with brown and has a darker red bill and legs. *Status*. A non-breeding summer migrant to the Park, sometimes abundant with numbers varying according to prevailing conditions. A very mobile species and therefore seen anywhere. *Call*. Usually silent. *Afrikaans*. Witooievaar.

✓African Spoonbill *Platalea alba* (95) 90 cm
The flattened, spatulate red and grey bill is diagnostic. Feeds with a characteristic side-to-side swinging motion, scything its bill through the water. In flight it differs from similar-sized 'white' egrets by flying with its head and neck outstretched, not tucked into the shoulders. *Status*. Restricted to the Park's water bodies – particularly the stiller backwaters of the larger dams. An uncommon irregular visitor but occasionally breeds in the Park. *Call*. Various grunts, bill-clapping at nest and a 'kaark' alarm call. *Afrikaans*. Lepelaar.

34

Openbilled Stork

Woollynecked Stork

White Stork

Yellowbilled Stork

African Spoonbill

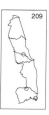

Crowned Crane *Balearica regulorum* (209) 105 cm
At rest the most startling feature of this large bird is the black and white head pattern which is topped with a golden, bristly crest. In flight the head and neck are held outstretched and slightly below body level and the large white upperwing patches are noticeable. Imm. lacks contrasting black and white face patch, and the bristly crest is less developed. *Status.* A very rare vagrant to the Park, with only three records from widely scattered localities.
Call. A trumpeting flight call 'mah hem' and a deep 'hum hum' when breeding.
Afrikaans. Mahem.

✓**Marabou Stork** *Leptoptilos crumeniferus* (89) 150 cm
The unusual pink, fleshy pouch that extends from the unfeathered neck and head, the large pale bill and black and white plumage make the Marabou unmistakable. In flight it might be mistaken for a vulture but the long legs projecting well beyond the end of its tail distinguish it. *Status.* A common species which may be seen in the vicinity of all the larger restcamps where it attends rubbish tips. Although present all year round, there are no confirmed breeding records. *Call.* Silent except for grunts and bill-clappering at nest.
Afrikaans. Maraboe.

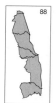

✓**Saddlebilled Stork** *Ephippiorhynchus senegalensis* (88) 145 cm
The long, slightly upturned, black and red bill with a yellow 'saddle' at the base renders this large black and white stork unmistakable. In flight the wing pattern is a contrasting black and white. Imm. is dowdier than ad., being grey rather than black, and lacks the bright yellow 'saddle' at the base of its bill. *Status.* A fairly common and conspicuous breeding resident. Occurs at pools on any of the larger rivers or at dams and seasonal pans. *Call.* Bill-clappering when breeding. *Afrikaans.* Saalbekooievaar.

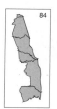

Black Stork *Ciconia nigra* (84) 97 cm
Distinguished from Abdim's Stork by its larger size, all-red bill and absence of a white rump. Imm. is a duller version of ad. and has a dull yellow bill and brownish legs. Occurs singly or in pairs and not in large concentrations as does Abdim's Stork. *Status.* An uncommon species whose numbers appear to be limited by a lack of suitable nesting sites. Out of the breeding season it may gather at suitable pools in groups of up to 20 birds. May be seen at any of the larger water bodies in the Park. *Call.* Normally silent unless breeding when whining and bill-clappering are given. *Afrikaans.* Grootswartooievaar.

Abdim's Stork *Ciconia abdimii* (85) 76 cm
Much smaller than the similar-coloured Black Stork, it differs further by having a dark bill, a lilac and red face, and a white lower back and rump. Imm. is dark brown and lacks the face colouring of ad. Normally seen in large groups feeding in open veld or spiralling on thermals on hot days. *Status.* A summer migrant to the Park which can occur in vast numbers. Birds have only occurred sporadically, and there are no records from recent years. Can occur anywhere.
Call. Silent in our region. *Afrikaans.* Kleinswartooievaar.

Crowned Crane

Marabou Stork

Saddlebilled Stork

Black Stork

Abdim's Stork

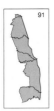

Sacred Ibis *Threskiornis aethiopicus* (91) 90 cm
The black, unfeathered neck and head, white plumage and long, decurved black bill are diagnostic. In flight the black-tipped flight feathers give the trailing edge a narrow black border. During the breeding season a scarlet unfeathered stripe is noticeable on the underwing. Imm. differs from ad. by having a feathered, white head and neck. *Status.* A rare vagrant to the area, staying nowhere for any length of time. Could be seen at any of the Park's water points. *Call.* Noisy croaking at breeding colonies.
Afrikaans. Skoorsteenveër.

Hamerkop *Scopus umbretta* (81) 56 cm
The peculiar hammer-shaped head profile of this large, dark brown bird renders it unmistakable. Often seen in the vicinity of its characteristic huge nest. In flight may be mistaken for a bird of prey because of its barred tail but the bill shape, and legs projecting beyond the tail readily identify it. *Status.* A common resident seen on all the Park's rivers (both perennial and with permanent pools). *Call.* A jumbled mixture of squeaks, hisses and frog-like croaks. *Afrikaans.* Hamerkop.

✓ Hadeda Ibis *Bostrychia hagedash* (94) 76 cm
A dull, greyish-brown ibis which in sunlight shows a bronzy, iridescent shoulder. A pale stripe is evident on the lower part of the face, running from the bill base to behind the eye. The bill has a broad base and is decurved, with a red stripe running along the ridge of the upper mandible. Imm. lacks red on the bill and bronze on the wing. *Status.* A common and conspicuous breeding resident attracting attention by its loud raucous calls. May be seen anywhere in the Park in the vicinity of water. *Call.* A diagnostic rendering of its name 'ha-ha ha-da-da'. *Afrikaans.* Hadeda.

Glossy Ibis *Plegadis falcinellus* (93) 65 cm
A small, slender ibis which from a distance appears all black. At closer range the dark chestnut brown plumage shows iridescent green and purple patches, especially on the wings and neck. Imm. is duller and less glossy than ad. *Status.* A very rare vagrant to the area, staying nowhere for long. Usually seen singly or in very small numbers. Could be seen at any of the Park's water points. *Call.* A low, guttural 'kok-kok-kok' emitted when breeding. *Afrikaans.* Glansibis.

38

Hamerkop

Sacred Ibis

Hadeda Ibis

Glossy Ibis

Whitefaced Duck *Dendrocygna viduata* (99) 48 cm
A duck with a very upright posture, a long neck, and a white face and throat
which are sometimes mud-stained brown. Also shows a chestnut breast, black
belly and finely barred flanks. Shape closely resembles that of the Fulvous
Duck which, however, lacks the white face and in flight shows a white rump.
Status. An uncommon to common breeding resident with numbers fluctuating
according to the availability of water, and so increasing after summer rains
have filled the temporary pans. *Call.* A shrill, three-note whistle
'wheet-wee-weeoo'. *Afrikaans.* Nonnetjie-eend.

Fulvous Duck *Dendrocygna bicolor* (100) 46 cm
Has an upright posture similar to that of Whitefaced Duck but is overall
chestnut in colour, lacks the white face and shows contrasting white stripes on
the flanks, and a white rump. Imm differs from imm. Whitefaced Duck by
having white-striped flanks and rump. *Status.* A very uncommon vagrant to the
Park having only a few widely scattered records. Appears to favour dams in
non-perennial watercourses. *Call.* A soft, hoarse whistle 'pe-chee'.
Afrikaans. Fluiteend.

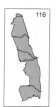

Spurwinged Goose *Plectropterus gambensis* (116) 100 cm
A large, black goose with variable amounts of white on the face, throat, neck
and belly. The bill is red and the forehead has brownish or reddish knobs. In
flight shows white shoulder patches. The bony spur on the wing is seen only at
close range. Imm. resembles ad. but the legs and bill are duller red.
Status. An uncommon vagrant to the Park occurring mainly in the summer
months when pans and dams hold water. May be seen at any of these water
bodies. *Call.* A raspy whistle given in flight. *Afrikaans.* Wildemakou.

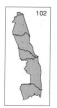

Egyptian Goose *Alopochen aegyptiacus* (102) 70 cm
A large, familiar water bird, easily recognized by the dark patch encircling the
eye and the dark spot on the breast which is especially visible in flight. Also
noticeable in flight are the large white patches on the forewing. *Status.* A very
common and conspicuous breeding resident. Occurs on nearly every
available stretch of water, even temporary pans. *Call.* Various honks and
hisses. *Afrikaans.* Kolgans.

Pygmy Goose *Nettapus auritus* (114) 33 cm
This diminutive duck is easily recognized by its white face, silky green ear
patch and orange underparts. The bill is bright yellow. Female is similar to
male but lacks the contrasting head pattern. In flight the bird appears very
dark above, showing patches of white on the wing. Hard to detect when sitting
among waterlilies. *Status.* A rare summer visitor which occasionally breeds in
the Park. May be seen on any of the smaller dams or large pans with lots of
lilies and sedges, particularly in years of above average rainfall. A species
which has apparently increased subsequent to the construction of dams in the
Park. *Call.* A soft whistle. *Afrikaans.* Dwerggans.

Whitefaced Duck

Fulvous Duck

Spurwinged Goose

Egyptian Goose

Pygmy Goose (♀ left, ♂ right)

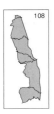

Redbilled Teal *Anas erythrorhyncha* (108) 48 cm
Easily distinguished from Cape Teal which also has a reddish-pink bill by its dark cap contrasting with buffy cheeks, and by the mottled beige and brown, not greyish body plumage. Hottentot Teal also has a dark cap but is much smaller and has a blue, not red bill. In flight shows a distinctive wing pattern of a pale speculum which in similar ducks is iridescent green or blue. *Status.* An uncommon summer visitor which occasionally breeds in the Park. Could be seen on any of the larger dams and pans. *Call.* Female quacks. Male gives a soft nasal whistle. *Afrikaans.* Rooibekeend.

Hottentot Teal *Anas hottentota* (107) 35 cm
A tiny duck which at long range vaguely resembles the more abundant Redbilled Teal, but the blue, rather than red bill and the dark spot on the creamy face should prevent confusion. In flight shows a green speculum which is broadly bordered with white on the trailing edge and quite unlike the buff speculum of Redbilled Teal. *Status.* A very rare visitor to the area, recorded from a few widely scattered points. Could be seen at any of the Park's water bodies. *Call.* In flight gives a series of soft whistles. *Afrikaans.* Gevlekte Eend.

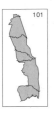

Whitebacked Duck *Thalassornis leuconotus* (101) 43 cm
A short, squat, hump-backed duck which skulks among floating vegetation, often with its body submerged in water, and showing only the neck and head. The plumage is a mottled brown and black with a dark cap and a diagnostic white spot at the bill base. The white back and white line running from the back on to the rump are rarely seen unless the bird is flushed and reluctantly takes flight. *Status.* A very rare vagrant, with only a few widely scattered records. Prefers well-vegetated dams and pans, where it is not easy to see. Occurs mainly in summers of above-average rainfall. *Call.* Normally silent but does have a soft whistle. *Afrikaans.* Witrugeend.

Cape Shoveler *Anas smithii* (112) 53 cm
A drab, mottled brown duck with both sexes showing a black spatulate bill, bright, yellow-orange legs, and powder-blue forewings which are most visible in flight. At long range the bird appears dark brown with a paler head and an all-black bill. *Status.* An extremely rare non-breeding vagrant to the Park which could turn up at any of the water bodies in the area. *Call.* 'Quack-quack'. *Afrikaans.* Kaapse Slopeend.

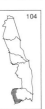

Yellowbilled Duck *Anas undulata* (104) 54 cm
A drab, mottled brown duck with a diagnostic chrome-yellow bill bisected on the upper mandible by a black patch. The bright green and blue iridescent speculum bordered with black and white is not often visible unless the bird is seen in flight. *Status.* A rare, sporadic vagrant mainly to the higher ground in the south-west of the Park with one breeding record in that area. *Call.* Female quacks and male hisses. *Afrikaans.* Geelbekeend.

Redbilled Teal

Hottentot Teal

Whitebacked Duck

Cape Shoveler

Yellowbilled Duck

Maccoa Duck *Oxyura maccoa* (117) 46 cm
The male is unmistakable with its matt-black head, cobalt-blue bill and deep chestnut body. The female is less distinct and could be confused with female Southern Pochard but has a pale face with a dark line running below the eye, not a white crescent behind the eye. Sits very low in the water with the tail flattened on the surface or cocked at a 45 degree angle. *Status.* A very rare visitor. Could occur at any of the larger pans or dams. *Call.* Male has a nasal 'prrrr' and a soft whistle. *Afrikaans.* Bloubekeend.

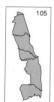

African Black Duck *Anas sparsa* (105) 56 cm
At long range might be mistaken for Yellowbilled Duck but is much darker with white spots on the back, and lacks the yellow bill. Sits very low in the water and appears long bodied. In flight shows a green-blue, iridescent speculum edged with white, and contrasting silvery-white underwings. *Status.* An uncommon winter-breeding resident occurring on the larger dams and perennial rivers. Shy, making observation difficult. *Call.* 'Quack-quack'. *Afrikaans.* Swarteend.

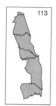

Southern Pochard *Netta erythrophthalma* (113) 50 cm
Male superficially resembles Maccoa Duck but has a dark brown, not black head, a pale blue rather than cobalt-blue bill, and a cherry-red eye. Female has dark brown plumage with a pale crescent on the face running below and behind the eye. In flight both sexes show a white wing bar, which differs from the all-dark wings of the Maccoa Duck. *Status.* A rare non-breeding visitor to the area, recorded from a few widely scattered points. Could be seen at any of the Park's water bodies. *Call.* The male whines, the female quacks. *Afrikaans.* Bruineend.

Maccoa Duck ♂

Maccoa Duck ♀

African Black Duck

Southern Pochard ♂

Southern Pochard ♀

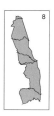

Dabchick *Tachybaptus ruficollis* (8) 20 cm
A tiny water bird which in breeding plumage has a dark cap, a chestnut neck and a pale creamy spot at the bill base. In non-breeding plumage the bird is grey and brown, and has a paler grey, fluffy vent, but the creamy bill spot is still evident. In flight it shows a white trailing edge to the wings.
Status. A breeding resident, common on the pans and dams throughout the Park. *Call.* A shrill, whinnying trill. *Afrikaans.* Kleindobbertjie.

African Jacana *Actophilornis africanus* (240) 28 cm
Unlikely to be mistaken for any other bird. The chestnut body, white throat and breast, yellow collar, and blue forehead and bill are diagnostic. The very long toes and toenails allow it to walk over floating vegetation and are conspicuous in flight. Imm. is paler than ad. and shows more white on the breast and belly.
Status. A very common breeding resident. Found on all the larger dams and rivers where floating vegetation occurs. *Call.* A sharp, ringing 'krrrek' and a 'krrrrk' flight call. *Afrikaans.* Grootlangtoon.

Lesser Jacana *Microparra capensis* (241) 15 cm
Considerably smaller than African Jacana, this species shows a chestnut crown and shoulder patches, and white underparts. Confusion might arise when the young African Jacana reaches the size of an ad. Lesser Jacana but the young bird can be distinguished as it has natal down, not feathers. In flight a white trailing edge to the wings is noticeable. *Status.* A very uncommon visitor with only two confirmed records for the Park. *Call.* A soft, often repeated 'krick'. *Afrikaans.* Dwerglangtoon.

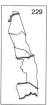

African Finfoot *Podica senegalensis* (229) 63 cm
When swimming, this species might be confused with a cormorant or the Darter but the neck is shorter and thicker and the bill is bright red. The white line that runs behind the eye and down the neck is diagnostic. When seen out of the water its bright red legs and feet are conspicuous. Swims very low in the water, often with its body submerged, and moves forward with jerky neck movements. *Status.* An uncommon breeding resident with a distribution limited to the permanent rivers on quiet pools with banks fringed with dense vegetation. May be more common than suspected. Patient observing of such pools in the Sabi, Crocodile and Luvuvhu rivers may be rewarded. *Call.* A soft, frog-like 'krok'. *Afrikaans.* Watertrapper.

Knobbilled Duck *Sarkidiornis melanotos* (115) 80 cm (male), 65 cm (female)
An almost goose-sized duck with contrasting black and white plumage. Male is larger than female and when breeding has a diagnostic black protruberance on the upper mandible. Both sexes show a pale head freckled with black, and in flight have completely dark wings which contrast with the white body.
Status. Fairly common, occurring mainly during the summer months when the pans and dams are full. Breeding has been recorded throughout summer.
Call. Usually silent but has a varied, whistled note. *Afrikaans.* Kobbeleend.

Dabchick (br.)

Dabchick (non-br.)

African Jacana (ad.)

African Jacana (imm.)

Lesser Jacana

African Finfoot ♀

Knobbilled Duck ♂

Knobbilled Duck ♀

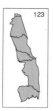

Whitebacked Vulture *Gyps africanus* (123) 95 cm
By far the most abundant vulture in the Park and easily confused with the
larger Cape Vulture. If seen, the white lower back will identify this species and
at closer range, its dark, not pale eye. Imm. is very much darker than ad. and
can only safely be distinguished from imm. Cape Vulture if the birds are seen
together when its smaller size can be determined. *Status.* Almost always
present at carcasses. A breeding resident. *Call.* Various cackles and hisses at
a carcass or when breeding. *Afrikaans.* Witrugaasvoël.

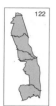

Cape Vulture *Gyps coprotheres* (122) 115 cm
Very difficult to distinguish from Whitebacked Vulture unless birds are seen
together when the much larger size of this species is evident. It is also far paler
and has black flight feathers which contrast more conspicuously with pale wing
linings. When seen at close range the pale, not dark eye and unfeathered
blue shoulder patches are diagnostic. Imm. not readily distinguished from
imm. Whitebacked Vulture unless seen together and size is comparable.
Status. A rare, non-breeding visitor to the Park. *Call.* Various cackles and
hisses when feeding and at nest. *Afrikaans.* Kransaasvoël.

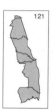

Hooded Vulture *Necrosyrtes monachus* (121) 70 cm
One of the smaller vultures in the Park and most likely to be confused with
imm. Egyptian Vulture but has a square, not wedge-shaped tail, and lacks the
bare facial skin and elongated nape feathers of that species. Imm. might be
confused with imm. Whiteheaded Vulture but lacks the distinctive white line
down base of flight feathers. Imm. Lappetfaced Vulture is almost twice the size
of the imm. Hooded Vulture. *Status.* A common vulture, it can be seen
throughout the Park. Attendant at almost all carcasses. *Call.* Silent except for
soft whistles at the nest. *Afrikaans.* Monnikaasvoël.

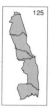

Whiteheaded Vulture *Trigonoceps occipitalis* (125) 80 cm
Both at rest and in flight shows very prominent white patches on the
secondaries, a white head, a red and blue bill, and a pink face. In flight the
white wing patches appear continuous with the white belly. Imm. could be
confused with imm. Lappetfaced and imm. Hooded vultures but shows a
diagnostic white line along the base of the flight feathers. *Status.* A fairly
common breeding species within the Park. Can be observed throughout and is
attendant at most kills. *Call.* Silent. *Afrikaans.* Witkopaasvoël.

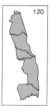

Egyptian Vulture *Neophron percnopterus* (120) 62 cm
Ad. is unmistakable with its white head and body, which may be tinged with
yellow, its long, white, wedge-shaped tail and its all-black flight feathers. At
close range the naked yellow face and elongated, shaggy nape feathers are
evident. *Status.* A rare vagrant to the northern sector of the Park. *Call.* Soft
grunts and hisses when excited. *Afrikaans.* Egiptiese Aasvoël.

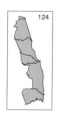

Lappetfaced Vulture *Torgos tracheliotus* (124) 100 cm
A very large, powerful vulture whose size, pinkish-red head and very dark
plumage facilitate identification. In flight shows white patches on the lower
belly which in fact are its thighs, and a white stripe along the leading edge of
the underwing from the body to the carpal joint. *Status.* Fairly common
throughout the Park and seen at most kills. A breeding resident.
Call. High-pitched whistles during display. *Afrikaans.* Swartaasvoël.

See also underwing patterns on pages 232-235

Whitebacked Vulture

Cape Vulture

Hooded Vulture

Whiteheaded Vulture

Egyptian Vulture

Lappetfaced Vulture

Yellowbilled Kite *Milvus migrans parasitus* 56 cm
The most obvious feature is the all-yellow bill and cere. Differs from African Marsh Harrier in bill colour and tail which is forked, not long or square-ended. Imm. has a black bill and is told from imm. Black Kite by the larger bill and overall darker appearance. *Status.* A conspicuous breeding summer migrant. *Call.* High-pitched squealing. *Afrikaans.* Geelbekwou.

Black Kite *Milvus migrans migrans* (126) 56 cm
Very similar to Yellowbilled Kite, but can be distinguished by its smaller black bill and its paler head. Seen more often in large gatherings than Yellowbilled Kite. Imm. not easy to separate from imm. Yellowbilled Kite except on the bill size and head features. *Status.* An uncommon, non-breeding summer migrant. *Call.* Silent in the region. *Afrikaans.* Swartwou.

Blackshouldered Kite *Elanus caeruleus* (127) 33 cm
A small grey and white bird of prey, easily identified by its diagnostic black shoulder and short, white tail. In flight appears very buoyant and the pointed wings show black tips below and black shoulders above. At close range the cherry-red eye and small, black bill can be seen. *Status.* An uncommon to common breeding visitor. *Call.* Various whistles and a harsher 'kek-kek-kek' sound. *Afrikaans.* Blouvalk.

African Marsh Harrier *Circus ranivorus* (165) 45-50 cm
Most likely to be mistaken for a Black or Yellowbilled Kite but has a thin, square-ended tail, and has noticeable barring on the underwings. Imm. has a variable amount of buff or white on the head and a buff bar across the breast. Distinguished from female and imm. Pallid and Montagu's harriers by its larger size and lack of a white rump. *Status.* A rare irregular visitor. May frequent the vleis below Nshawu Dam. *Call.* When breeding gives a 'woop' and 'chuk-chuk' notes. *Afrikaans.* Afrikaanse Paddavreter.

Montagu's Harrier *Circus pygargus* (166) 41-46 cm
Ad. male told from ad. male Pallid Harrier by being darker, slightly larger, and by the rust streaking on the belly and flanks, and the black bar on the secondaries. Female and imm. not readily distinguished from female and imm. Pallid Harrier. *Status.* A rare summer migrant. Viewing possibilities are as for the Pallid Harrier. *Call.* Silent. *Afrikaans.* Bloupaddavreter.

European Marsh Harrier *Circus aeruginosus* (164) 48-55 cm
Ad. male is unmistakable with its ashy grey tail and black-tipped flight feathers. Female and imm. show a creamy-white head and a dark mask and are best distinguished from similarly plumaged African Marsh Harrier by their larger size and lack of barring on tail and flight feathers. *Status.* A very rare summer vagrant. *Call.* A plover-like 'clee-aa'. *Afrikaans.* Europese Paddavreter.

Pallid Harrier *Circus macrourus* (167) 38-46 cm
Much paler than the slightly larger Montagu's Harrier, having pale grey and white plumage, black wing tips, and lacking the streaking on the belly and flanks and the black bar on the secondaries. Female and imm. very difficult to distinguish from female and imm. Montagu's Harrier. *Status.* A very rare summer migrant, frequenting only the open, grass plains in the eastern half of the Park. *Call.* Silent. *Afrikaans.* Witborspaddavreter.

See also underwing patterns on pages 232–235

Yellowbilled Kite

Black Kite

Blackshouldered Kite

African Marsh Harrier

Montagu's Harrier ♂

European Marsh Harrier ♂

Pallid Harrier ♂

Pallid Harrier ♀

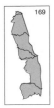

Gymnogene *Polyboroides typus* (169) 60-66 cm
One of the easiest birds of prey to identify with its overall greyish appearance, very finely barred underparts and bare yellow face. In flight the long, black tail shows a broad white bar across the centre and the wings show a narrow black trailing edge. The Dark Chanting Goshawk bears a vague resemblance but has long, red legs and lacks the black tail with a white tail bar. Imm. is dark brown but has few diagnostic features other than the small head, long tail and generally lazy, floppy flight typical of the ad. *Status.* A fairly common and widespread breeding resident. Occurs mainly along riverine habitats but also in areas of tall trees. *Call.* Utters a whistled 'suuu-eeee-oooo' during breeding. *Afrikaans.* Kaalwangvalk.

African Fish Eagle *Haliaeetus vocifer* (148) 63-73 cm
The call of this bird can be heard throughout the Park in suitable areas and makes it one of the more familiar birds of prey. The white head and breast, chestnut belly and forewings, black wings, and short, white tail make it easy to identify. Imm. is brown with white blotches on the head and breast, and shows a short, white tail with a black tip. In flight the broad wings and short tail give it a distinctive silhouette. *Status.* A common and conspicuous breeding resident, present along all the major watercourses and dams in the Park. *Call.* A gull-like yelping. *Afrikaans.* Visarend.

Bat Hawk *Macheiramphus alcinus* (129) 45 cm
A large bird of prey, approaching a buzzard in size but resembling a falcon in shape. From a distance its dark brown plumage appears black. Has a white throat and variable amounts of white on the belly and breast. At closer range the large yellow eye is obvious and if partially closed shows a large, white patch above and below it. Hunts mostly at dusk and is extremely fast and agile, out-manoeuvring its prey with ease. *Status.* Rare but probably resident, although breeding has not been recorded. Usually seen at sunrise and sunset along riverine habitats and particularly at the larger bridges (such as that over the Sabie River near Nkuhlu Picnic Spot, and the bridges over the Olifants, Letaba and Luvuvhu rivers) which seasonally house bats. The seasonality of these bats may influence numbers and distribution in the Park.
Call. A high-pitched, kestrel-like 'kek-kek-kek-kek'. *Afrikaans.* Vlermuisvalk.

Osprey *Pandion haliaetus* (170) 55-69 cm
An unmistakable bird of prey which has a white head bisected by a dark eye-stripe, white underparts with a streaked breast band, and white underwings which show a black carpal patch. The wings are long and narrow, and show a distinct bend at the carpals. Occurs in the same habitat as African Fish Eagle and might be mistaken for its imm. but is smaller, and lacks the broad wings and short tail. *Status.* A rare summer migrant and vagrant, recorded in both summer and winter on the major rivers and dams. *Call.* Silent in our region. *Afrikaans.* Visvalk.

See also underwing patterns on pages 232-235

Gymnogene (imm.)

Gymnogene (ad.)

African Fish Eagle (imm. left, ad. right)

Bat Hawk

Osprey

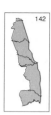

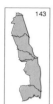

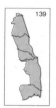

Brown Snake Eagle *Circaetus cinereus* (142) 70-76 cm
A nondescript brown eagle which, when perched, is best told from other brown eagles by its unfeathered whitish legs, its unusually large, round head and its large, yellow eyes. In flight the dark body and wing linings contrast with the paler flight feathers and the tail has three, narrow, pale bars. Imm. is very like ad. but shows variable amounts of white flecking on the underparts. *Status.* One of the more common eagles of the Park. Conspicuous as it hunts from prominent perches. A widespread breeding resident. *Call.* A croaking 'hok-hok-hok' sometimes uttered in flight. *Afrikaans.* Bruinslangarend.

Blackbreasted Snake Eagle *Circaetus gallicus* (143) 63-68 cm
When perched might be mistaken for the much larger Martial Eagle (p. 58) but the large, round head showing large, yellow, owl-like eyes, and the unfeathered whitish legs should rule out confusion. In flight differs from Martial Eagle by having white, not dark underwings and black barring on the flight feathers. Imm. is quite unlike ad., being rich rufous-brown with an almost uniform brown tail. *Status.* Less common than the Brown Snake Eagle. Also less conspicuous due to its habit of hunting on the wing. *Call.* A melodious 'kwo-kwo-kwo-kweeu'. *Afrikaans.* Swartborsslangarend.

Longcrested Eagle *Lophaetus occipitalis* (139) 52-58 cm
A small, very dark brown eagle easily recognized by its white feathered legs and long wispy crest. When the bird is perched the long crest may be wind-blown and then curls forward over the head. In flight shows conspicuous white patches in the wings and a black and white barred tail. *Status.* A rare vagrant to the area probably moving down to the Lowveld from the escarpment in the west. Recorded from widely scattered localities throughout. *Call.* A high-pitched 'kee-ah' given during display, in flight or when perched. *Afrikaans.* Langkuifarend.

Bateleur *Terathopius ecaudatus* (146) 55-70 cm
The sight of this strikingly patterned eagle gliding in a straight line with its head down and wings held slightly angled, and swaying from side to side in the breeze is a familiar one in the bushveld. From below the bird shows a uniform black body, a very short, chestnut tail and predominantly white underwings with a narrow, black trailing edge which is broader in the male. Imm. is uniform dark brown and has the same outline as ad., but has a slightly longer tail. *Status.* A very common and conspicuous breeding resident throughout the Park. *Call.* A loud, barking crow 'kow-wah'. *Afrikaans.* Berghaan.

See also underwing patterns on pages 232-235

Brown Snake Eagle

Blackbreasted Snake Eagle (ad.)

Blackbreasted Snake Eagle (imm.)

Longcrested Eagle

Bateleur (♂ left, imm. right.)

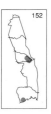

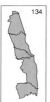

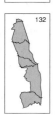

Jackal Buzzard *Buteo rufofuscus* (152) 45-53 cm

Appears very dark at rest, and at close range the slaty black upperparts, chestnut breast and tail, and belly bisected by an irregular white bar are conspicuous. In flight the white underwing shows a broad, black wing lining and a narrow, black trailing edge, and the short, rufous tail is conspicuous. Could be mistaken for Bateleur (p. 54) in flight but Bateleur lacks chestnut tail, and the underwing shows a different black and white pattern. Imm. has very rufous plumage but still shows short tail and broad wings with white flight feathers. *Status.* A vagrant to the Park, occurring widely with recent sightings near Malelane. *Call.* A loud, drawn-out 'weeah-ka-ka-ka' much like the yelp of a Blackbacked Jackal. *Afrikaans.* Rooiborsjakkalsvoël.

Steppe Eagle *Aquila nipalensis* (133) 65-80 cm

So closely resembles Tawny Eagle that some authorities consider them to be the same species. Very difficult to tell apart in the field except in that ad. Steppe Eagle lacks any tawny markings on its dark brown plumage. Best identified at close range when the gape is visible: in this species the gape extends behind the eye while on the Tawny it stops just below the eye. In summer the Steppe Eagle may be seen in large flocks, often comprised of other eagles. In flight, it shows a more curved 'S' trailing edge to the wing than the Tawny Eagle. *Status.* An uncommon non-breeding summer migrant. Usually occurs in flocks of up to several hundred birds, sometimes in company of the Lesser Spotted Eagle. *Call.* Silent. *Afrikaans.* Steppe-arend.

Steppe Buzzard *Buteo buteo* (149) 45-50 cm

Plumage is very variable ranging from light to blackish-brown but the most common pattern is dark brown with a pale crescent across the breast. Although many intermediate forms occur, most birds show the pale crescent. Perches in trees along roadsides. *Status.* A very rare summer vagrant which is probably only seen while passing through the Park. *Call.* A gull-like 'pee-oo'. *Afrikaans.* Bruinjakkalsvoël.

Lesser Spotted Eagle *Aquila pomarina* (134) 61-66 cm

Smaller than both Steppe and Tawny eagles and distinguished in flight by its broad white rump, longer tail, white bars on wings, and spotting on forewings. When perched the short leg feathers impart a thin-legged appearance, and at close range the round, not oval nostril is visible. *Status.* A migrant eagle, less common than the Steppe Eagle and usually, though not always, found singly or in small groups. Sometimes occurs in larger numbers in mixed flocks with Steppe Eagles, particularly when feeding on termite alates. Active Quelea breeding colonies offer good opportunities for seeing this and other raptor species. *Call.* Silent in this region. *Afrikaans.* Gevlekte Arend.

Tawny Eagle *Aquila rapax* (132) 65-80 cm

Not easily distinguished from Steppe Eagle during summer when both species are present in the Park. Birds seen during winter will almost certainly be this species. At close range the gape is seen to extend to just below the eye and not behind it as in Steppe Eagle. Ad. has a yellow, not dark eye. Ad. plumage is a rich tawny colour on the head and body with a darker back and wings. Imm. is sometimes very pale. *Status.* A fairly common breeding resident found throughout the Park. *Call.* Grunts and croaks during display flight. *Afrikaans.* Roofarend.

See also underwing patterns on pages 232-235

Jackal Buzzard (ad.)   Jackal Buzzard (imm.)

Steppe Eagle   Steppe Buzzard

Lesser Spotted Eagle   Tawny Eagle

Martial Eagle *Polemaetus bellicosus* (140) 78-83 cm
A very large eagle with similar colouring to Blackbreasted Snake Eagle though
its size and uniform dark, not white underwing should rule out confusion. Imm.
appears very pale with white underparts; differs from similar imm. Crowned
Eagle by having no spotting on flanks and legs and less heavily barred flight
feathers. *Status.* A fairly common breeding resident found throughout the Park.
Call. Display call consists of a rapid 'klooee-klooee-klooee'.
Afrikaans. Breëkoparend.

Crowned Eagle *Stephanoaetus coronatus* (141) 80-90 cm
An enormous eagle easily recognized by its very dark plumage with a rufous-
and black-mottled breast. When the bird is perched the elongated head
feathers can be raised to form an impressive crest. Unmistakable in flight
showing a long tail and broad, rounded wings which have rufous linings and
barred flight feathers. Imm. is white below and resembles imm. Martial Eagle
but has black spotting on flanks and legs, and heavily barred flight feathers.
Status. Seen regularly only along the Luvuvhu River where it is a breeding
resident. The best opportunity of seeing this species is on the Nyalaland Trail
which operates along this river. Has been seen a few times on the Sabie River.
Call. In display flight over forests gives a high-pitched 'kewee-kewee-kewee'
call. *Afrikaans.* Kroonarend.

Black Eagle *Aquila verreauxii* (131) 75-95 cm
In flight this large, very dark eagle shows a white rump and a white lower back
which forms a diagnostic 'V'. When viewed from below, white 'windows' at the
primary bases are visible. At rest the black plumage is relieved only by the
white 'V' on the back, the bright yellow cere, and the naked skin around the
eyes and on the feet. Imm., although also very dark, is brown, not black and
has a conspicuous rust-coloured crown and nape, which differentiate it from
other large brown eagles. *Status.* As with the Crowned Eagle only regularly
seen along the Luvuvhu River where it is a breeding resident. Again, the best
opportunity of seeing this species is on the Nyalaland Trail which operates
along this river. Has been seen a few times – mainly juveniles – further south,
particularly at Masorini Hill near Phalaborwa. *Call.* A yelping 'keee-uup'.
Afrikaans. Witkruisarend.

See also underwing patterns on pages 232-235

Martial Eagle (ad.)

Martial Eagle (imm.)

Crowned Eagle (ad.)

Crowned Eagle (imm.)

Black Eagle

Black Eagle

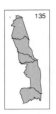

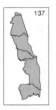

Wahlberg's Eagle *Aquila wahlbergi* (135) 55-60 cm
A small eagle, normally brown but also occurring in paler forms from very light to intermediate. Fairly nondescript at rest except for the small, pointed crest, but in flight is easily identified by the long, straight-edged wings and long, narrow, square-ended tail. Pale form birds might be confused with pale form Booted Eagle but the narrow, pencil-thin tail should help distinguish it. *Status.* A common breeding summer migrant arriving in August and starting to breed almost immediately. Possibly the most common eagle present in the Park during summer. *Call.* A loud 'keee-eeee' is given in flight. *Afrikaans.* Bruinarend.

Booted Eagle *Hieraaetus pennatus* (136) 46-53 cm
A small eagle which occurs in two colour forms, both similar to Wahlberg's Eagle. Differs mainly by having a shorter, broader tail, broader wings and, when seen from above, by the small pale area at the base of the forewing which gives the impression of a pair of pale 'braces'. The dark colour on the head extends well below the eye. *Status.* A rare vagrant to the area, but occurring in both summer and winter. Recorded from a few widely scattered points throughout the Park. There are no breeding records. *Call.* A high-pitched 'kee-keee' or 'pee-pee-pee'. *Afrikaans.* Dwergarend.

African Hawk Eagle *Hieraaetus fasciatus* (137) 66-74 cm
When perched appears black and white with a heavily spotted breast and a dark cap. Easily identified in flight by the dark bar on the underwing running from the wing base to the carpals, and contrasting with the white leading and trailing edges. Differs from Ayres' Eagle by being less boldly spotted on the underparts and showing pale bases to the primaries. Imm. is rufous but still shows underwing pattern of ad. *Status.* A fairly rare breeding resident recorded throughout the Park. *Call.* A musical 'klee-klee-klee' given during display. *Afrikaans.* Grootjagarend.

Ayres' Eagle *Hieraaetus ayresii* (138) 45-55 cm
Very much darker than the similar African Hawk Eagle and more boldly spotted below with spots extending on to the belly and flanks. The dark brown colouring on the head extends well below the eye and at long range gives the effect of a dark head. In flight the underwing appears much darker and lacks diagnostic pattern of African Hawk Eagle. More importantly, when seen from above, it lacks the pale primary bases of African Hawk Eagle. Imm. is darker rufous than imm. African Hawk Eagle but this is too variable to be a reliable identification feature. *Status.* Very rare in the Park and recorded as a non-breeding summer visitor. Most records are from the northern parts. *Call.* When displaying utters a shrill 'pueep-pip-pip-pueep'. *Afrikaans.* Kleinjagarend.

Honey Buzzard *Pernis apivorus* (130) 56 cm
Plumage coloration is as variable as in Steppe Buzzard (p. 56) with which it is most likely to be confused. Differs by having a smaller, more pointed head, heavily barred flight feathers and a diagnostically barred tail which shows a dark tip and two black bars near the base (often difficult to see). At close range the head appears small with a small, weak bill and has tiny feathers encircling the face and the eyes. *Status.* An extremely rare summer migrant. *Call.* A higher-pitched 'pee-oo' than Steppe Buzzard. *Afrikaans.* Wespedief.

See also underwing patterns on pages 232–235

Wahlberg's Eagle (dark form)   Booted Eagle (pale form)

African Hawk Eagle   Ayres' Eagle

Honey Buzzard

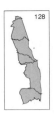

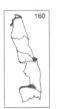

Cuckoo Hawk *Aviceda cuculoides* (128) 40 cm
Might be mistaken for the similar male African Goshawk but has a grey breast and throat, a slightly pointed crest, shorter legs, and chestnut barring on the lower breast and belly. In flight shows pointed, not rounded wings and conspicuous chestnut wing linings. Imm. similar to imm. African Goshawk but is much paler and differs in shape, having a shorter tail, pointed wings and shorter legs; also, lacks the black stripe on the throat. *Status.* Recorded occasionally and widely in the Park. Probably resident but then only in riverine vegetation zones with gallery forest canopies. *Call.* A loud, far-carrying 'teee-ooo' whistle and a shorter 'tittit-eooo'. *Afrikaans.* Koekoekvalk.

Lizard Buzzard *Kaupifalco monogrammicus* (154) 35-37 cm
A stocky bird of prey most frequently confused with Gabar Goshawk (p. 66) which is more slender, longer tailed and lacks the obvious black stripe down the throat. In flight shows a broad white rump and a distinctive white band across the centre of the tail. The legs and cere are orange. Imm. resembles ad. but has buff edging to the mantle feathers. *Status.* Not common but a widespread breeding resident. *Call.* A whistled 'peeoo' and a trilling 'klioo-klu-klu-klu'. *Afrikaans.* Akkedisvalk.

African Goshawk *Accipiter tachiro* (160) 36-39 cm
Male is most likely to be confused with Cuckoo Hawk but has much finer barring on the underparts, longer, thinner legs, and lacks a small crest. In flight it shows rounded wings which lack the chestnut wing linings of the Cuckoo Hawk. Female is much larger than male and has brown, not chestnut barring on the underparts. Imm. has a diagnostic black stripe on the throat which rules out confusion with all other similar small hawks. *Status.* Not common except for a few scattered localities where suitable habitat occurs. Essentially a forest species, it is recorded regularly only in the riverine vegetation of the Limpopo, Luvuvhu and Sabie rivers (west of Nkuhlu Picnic Spot) and in the thickly wooded parts around Punda Maria and the Bangu Gorge. *Call.* A short, sharp 'whit' or 'chip' given in flight. *Afrikaans.* Afrikaanse Sperwer.

Dark Chanting Goshawk *Melierax metabates* (163) 50-56 cm
This large bird of prey is unmistakable with its dark grey plumage, very finely barred underparts, long red legs and red cere. Might be confused with the very much smaller Gabar Goshawk (p. 66) but the size difference is significant. Imm. is a brown, streaked version of ad., also has long legs, and is distinguished from any 'ringtail' harrier by its lack of a white rump. *Status.* Not common but a widespread breeding resident. Prefers the thicker bush in the western half of the Park and more particularly the south-western parts around Pretoriuskop and in the north-east around the Nwambiya Sandveld.
Call. A piping 'kleeu-kleeu-klu-klu'. *Afrikaans.* Donkersingvalk.

See also underwing patterns on pages 232-235

Cuckoo Hawk

Lizard Buzzard

African Goshawk (ad.)

African Goshawk (imm.)

Dark Chanting Goshawk (ad.)

Dark Chanting Goshawk (imm.)

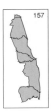

Little Sparrowhawk *Accipiter minullus* (157) 23-25 cm
This little bird of prey, especially the female, can be identified by size alone. In its plumage details it most closely resembles the Little Banded Goshawk and African Sparrowhawk but is readily identified by its white rump and diagnostic white spots on the uppertail. Imm. resembles imm. African Goshawk (p. 62) but is very much smaller, shows the white spots on its uppertail, and lacks the black stripe down the centre of the throat. *Status.* Uncommon and not conspicuous, but a breeding resident throughout the Park. *Call.* A high-pitched 'kek-kek-kek-kek' uttered by the male. Female has a softer 'kew-kew-kew'. *Afrikaans.* Kleinsperwer.

Little Banded Goshawk *Accipiter badius* (159) 28-30 cm
Most closely resembles Little Sparrowhawk but is stouter in build, and lacks the white rump and uppertail spots of that species. It can be distinguished from the larger but similar Ovambo Sparrowhawk (p.66) by having russet, not grey barring on the underparts, and yellow, not orange legs and cere. Imm. differs from imm. Little Sparrowhawk by lacking the white rump and tail spots. *Status.* Fairly common throughout the Park. A breeding resident, more common than the previous species but also not conspicuous. *Call.* Male's call is a high-pitched 'keewik-keewik-keewik'. Female's is a softer mewing 'kee-uu'. *Afrikaans.* Gebande Sperwer.

Black Sparrowhawk *Accipiter melanoleucus* (158) 46-58 cm
A round-winged hawk readily identified by its black and white plumage and its large size. A very rare black form with a small white throat occurs and could then be confused with black forms of Gabar Goshawk or Ovambo Sparrowhawk (p. 66), but its large size and the small white patch on the throat should aid identification. Imm. occurs in both a pale and rufous phase, the latter often confused with the much larger imm. African Hawk Eagle (p. 60), but distinguished by its different shape and lack of heavy streaking on the underparts. Imm. pale phase is easily confused with imm. African Goshawk (p. 62) but lacks the black stripe down the throat of that species. *Status.* Very uncommon and restricted to the forest-like vegetation along larger rivers – particularly the Sabie and Luvuvhu rivers and the well-wooded gulleys in the hilly south-west of the Park. Probably resident as there is a breeding record near Newu Dam in the Wolhuter Trails area. *Call.* A high-pitched 'kee-kee-kee' or 'pee-pee-pee'. *Afrikaans.* Swartsperwer.

See also underwing patterns on pages 232-235

Little Sparrowhawk (ad.)

Little Sparrowhawk (imm.)

Little Banded Goshawk (ad.)

Little Banded Goshawk (imm.)

Black Sparrowhawk (ad.)

Black Sparrowhawk (imm.)

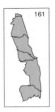

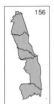

Gabar Goshawk *Micronisus gabar* (161) 30-34 cm
This small grey goshawk has red legs and cere, and in flight shows a diagnostic white rump. When perched, differs from Ovambo Sparrowhawk by having the upper breast and throat uniform grey, not barred, and by its red, not orange legs and cere. The black (or melanistic) form could be confused with black form of Ovambo Sparrowhawk but can be distinguished by the red, not orange cere and legs. Imm. differs from other similar imm. sparrowhawks and goshawks by having a white rump. *Status.* A fairly common and widespread breeding resident. Probably the most common of the small goshawks in the Park. *Call.* A high-pitched 'kik-kik-kik-kik-kik'. *Afrikaans.* Witkruissperwer.

Ovambo Sparrowhawk *Accipiter ovampensis* (156) 33-40 cm
A small hawk most likely to be confused with Little Banded Goshawk (p. 64) but differs by having grey, not rufous barring on the underparts and orange, not yellow legs, feet and cere. Also resembles Gabar Goshawk but has a dark, not white rump, lacks the grey throat and breast of that species, and has barring continuing up on to the breast and throat. The black form differs from black form of Gabar Goshawk by having much darker flight feathers and less noticeable barring on the tail. Imm. has a pale and a rufous phase; in the latter, it shows a very pale head with a dark spot behind the eye. *Status.* Very rare in the Park which, in conjunction with the lack of breeding records, suggests that it is vagrant to the area. *Call.* A soft 'keeep-keeep-keeep' given when breeding. *Afrikaans.* Ovambosperwer.

See also underwing patterns on pages 232-235

66

Gabar Goshawk (ad.)   Gabar Goshawk (imm.)

Gabar Goshawk (melanistic form)

Ovambo Sparrowhawk (ad.)   Ovambo Sparrowhawk (imm.)

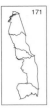

Peregrine Falcon *Falco peregrinus* (171) 34-38 cm
A dark, medium-sized falcon most likely to be confused with Lanner Falcon but distinguished by its black crown, very broad black moustachial stripes, and white underparts finely barred and spotted with black. Imm. differs from imm. Lanner Falcon by its darker plumage and brown, not pale to rufous crown. Altogether more powerful and streamlined than Lanner Falcon, much darker in appearance, and has a swifter and more dynamic flight action. *Status.* Very rare in the Park and resident only in the extreme north where there are suitable cliffs for breeding. The only reasonable chance of seeing this bird is along the Nyala Drive at Pafuri. *Call.* A loud, fast 'kek-kek-kek-kek-kek' is uttered over breeding territory. *Afrikaans.* Swerfvalk.

Lanner Falcon *Falco biarmicus* (172) 40-45 cm
Most likely to be confused with Peregrine Falcon but differs by having a pale rufous crown, thinner, less distinct moustachial stripes, and unmarked, off-white to pinkish underparts. Imm. is similar to imm. Peregrine Falcon but has a pale, not dark crown and is very much paler overall with less heavily marked underparts. Although very fast and dynamic in flight, it has a slower and floppier flight than the Peregrine, and its wings are broader-based and not as long and pointed. *Status.* Uncommon but widespread and believed to be resident in the Park. *Call.* A harsh 'kek-kek-kek-kek-kek', not unlike the Peregrine's call. *Afrikaans.* Edelvalk.

See also underwing patterns on pages 232-235

Peregrine Falcon (ad.)

Peregrine Falcon (imm.)

Lanner Falcon (ad.)

Lanner Falcon (imm.)

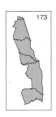

European Hobby *Falco subbuteo* (173) 28-35 cm
Easily confused with female and imm. Eastern Redfooted Falcon but has much whiter underparts heavily streaked with black, a richer chestnut vent, and a black patterned head which contrasts strongly with the white throat. Might also be confused with African Hobby, but African Hobby is much darker and has rufous underparts heavily streaked with black. *Status.* A fairly common non-breeding summer migrant. The best opportunity of seeing these birds is by skywatching at dusk at Skukuza (where the buildings house large numbers of bats). The large bridges over the Luvuvhu, Letaba, Olifants and Sabie rivers also often attract hobbies to their bat colonies. *Call.* Normally silent in Africa. *Afrikaans.* Europese Boomvalk.

African Hobby *Falco cuvierii* (174) 28-30 cm
This small, powerful falcon is more active during twilight hours, especially in the evening, when plumage details are not clearly visible. If seen, the rufous face, throat and underparts are diagnostic. Shape and flight pattern resemble that of the European Hobby but the darker underparts and rufous face distinguish it. *Status.* A rare summer vagrant to the Park. *Call.* A high-pitched 'kik-kik-kik-kik' given during display. *Afrikaans.* Afrikaanse Boomvalk.

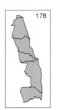

Rednecked Falcon *Falco chicquera* (178) 30-36 cm
Unmistakable if clearly seen, having a chestnut crown and nape, and brown moustachial stripes which contrast with the creamy face, throat and upper breast. Upperparts are pale grey and finely barred with black, and remaining underparts are white, finely barred with black and grey. *Status.* A rare vagrant. *Call.* A shrill 'ki-ki-ki-ki-ki' during the breeding season. *Afrikaans.* Rooinekvalk.

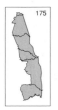

Sooty Falcon *Falco concolor* (175) 32-35 cm
Much slimmer, longer tailed and longer winged than Western Redfooted Falcon and Dickinson's Kestrel. Also, lacks any chestnut on the vent, and the head and body are a uniform grey. Imm. has pale grey underparts streaked with black, and at rest the wings reach almost to the tail tip. *Status.* A very rare summer vagrant recorded from scattered localities. *Call.* Silent in Africa. *Afrikaans.* Roetvalk.

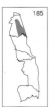

Dickinson's Kestrel *Falco dickinsoni* (185) 28-30 cm
The contrasting pale grey head and dark back and wings distinguish this small falcon from Sooty Falcon. In flight shows a pale rump which contrasts with the barred tail and dark upperparts. Imm. has white barring on the flanks. *Status.* A fairly common localized breeding resident. Restricted mainly to the eastern plains north of the Shingwedzi River, but has been recorded further south. The tarred road to the north of Shingwedzi and the new Hlamalala loop to the east of this road offer the best chances of a sighting. *Call.* A high-pitched 'keee-keee-keee'. *Afrikaans.* Dickinsonse Grysvalk.

Greater Kestrel *Falco rupicoloides* (182) 36-40 cm
Much paler than other kestrels, lacks moustachial stripes, and at close range shows a diagnostic pale eye. Differs from imm. Rock and Lesser kestrels by having an obvious grey barred tail and in flight a white or silvery underwing. *Status.* A very rare vagrant to the Park apparently restricted to the northern parts. *Call.* During display a shrill 'kwirr' or 'kweek' is given. *Afrikaans.* Grootrooivalk.

See also underwing patterns on pages 232-235

70

European Hobby

African Hobby (imm.)

Rednecked Falcon

Sooty Falcon

Dickinson's Kestrel

Greater Kestrel

Rock Kestrel *Falco tinnunculus* (181) 33-39 cm
Male differs from male Lesser Kestrel by having a black-spotted chestnut back, and spotted and barred, not silvery-white underwings; also, it lacks grey on the secondaries. Female and imm. are very similar to female and imm. Lesser Kestrel and not readily distinguished although the flocking behaviour of Lesser Kestrel should help separate the two species. Differs from the larger Greater Kestrel (p. 70) by having a spotted, not barred back and a more heavily marked underwing. *Status.* An uncommon breeding resident. Mainly restricted to the grass flats north of the Shingwedzi River though also recorded in the Crocodile Bridge area. *Call.* A high-pitched 'kee-kee-kee' or 'kik-kik-kik'. *Afrikaans.* Rooivalk.

Lesser Kestrel *Falco naumanni* (183) 30 cm
Ad. male is distinguished from Rock Kestrel by its uniform chestnut back, its pale, blue-grey secondaries and its almost silvery underwing. Female and imm. are very difficult to separate from female and imm. Rock Kestrel but habitat preference and flocking behaviour of this species should help identify it. At very close range the diagnostic white toenails may be seen. *Status.* An uncommon non-breeding summer migrant to the Park. Occurs mainly on the grass flats in the north. *Call.* Various high-pitched squeals at their communal roosts. *Afrikaans.* Kleinrooivalk.

Eastern Redfooted Falcon *Falco amurensis* (180) 30 cm
A small grey falcon with red legs, feet and cere, and easily identified in flight by its conspicuous white wing linings which contrast with the dark slate plumage. The female is easily confused with European Hobby (p. 70) but differs by having thinner black moustachial stripes, buff streaking on the dark head, less distinct spotting below, and a weaker, less dynamic flight action. *Status.* A common and widespread non-breeding summer migrant to the Park. Nearly always occurs in large flocks. *Call.* High-pitched trills at communal roosts. *Afrikaans.* Oostelike Rooipootvalk.

Western Redfooted Falcon *Falco vespertinus* (179) 30 cm
A small grey falcon distinguished from Eastern Redfooted Falcon by having dark, not white wing linings. Differentiated from the larger and more slender Sooty Falcon (p. 70) by having a chestnut, not grey vent, and from Dickinson's Kestrel (p. 70) by its overall more uniform dark colouring. Female and imm. differ from female and imm. Eastern Redfooted Falcon by having rufous heads, and slightly black-streaked underparts. Imm. might be confused with African Hobby (p. 70) but has paler underparts and underwings, and its flight is nowhere near as fast and dynamic. *Status.* Similar in status and habits to Eastern Redfooted Kestrel but much less common and found in smaller flocks. Sometimes joins flocks of other migrant kestrels. *Call.* High-pitched trills at communal roost. *Afrikaans.* Westelike Rooipootvalk.

See also underwing patterns on pages 232-235

Rock Kestrel ♂   Rock Kestrel ♀

Lesser Kestrel ♂   Lesser Kestrel ♀

Eastern Redfooted Falcon ♂   Eastern Redfooted Falcon ♀

Western Redfooted Falcon ♂   Western Redfooted Falcon ♀

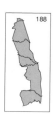

Coqui Francolin *Francolinus coqui* (188) 28 cm
Although very small this francolin is not likely to be confused with any quail species. Male has a buffy-orange head with a darker cap and its body is heavily barred below. Female might be confused with the larger Shelley's Francolin but lacks rufous striping on the breast and has yellowish legs. *Status.* An uncommon breeding resident which has been recorded throughout the Park. A secretive bird which is most easily located by its call. *Call.* A creaky, jangled 'kenk-enkenkenk' and a repeated 'kok-eee, kok-eee'. *Afrikaans.* Swempie.

Crested Francolin *Francolinus sephaena* (189) 33-35 cm
The dark cap with contrasting broad, creamy eyebrow stripe and dark-streaked breast are diagnostic. The only francolin in the Park to hold its tail cocked like a bantam, and invariably erects its crown feathers to form a crest. *Status.* A very common breeding resident. Found mainly in the riverine bush and thickets along watercourses, a habitat it shares with the Natal Francolin. *Call.* A rattling 'chee-chakla, chee-chakla'. *Afrikaans.* Bospatrys.

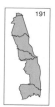

Shelley's Francolin *Francolinus shelleyi* (191) 33 cm
The bright rust or chestnut-streaked breast and flanks, and the black and white barred belly aid identification. Female superficially resembles female Coqui Francolin but is larger and has chestnut streaking on the breast and flanks. *Status.* An uncommon breeding resident which occurs throughout the Park. Most easily located by its call in the early morning and evening, but difficult to observe due to its relative scarcity and secretive nature. *Call.* A 'klee-klee-kleer' given mostly at dawn and dusk. *Afrikaans.* Laeveldpatrys.

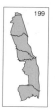

Swainson's Francolin *Francolinus swainsonii* (199) 38 cm
The bare red skin encircling the eyes and on the throat combined with the drab brown plumage and blackish-brown legs help to identify this large francolin. It could be mistaken for Rednecked Francolin but has dark, not red legs and lacks the bold black and white striping on the flanks. *Status.* An extremely common breeding resident recorded throughout the Park. Prefers well-grassed areas particularly the basalt plains in the eastern half of the Park, and tends to avoid the thicker bush of watercourses. *Call.* A raucous crowing 'krraae-krraae-krraae' in the early morning and evening. *Afrikaans.* Bosveldfisant.

Natal Francolin *Francolinus natalensis* (196) 35 cm
A large, drab francolin which might be confused with both Swainson's and Rednecked francolins but lacks bare red skin on the face and throat. The underparts are boldy patterned with black and white scaling, most obviously on the flanks and belly. Imm. is dowdier than ad. and has underparts washed with buff. *Status.* A very common and widespread breeding resident. Prefers the thicker bush along watercourses. *Call.* A ringing 'kwali-kwali-kwali' given at dawn and dusk. *Afrikaans.* Natalse Fisant.

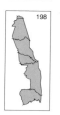

Rednecked Francolin *Francolinus afer* (198) 36 cm
Shows the same amount of bare red skin around the eyes and throat as Swainson's Francolin but differs by having red, not dark legs and by having very obvious black and white striping on the flanks. It may also show a variable amount of white on the head. *Status.* Has been recorded once only in the Park. *Call.* A loud, crowing 'kwoor-kwoor-kwoor-kwaaa'. *Afrikaans.* Rooikeelfisant.

74

Coqui Francolin ♀

Coqui Francolin ♂

Crested Francolin

Shelley's Francolin

Swainson's Francolin

Natal Francolin

Rednecked Francolin

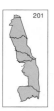

Doublebanded Sandgrouse *Pterocles bicinctus* (347) 25 cm
This small sandgrouse appears almost legless as it scuffles along the ground.
Male is easily recognized by the black and white markings on the forehead
and crown and by the thin, black and white breast band. Female and imm.
lack head markings and show a cryptic, buff and brown mottled pattern on the
back. *Status.* A common and widespread breeding species, more common in
the north and on the eastern plains further south. In winter large numbers can
sometimes be seen coming to drink at waterholes at sunset. *Call.* A whistled
'chwee-chee-chee' and a soft 'wee-chee-choo-chip-chip' flight call.
Afrikaans. Dubbelbandsandpatrys.

Kurrichane Buttonquail *Turnix sylvatica* (205) 14 cm
This tiny quail is difficult to distinguish on the ground and is most often seen
when flushed from grassland. It appears quite heavily streaked and mottled in
flight and its greyish wings contrast with the pale rump. Much smaller and
paler than Common Quail, and has pale-coloured eyes. *Status.* A breeding
resident, its numbers in the Park fluctuating markedly in accordance with the
availability of cover and food. Although sometimes abundant, difficult to see as
it remains hidden in long grass unless flushed. Can sometimes be seen as it
crosses the road. More common on the basalt plains where the grass cover is
greater than in the west. *Call.* A soft, two-note 'dooo-dooo'.
Afrikaans. Bosveldkwarteltjie.

Harlequin Quail *Coturnix delegorguei* (201) 18 cm
Darker than Common Quail from which it is not easily distinguished. Unless
the chestnut underparts and black belly are clearly seen, identification cannot
be certain. It also shows a white and black patterned throat which may be
more obvious than the dark underparts. Female and imm. are almost
indistinguishable from Common Quail. *Status.* Occurrence variable and
dependent on rainfall. Can be abundant in seasons of high rainfall, but difficult
to see unless flushed. A breeding visitor. *Call.* Very similar to Common Quail's
but sharper. *Afrikaans.* Bontkwartel.

Common Quail *Coturnix coturnix* (200) 18 cm
A small, rotund ground bird which creeps, rodent-like, through the grass and is
more often heard than seen. Most frequently encountered in grassland when
startled into flight, when it flies rapidly on buzzing wings. Male has a black
throat and is often difficult to distinguish from Harlequin Quail unless the black
underparts of the latter are clearly seen. *Status.* Occurrence variable and
dependent on rainfall. Can be abundant in seasons of high rainfall, but difficult
to see unless flushed. A breeding visitor. *Call.* A sharp 'whit-tit-tit' and a
'crwee-crwee' flight call. *Afrikaans.* Afrikaanse Kwartel.

Doublebanded Sandgrouse ♂

Doublebanded Sandgrouse ♀

Kurrichane Buttonquail

Harlequin Quail

Common Quail

Black Crake *Amaurornis flavirostris* (213) 20 cm
More frequently seen than other crakes and rails, and easily identified by the combination of its matt-black plumage, bright yellow bill and red legs. Imm. shows a dark bill and dull red legs. *Status.* A common breeding resident. Found on all the dams and permanent rivers and pools. *Call.* A throaty 'chrrooo-chrrooo' and a rippling trill 'weeet-eet-eet'. *Afrikaans.* Swartriethaan.

African Rail *Rallus caerulescens* (210) 37 cm
Like many small crakes and rails, this species shows conspicuous barring on the flanks but it is the only species to have a long, slightly decurved red bill and red legs. The throat and breast are greyish-blue, the back warm brown, and there is black and white barring on the flanks and undertail. *Status.* Very secretive and thus may be more common than suspected. Recorded mostly near Punda Maria. *Call.* A high-pitched 'trrreee-tee-tee-tee'. *Afrikaans.* Grootriethaan.

Baillon's Crake *Porzana pusilla* (215) 17 cm
Resembles mostly the larger African Crake, having similar greyish underparts with black and white barring confined to the flanks, but its smaller size and warm brown upperparts, speckled and flecked with white, should distinguish it. *Status.* Only two records exist for the Park: one in the Nwanetsi area and the other near Punda Maria. *Call.* A soft 'qurrr-qurrr' and various frog-like croaks. *Afrikaans.* Kleinriethaan.

African Crake *Crex egregia* (212) 22 cm
Smaller than Corncrake and darker, with a grey breast, and black barring on the flanks. In flight is more sluggish than Corncrake and lacks the bright chestnut wing coverts. *Status.* There are three records from the Stolsnek area. *Call.* A high-pitched whistling. *Afrikaans.* Afrikaanse Riethaan.

Corncrake *Crex crex* (211) 35 cm
Larger, and a much paler sandy colour than the African Crake, and has chestnut, not black barring on the flanks. Easily flushed and flies away on whirring wings, legs dangling, and showing bright chestnut wing coverts. *Status.* A rare non-breeding migrant, with most birds being present in summers of above-average rainfall. Frequents watercourses where grass tends to be at its most rank. *Call.* Silent in Africa. *Afrikaans.* Kwartelkoning.

Buffspotted Flufftail *Sarothrura elegans* (218) 16 cm
The combination of a chestnut head and breast, and a dark brown to black body liberally spotted with buff identifies the male. Female and imm. are drab brown with buffish throats and breasts. *Status.* A very rare vagrant to the Park. *Call.* A foghorn-like 'doooooo' is diagnostic and given mostly at night and on overcast days. *Afrikaans.* Gevlekte Vleikuiken.

Redchested Flufftail *Sarothrura rufa* (217) 16 cm
Male is similar to male Buffspotted Flufftail but has more extensive chestnut on the breast, and the black body is streaked and flecked with white, not spotted with buff. Female and imm. differ from female and imm. Buffspotted Flufftail by their greyish to white, not buffish throats and breasts, and by their dark brown upperparts which are finely flecked and spotted with buff. *Status.* Status is unclear, although a few records exist from scattered localities. It frequents marshes and vleis and it may occur only in the wetter years. *Call.* A low 'oooup-oooup' and a ringing 'klee-klee-klee'. *Afrikaans.* Rooiborsvleikuiken.

Black Crake (ad.)

Black Crake (imm.)

African Rail

Baillon's Crake

African Crake

Corncrake

Buffspotted Flufftail

Redchested Flufftail

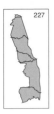

Lesser Moorhen *Gallinula angulata* (227) 24 cm

Similar to Moorhen but is more grey than sooty black and has a diagnostic yellow, not red bill. More skulking than Moorhen, keeping to the deeper recesses of marshes. Its legs and toes are reddish-brown, not green as in Moorhen. *Status.* A very rare and irregular visitor to the Park. Recorded throughout the area on large seasonal pans only. *Call.* A sharp 'krrrik', higher-pitched than that of the Moorhen. *Afrikaans.* Kleinwaterhoender.

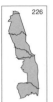

Moorhen *Gallinula chloropus* (226) 32 cm

Smaller than Purple Gallinule, this species has sooty black, not green and purple plumage. It is further distinguished by the yellow-tipped bill, the green, not red legs and the white horizontal stripe on its flanks. The undertail is white with a black centre. Imm. is greyish and differs from imm. Lesser Moorhen by having green, not brown legs and a grey head and throat. Bolder than Lesser Moorhen and Purple Gallinule, swimming over open water more often. *Status.* More common and less secretive than the Lesser Moorhen. A breeding resident in wetter years, though absent during droughts. Could be seen on any of the more permanent pools (such as Klopperfontein). *Call.* A sharp 'krrik'. *Afrikaans.* Waterhoender.

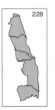

Redknobbed Coot *Fulica cristata* (228) 44 cm

A black, duck-like bird with a diagnostic white bill and a white, unfeathered forehead. The small red knobs on top of the frontal shield are more conspicuous during the breeding season. Imm. is greyish-brown and differs from imm. Moorhen by being larger and lacking a white undertail. *Status.* A very rare vagrant to the Park recorded from widely scattered points. Appears to visit the larger dams only but does not stay for long. *Call.* A harsh, metallic 'claak'. *Afrikaans.* Bleshoender.

Purple Gallinule *Porphyrio porphyrio* (223) 46 cm

A chicken-sized, reed-dwelling bird with a conspicuous large red bill and frontal shield, red legs and toes, and brightly coloured purple and green plumage. At long range might be mistaken for Lesser Gallinule but shows a red, not green frontal shield and is almost twice the size. Imm. is a duller version of ad. *Status.* A very rare vagrant to the Park with no breeding records. Could be seen anywhere at pans or marshy headwaters of dams where reeds or rushes occur. *Call.* A variety of harsh shrieks, booming notes and a 'keyik' contact call. *Afrikaans.* Grootkoningriethaan.

Lesser Gallinule *Porphyrula alleni* (224) 25 cm

Ad. might be mistaken for Moorhen but is noticeably smaller, has a greenish-blue, not red frontal shield, lacks Moorhen's white flank stripe and has bright red, not greenish-brown legs and feet. Imm. is very similar to imm. Moorhen but has pale flesh-coloured, not greenish-brown legs. *Status.* A very rare summer visitor to the northern and eastern pans. *Call.* A metallic 'klaark' and other frog-like noises. *Afrikaans.* Kleinkoningriethaan.

Lesser Moorhen

Moorhen (ad.)

Moorhen (imm.)

Redknobbed Coot (ad.)

Redknobbed Coot (imm.)

Purple Gallinule

Lesser Gallinule

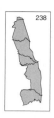

Blackbellied Korhaan *Eupodotis melanogaster* (238) 64 cm
Much larger than Redcrested Korhaan with which it might be confused.
Further differs by having a much longer, thinner neck, longer legs and has the
black on the belly extending upwards into a thin, black line on the throat. In
flight the black underwing contrasts with the large, white patches on the
upperwing. During display flight the male flies high in the air over its territory
and slowly glides to earth dangling its legs. *Status.* An uncommon but
widespread breeding resident. *Call.* A short, sharp 'chikk' followed by a 'pop',
given from a mound or antheap. *Afrikaans.* Langbeenkorhaan.

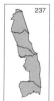

Redcrested Korhaan *Eupodotis ruficrista* (237) 50 cm
Smaller than the similar Blackbellied Korhaan, has a shorter, thicker neck and
lacks the black line running down the throat. In flight does not show any white
on the upperwing but has a white patch on either side of the upper breast. The
red crest is visible only during display. In display flight the male makes a
spectacular vertical ascent and then suddenly tumbles and plummets
earthwards. *Status.* A common, widespread breeding resident. *Call.* A loud,
whistled 'chew-chew-chew'. *Afrikaans.* Boskorhaan.

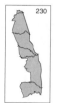

Kori Bustard *Ardeotis kori* (230) 135 cm
This large bustard is unmistakable and of the terrestrial birds in the Park is
second in size only to the Ostrich. The female is noticeably smaller than the
male. Flies slowly with ponderous wing beats and usually no higher than the
tree tops. Strides across the veld swinging its head with a peculiar backwards
and forwards motion. *Status.* An uncommon breeding resident. Occurs mainly
on the eastern side of the Park on open plains. *Call.* A deep, resonant
'oom-oom-oom' given during the breeding season. *Afrikaans.* Gompou.

Stanley's Bustard *Neotis denhami* (231) 104 cm
Could only be mistaken for the Kori Bustard in the Park but is smaller and
shows a rich chestnut stripe on the hind neck which broadens on to the lower
neck. In flight shows much more white on the wings than Kori Bustard.
Status. There are only two records of this bird in the Park. It is essentially a bird
of the highveld grasslands and may thus occur in the Park only as a very rare
non-breeding winter vagrant. If and when it occurs in the Park, it is likely to be
on the flat eastern grasslands. *Call.* A 'wak-wak' and a booming 'oomp-oomp'
are given. *Afrikaans.* Veldpou.

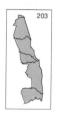

Helmeted Guineafowl *Numida meleagris* (203) 56 cm
This chicken-sized bird with a grey body flecked with white, and an
unfeathered blue and red head is unmistakable. The horny, red casque on the
crown varies in size. Imm. has a less-developed casque and duller head
colouring. *Status.* A common and widespread breeding resident. *Call.* A loud,
repeated 'krrdi-krrdi-krrdi' and a 'kek-kek-kek'. *Afrikaans.* Gewone Tarentaal.

Crested Guineafowl *Guttera pucherani* (204) 50 cm
Differs from Helmeted Guineafowl by having black plumage finely spotted with
pale blue-grey. The naked grey head, black ruff around the neck, and thatch of
short, curly, black feathers on the crown also distinguish it. The wings show
pale buffy primaries. *Status.* Fairly common only at Pafuri where it is quite easy
to observe. Also occurs in the denser vegetation types of the Lebombo range
and in the Bangu area. A breeding resident at Pafuri. *Call.* A 'chick-chick-
chick-chirrr' given by the male. *Afrikaans.* Kuifkoptarentaal.

Blackbellied Korhaan

Redcrested Korhaan

Kori Bustard

Stanley's Bustard

Helmeted Guineafowl

Crested Guineafowl

Caspian Plover *Charadrius asiaticus* (252) 22 cm
A fairly nondescript bird, greyish-brown above and paler below with a short bill, but much larger than other similar plovers found in the Park. Might be confused with imm. Kittlitz's Plover which is very much smaller and has a pale, buffy collar, and with imm. Whitefronted Plover which is white, not buff below. Found away from water on short-grassed or recently burnt areas.
Status. A rare summer visitor to the Park with a few widely scattered records. Has been seen a few times at Nshawu Dam. Prefers well- or overgrazed areas.
Call. Usually silent. *Afrikaans.* Asiatiese Strandkiewiet.

Chestnutbanded Plover *Charadrius pallidus* (247) 15 cm
Smaller than Whitefronted Plover and very much paler on the back. Ad. has a diagnostic thin chestnut band on the breast and a dark line across the forehead. Imm. lacks chestnut bar but the dark brown markings on either side of the breast show the beginnings of it. *Status.* A very rare plover, the few records being from localities down the length of the Park. Prefers rivers when water levels are low. *Call.* A single 'tooit'. *Afrikaans.* Rooibandstrandkiewiet.

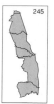

Ringed Plover *Charadrius hiaticula* (245) 16 cm
Larger than Chestnutbanded Plover and darker above, with a white collar, a broad, dark brown or black breast band which is sometimes incomplete, and bright orange legs. Differs from Threebanded Plover by having only one, not two dark bars across the breast. *Status.* A very rare summer vagrant. Could be seen at any of the Park's rivers and dams. *Call.* A fluty 'tooi'.
Afrikaans. Ringnekstrandkiewiet.

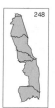

Kittlitz's Plover *Charadrius pecuarius* (248) 16 cm
The buffy, unmarked underparts and clearly defined black line running through the eye on to the nape readily identify this small wader. Confusion may arise in imm. plumage when it resembles Whitefronted Plover but even then the uniform buffy underparts distinguish it. *Status.* A rare breeding resident recorded from a few widely scattered localities. Seen mostly at Nshawu Dam and may be resident there. *Call.* A short, clipped, trill 'kittip'.
Afrikaans. Geelborsstrandkiewiet.

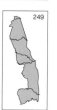

Threebanded Plover *Charadrius tricollaris* (249) 18 cm
The black double breast band is diagnostic, and at close range the bright red eye-ring and red base to the bill are distinct. Its long, attenuated shape is quite unlike that of any other small plover. In flight the tail shows a white terminal bar. Imm. is duller version of ad., showing brown breast bands which are sometimes incomplete. *Status.* An abundant breeding resident. Occurs at nearly every water body in the Park. *Call.* A clear, penetrating 'weet weet' whistle. *Afrikaans.* Driebandstrandkiewiet.

Whitefronted Plover *Charadrius marginatus* (246) 18 cm
A very pale plover which might be confused with imm. Chestnutbanded Plover but is larger and shows a pale collar. Differs from imm. Kittlitz's Plover by having clear white, not buff underparts, though belly is sometimes buffy or cinnamon tinged. *Status.* An uncommon plover which probably breeds in the Park. Occurs mainly at the larger dams on rivers, such as the Kanniedood Dam on the Shingwedzi River and the Engelhard Dam on the Letaba River. Also can be seen on sandbanks on any of the larger rivers. *Call.* A clear 'wiiit' and a 'tukut' alarm call. *Afrikaans.* Vaalstrandkiewiet.

Caspian Plover

Chestnutbanded Plover

Ringed Plover

Kittlitz's Plover

Threebanded Plover

Whitefronted Plover

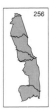

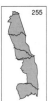

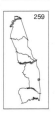

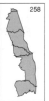

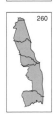

Lesser Blackwinged Plover *Vanellus lugubris* (256) 22 cm
A large plover which might be found in company with either the Caspian or Crowned Plover, well away from water and especially on recently burnt grassveld. Identified by its grey breast edged with black and contrasting with the white belly, the small white forehead and pale eye. In flight the upperwing pattern is distinct and shows the white secondaries contrasting with the black primaries. *Status.* Uncommon and erratic, occurring mainly in middle to late winter. Breeds occasionally in the Park. Occurs throughout the area on well- or overgrazed veld or on recently burnt veld. *Call.* A clear, double-note 'tee-yoo tee-yoo'. *Afrikaans.* Kleinswartvlerkkiewiet.

Crowned Plover *Vanellus coronatus* (255) 30 cm
A familiar bird, easily identified by its black cap encircled with a white 'halo', and by its bright red legs and basal part of bill. Has a very upright stance and in flight shows conspicuous white wing patches. Imm. is duller version of ad. and with less distinct markings. *Status.* A very common breeding resident. Occurs throughout the Park on all well-grazed areas and bare ground, even roadsides. *Call.* An extremely noisy bird, uttering a loud, grating 'krreeep' or 'keefeeet' both day and night. *Afrikaans.* Kroonkiewiet.

Whitecrowned Plover *Vanellus albiceps* (259) 30 cm
Most likely to be confused with Wattled Plover but has a grey head, a white, not brown breast and longer, more obvious yellow wattles. The white stripe running over the crown is not always conspicuous. In flight the wings appear almost entirely white. *Status.* A common breeding resident on the Olifants, Limpopo and Luvuvhu rivers though absent from the Letaba River which has its confluence with the Olifants River inside the Park. A few have settled on the Sabie River near the Nwatimhiri Causeway and can often be seen there. Also occurs on the Crocodile River and the Sweni Causeway. The Olifants Trail offers a certain chance of seeing this bird. *Call.* An often-repeated 'peek-peek'. *Afrikaans.* Witkopkiewiet.

Blacksmith Plover *Vanellus armatus* (258) 30 cm
This very vocal, black, white and grey wader is one of the easiest to identify in the Park. In flight shows a black saddle and grey wings with black primaries. Imm. has brown in place of black plumage in ad. *Status.* A very common breeding resident, occurring throughout the Park in association with water. Can easily be seen on any of the Park's rivers or dams. *Call.* A loud, ringing 'tink-tink-tink' alarm note. *Afrikaans.* Bontkiewiet.

Wattled Plover *Vanellus senegallus* (260) 35 cm
A very large plover which is often heard before it is seen. The long yellow wattles extending from the bill base are very noticeable but are smaller than those of the Whitecrowned Plover with which it might be confused. It is also distinguished from the Whitecrowned Plover by its brown, not white breast. In flight shows white wing patches. Imm. has less developed wattles than ad. *Status.* An uncommon species occurring throughout the area, it may or may not be resident. *Call.* A high-pitched, ringing 'keep-keep'. *Afrikaans.* Lelkiewiet.

Lesser Blackwinged Plover

Blacksmith Plover

Crowned Plover

Whitecrowned Plover

Wattled Plover

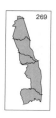

Marsh Sandpiper *Tringa stagnatilis* (269) 23 cm
A very pale wader, smaller and paler than the similar Greenshank. Differs further by having a finer, needle-like bill quite unlike the thicker, upturned bill of Greenshank. Also, has slimmer proportions and longer legs which extend well beyond the tail in flight. In flight shows a white rump and no wing bar. *Status.* An uncommon but widespread summer migrant. Could be seen on any of the Park's water bodies. *Call.* A single, shrieked 'tchuck'. *Afrikaans.* Moerasruiter.

Greenshank *Tringa nebularia* (270) 32 cm
A large wader most closely resembling Marsh Sandpiper but altogether larger and darker. It also has a much heavier bill which is slightly upturned and is bicoloured grey and black. In flight the wings are dark and contrast markedly with the white rump which continues up the back in a white wedge. *Status.* A common and conspicuous wader on all of the Park's waters. A summer migrant though a few birds overwinter. *Call.* A loud, ringing 'chew-chew-chew'. *Afrikaans.* Groenpootruiter.

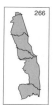

Wood Sandpiper *Tringa glareola* (266) 20 cm
A small sandpiper with greenish or yellowish legs, a dark, buff-speckled back and a thin, medium-length bill. Differs from Marsh Sandpiper and Greenshank by being smaller and darker, and from the similar Green Sandpiper by having a paler back and less contrasting underwing. Common Sandpiper is smaller and has a more uniformly coloured back, an obvious white shoulder and a peculiar flight action. *Status.* Probably the most common of the sandpipers occurring in the Park. A summer migrant that could be seen on any of the water bodies, large or small. *Call.* A 'chiff-iff-iff' flight call. *Afrikaans.* Bosruiter.

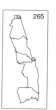

Green Sandpiper *Tringa ochropus* (265) 23 cm
Likely to be confused only with the similar Wood Sandpiper but is larger, more robust and has a darker plumage. In flight the underwings are very dark, imparting a highly contrasting black and white pattern. *Status.* An extremely rare summer migrant with only two records for the Park, the latest being at Pafuri. *Call.* A fluty, whistled 'tew-a-tew'. *Afrikaans.* Witgatruiter.

Ruff *Philomachus pugnax* (284) 30 cm (male), 24 cm (female)
A variably sized wader, the male (Ruff) much larger than the female (Reeve) but both sexes showing a very noticeably scaled back. Leg colour varies greatly from green to bright orange. In flight, the Ruff shows a dark rump with two white oval marks at the base of the tail. *Status.* A fairly common summer migrant. Could be seen on mudflats at any of the larger dams. *Call.* Silent. *Afrikaans.* Kemphaan.

Marsh Sandpiper

Greenshank

Wood Sandpiper

Green Sandpiper

Ruff

Turnstone *Arenaria interpres* (262) 23 cm
A small, dumpy wader with relatively short, orange legs and a short, slightly upturned bill. The plumage is mottled brown and black with irregular black markings across the breast. In breeding plumage a rich chestnut colour is apparent on the back and wings. In flight in all plumages, the upperwing shows two distinctive white patches. *Status.* A rare vagrant to the Park. *Call.* A sharp, rattled 'kuttuck'. *Afrikaans.* Steenloper.

Sanderling *Calidris alba* (281) 19 cm
A small, very pale wader which has a short, thick, black bill and a dark shoulder patch. It is larger and paler than Little Stint and in flight shows a broad white wing bar. In breeding plumage the back and head become heavily marked with rufous. *Status.* An uncommon summer migrant to the Park usually seen on the mudflats of dams. Recorded throughout the area. *Call.* A single flight note 'wick'. *Afrikaans.* Drietoonstrandloper.

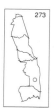

Dunlin *Calidris alpina* (273) 18 cm
This very rare wader is easily confused with the Curlew Sandpiper in the Park but is smaller, has a shorter, less decurved bill and a dark, not white rump. In breeding plumage shows rusty upperparts and a black belly patch. *Status.* Has occurred only once in the Park, at Mazithi Dam. *Call.* A weak 'trreep' note given mostly in flight. *Afrikaans.* Bontstrandloper.

Curlew Sandpiper *Calidris ferruginea* (272) 19 cm
The long, decurved bill is distinctive on this small wader and this, combined with the white rump which is visible in flight, is diagnostic. In breeding dress the rump becomes finely barred and the underparts deep rust in colour. The Dunlin is very similar but lacks the white rump and has a shorter, less decurved bill. *Status.* A fairly common summer migrant to the Park which could be seen on any of the dams with exposed mudflats. *Call.* A short, trilled 'chirrup'. *Afrikaans.* Krombekstrandloper.

Little Stint *Calidris minuta* (274) 14 cm
As the smallest wader in the Park it is easily identified by size alone but its overall grey and white plumage and short, thin bill further aid identification. An extremely active bird, busily running back and forth, probing the mud with its short bill. *Status.* An uncommon summer migrant. Could be seen at any of the water points in the Park. *Call.* A short, weak 'peep'. *Afrikaans.* Kleinstrandloper.

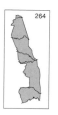

Common Sandpiper *Tringa hypoleucos* (264) 19 cm
Might be mistaken for Wood Sandpiper (p. 88) but normally shows a white shoulder in front of the closed wing, has shorter legs, and lacks pale speckling on the back. Has a peculiar teetering motion, bobbing backwards and forwards as it stands. Typically bobs its tail while feeding. In flight holds wings slightly bowed and gives flicking wing beats low over the water, showing a white wing bar and white, barred sides to the tail. *Status.* A common wader which may be seen at any of the dams or natural water points in summer. Sometimes frequents the lawns of restcamps. *Call.* A shrill, high-pitched 'ti-ti-ti-ti'. *Afrikaans.* Gewone Ruiter.

Turnstone

Sanderling

Dunlin

Curlew Sandpiper

Little Stint

Common Sandpiper

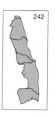

Painted Snipe *Rostratula benghalensis* (242) 24-28 cm

An unusual wading bird in which the female is larger and brighter in colour than the male, and easily identified by the chestnut neck and breast, and white eye-patch. The breast and head pattern should immediately distinguish it from the Ethiopian Snipe. *Status.* An uncommon but widely recorded species, difficult to see due to its shy nature. There are no breeding records but it may be resident at some of the more permanent waters. *Call.* Not very vocal but the female utters a 'kook' call and the male trills. *Afrikaans.* Goudsnip.

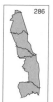

Ethiopian Snipe *Gallinago nigripennis* (286) 32 cm

This skulking, furtive wader is readily identified by its very long bill, markedly striped head and buff striping on the back. When flushed it has a rapid, jerky flight. It displays in a shallow swoop, spreading its tail feathers and producing a humming sound. *Status.* A rare vagrant to the Park, its numbers probably dependent on rainfall and the resulting availability of suitable marshy habitat. Isolated records exist for localities down the length of the Park. *Call.* A short, sharp grunt when flushed. *Afrikaans.* Afrikaanse Snip.

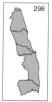

Water Dikkop *Burhinus vermiculatus* (298) 40 cm

Easily confused with Spotted Dikkop but this species is mostly found near water. At rest it shows grey panels on the folded wing bordered by a white stripe, and has a less spotted and vermiculated plumage than Spotted Dikkop. In flight an obvious white wing bar is evident, which further distinguishes it from Spotted Dikkop. *Status.* A common water bird occurring all year round at permanent water points. Difficult to see because of its excellent camouflage but careful scanning of water lines at dams and rivers will usually reveal its presence. *Call.* An eerie, whistled 'ti-ti-tee-teee-too', slowing and dropping in pitch at the end. *Afrikaans.* Waterdikkop.

Spotted Dikkop *Burhinus capensis* (297) 44 cm

Larger and bulkier than Water Dikkop, this species also has more heavily marked plumage and less pronounced white markings around the eye. Folded wing shows no grey panel or white stripe. In flight the two obvious white patches in each wing are quite unlike the white wing bar of Water Dikkop. *Status.* Fairly common and resident in the Park though difficult to observe on account of its nocturnal habits and excellent camouflage. On quiet moonlit nights can often be heard giving its characteristic call. *Call.* A whistled 'whiw-whiw-whiw' given at dusk and during the night. *Afrikaans.* Dikkop.

Painted Snipe ♀

Ethiopian Snipe

Water Dikkop

Spotted Dikkop

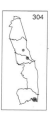

Redwinged Pratincole *Glareola pratincola* (304) 27 cm
In flight its long thin wings and forked tail sometimes give this species the appearance of a huge swallow. At rest it shows a warm, creamy throat which is bordered by a black line. Sometimes in display it raises its wings over its back, showing the diagnostic rust-coloured wing linings which are not easily seen in flight. Imm. resembles ad. but lacks throat pattern. *Status.* An uncommon breeding summer visitor to a few isolated points in the Park. Regularly seen (and nesting recorded) each year at the Engelhard and Nshawu dams. *Call.* A sharp 'kik-kik' alarm note. *Afrikaans.* Rooivlerksprinkaanvoël.

Bronzewinged Courser *Rhinoptilus chalcopterus* (303) 25 cm
A mostly nocturnal species which usually hides in the shelter of a bush during the day. Easily recognized by the single dark bar across the breast, the red legs, and the white marking across the head which gives it a close resemblance to the larger Crowned Plover (p. 86). In flight shows a conspicuous white rump and wing bar. *Status.* A fairly common and widespread breeding resident. Its nocturnal habits make it extremely difficult to observe in the Park. *Call.* A ringing 'ki-kooi'. *Afrikaans.* Bronsvlerkdrawwertjie.

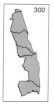

Temminck's Courser *Cursorius temminckii* (300) 20 cm
Much smaller than other coursers and most closely resembles Burchell's Courser from which it is distinguished by the dark belly patch which extends between the legs. Further differs by having a chestnut, not blue-grey nape and a chestnut lower breast. Found on short grassy areas and in recently burnt veld in moister areas than Burchell's Courser. *Status.* A fairly common bird, it has been recorded in all months in open, overgrazed areas, particularly the flatter areas in the eastern half of the Park. It breeds in the Park but is nomadic in habits. *Call.* A sharp, piercing 'keer-keer'. *Afrikaans.* Trekdrawwertjie.

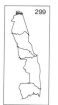

Burchell's Courser *Cursorius rufus* (299) 23 cm
Very similar to the smaller Temminck's Courser but shows a dark bar not a black belly patch, a blue-grey nape and a distinct black and white eye-stripe extending backwards from the eye. In flight shows dark primaries and a narrow white trailing edge to the wing. *Status.* Occurs only in the extreme north at Pafuri. A very rare visitor to the Park, probably only in years of extreme drought. *Call.* A harsh, often repeated 'wark'. *Afrikaans.* Bloukopdrawwertjie.

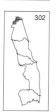

Threebanded Courser *Rhinoptilus cinctus* (302) 28 cm
Mostly nocturnal, resting during daylight hours under thick scrub. A fairly large and robust courser, easily identified by its rufous throat and lower breast band. The upperparts are well marked brown and buff giving the bird protective camouflage. In flight it shows a white rump but dark wings. *Status.* A very rare vagrant seen only twice in the Park in the extreme north at Pafuri. Both sightings were in early summer and on the second occasion adults with a chick were seen. *Call.* A repeated 'kika-kika-kika'. *Afrikaans.* Driebanddrawwertjie.

Redwinged Pratincole

Bronzewinged Courser

Temminck's Courser

Burchell's Courser

Threebanded Courser

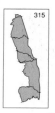

Greyheaded Gull *Larus cirrocephalus* (315) 42 cm
The only gull likely to be seen in the Park. Ad. shows distinctive grey hood.
Imm. and non-breeding ad. lack grey hood but have dusky markings behind
and below the eye. In flight shows a white wedge down the forewing and a
dark underwing. *Status.* A rare non-breeding summer vagrant to the Park.
Records are widely distributed and birds may be expected on any of the
larger water bodies. *Call.* A typical small-gull 'kaarrh' and a 'pok-pok'.
Afrikaans. Gryskopmeeu.

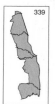

Whitewinged Tern *Chlidonias leucopterus* (339) 23 cm
A very distinctive bird in breeding dress with a sooty black body contrasting
with pale, almost silvery upperwings. Nondescript in non-breeding plumage
and easily confused with non-breeding Whiskered Tern but shows more black
on the crown and nape, often has irregular black markings on the underwing,
and has a white rump and tail which contrast with the grey back. *Status.* An
uncommon non-breeding summer visitor which may be seen at any of the
larger dams in the area. *Call.* Mostly silent except for a short 'kek-kek'.
Afrikaans. Witvlerksterretjie.

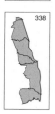

Whiskered Tern *Chlidonias hybridus* (338) 25 cm
Unmistakable in breeding plumage with a dark cap, an all-grey body plumage
and a conspicuous white stripe across the cheek. Non-breeding bird is easily
confused with Whitewinged Tern but is paler overall with very little black on the
head, and has a stouter bill and a grey tail. Also shows a more laboured flight
action. *Status.* A rare non-breeding visitor which could occur on any of the
larger dams. *Call.* A repeated, hard 'zizz'. *Afrikaans.* Witbaardsterretjie.

Greyheaded Gull (ad.)

Greyheaded Gull (imm.)

Whitewinged Tern (br.)

Whitewinged Tern (non-br.)

Whiskered Tern (br.)

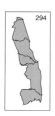

Avocet *Recurvirostra avosetta* (294) 42 cm
Unlikely to be confused with any other wading bird. The black and white plumage combined with a long, very thin, upturned bill is diagnostic. In flight legs project well beyond tail and the pied pattern on the wings is obvious. Frequently swims in deep water when not wading. *Status.* A very rare vagrant recorded down the length of the Park. Has been seen at a wide variety of water bodies from dams to gravel pits holding rainwater. *Call.* A clear, whistled 'kooit' and a sharper 'kik-kik' alarm note. *Afrikaans.* Bontelsie.

Blackwinged Stilt *Himantopus himantopus* (295) 38 cm
A black and white wading bird with extremely long, red legs and a long, thin, black bill. In flight the legs project almost 20 cm beyond the tail and the wings are uniform black and pointed. Breeding male has a black nape as opposed to the greyish nape of non-breeding bird. Imm. has brownish-grey plumage in place of black and has duller legs. *Status.* Common only along the western reaches of the Olifants River where it appears to be resident, though no breeding records exist. May be seen at any of the rivers, dams and pans. *Call.* A short, harsh 'kik-kik' especially when alarmed. *Afrikaans.* Rooipootelsie.

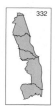

Sooty Tern *Sterna fuscata* (332) 44 cm
A black and white tern which shows a small white forehead and a deeply forked tail with white outer tail feathers. Imm. is dusky brown except for a white vent and buff freckling on the back. A very rare vagrant to the Park having been blown inland by cyclones from the Indian Ocean. *Status.* Six of these birds were recorded between Satara and Skukuza after Cyclone Danae passed through the area in January 1976, and another two were recorded near Letaba after a gale in January/February 1984. *Call.* 'Wick-a-wick'. *Afrikaans.* Roetsterretjie.

Arctic Skua *Stercorarius parasiticus* (307) 46 cm
A gull-like bird with very variable plumage: pale, dark and intermediate phases occur. It always shows white patches at base of the primaries and, if present, tail projections are pointed. *Status.* Has occurred once only, to the north of Orpen Gate after Cyclone Danae moved through the Park in January 1976. *Call.* Silent in our region. *Afrikaans.* Arktiese Roofmeeu.

Avocet

Blackwinged Stilt

Sooty Tern

Arctic Skua

Mourning Dove *Streptopelia decipiens* (353) 30 cm
Might be confused with the slightly smaller Cape Turtle Dove but has a grey head, a pale yellow eye encircled with bare red skin, and a bluish shoulder. Redeyed Dove is much larger, has a paler head, a dark red eye, and a dark tail without a white tip or white outer tail feathers. *Status.* This dove shows distinct affinities with man in the Park, and its distribution is limited almost entirely to certain restcamps. It is common in Shingwedzi, Letaba and Satara where it has become very tame. Occasionally recorded away from these restcamps and then usually in well-wooded areas. A breeding resident. *Call.* A soft, dove-like 'coooc-currr'. *Afrikaans.* Rooioogtortelduif.

Redeyed Dove *Streptopelia semitorquata* (352) 35 cm
By far the largest and darkest of the 'ringneck doves', with a black bar on the tip of the undertail, but lacking any white on tail tip or outer tail feathers as seen in the Mourning Dove and Cape Turtle Dove. At close range the dark red eye encircled by a thin red line of bare skin is visible. *Status.* Shows a marked preference for well-wooded areas, particularly riverine habitats with tall, broadleaved trees. Common also in most restcamps where its preferred habitat has been created by the planting of trees. A common breeding resident. *Call.* Alarm call is a 'chwaa'. Other calls are variable but a dove-like 'coo-coo, kook-co-co' is typical. *Afrikaans.* Grootringduif.

Cape Turtle Dove *Streptopelia capicola* (354) 28 cm
The smallest and palest of the 'ringneck doves', this species shows a dark brown eye without any bare skin encircling it. When seen in flight or display, it shows white outer tail feathers and a white tail tip. *Status.* A very common breeding resident throughout the Park. *Call.* A harsh 'kurrr' when alarmed, and the well-known dove call of Africa: 'kuk-cooo-kuk'. *Afrikaans.* Gewone Tortelduif.

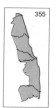

Laughing Dove *Streptopelia senegalensis* (355) 26 cm
Differs from the similarly coloured 'ringneck doves' by lacking the black bar on the hind neck and by having a pinkish breast freckled with black, and a pale blue forewing. In flight shows much more white in the tail than the larger Cape Turtle Dove and also an extensive blue forewing which contrasts with the cinnamon-coloured back. *Status.* A very common breeding resident found throughout the Park. *Call.* Common call is a distinctive rising and falling 'ooo-coooc-coooc-coo-coo'. *Afrikaans.* Rooiborsduifie.

Greenspotted Dove *Turtur chalcospilos* (358) 22 cm
A common, small dove which, when flushed, shows chestnut patches on the wings and two black bars on the lower back and rump. Distinguished from Bluespotted Dove at close range when the bill is seen to lack the red and yellow colouring, and wing spots show iridescent emerald green in direct sunlight. *Status.* A common and widespread breeding resident, easily seen throughout the Park. *Call.* One of the most characteristic calls of the bushveld: a series of low 'du-du-du-du' notes which descends in scale and quickens towards the end. *Afrikaans.* Groenvlekduifie.

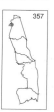

Bluespotted Dove *Turtur afer* (357) 22 cm
Not likely to be distinguished from Greenspotted Dove unless seen at close range when the red bill with its bright yellow tip is evident and, in direct sunlight, the iridescent blue spots on the wings. *Status.* Very rare in the Park, recorded only in the Punda Maria area. *Call.* A series of muffled 'du-du-du-du' call notes, similar to those of Greenspotted Dove. *Afrikaans.* Blouvlekduifie.

Mourning Dove

Redeyed Dove

Greenspotted Dove

Cape Turtle Dove

Laughing Dove

Bluespotted Dove

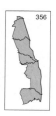

Namaqua Dove *Oena capensis* (356) 28 cm
The long, pointed tail (seen in all plumages) renders this diminutive dove unmistakable. Male has a black face, bib and breast, a bright red and yellow bill, and pale underparts which, combined with the long tail, render it unmistakable in flight. Female and imm. lack the black face and bib of the male, and while the tail is not as long, it is still noticeably pointed.
Status. Occurs erratically in the Park showing no seasonal pattern. Appears to favour well- or overgrazed areas though can occur anywhere. Breeding suspected. *Call.* A soft, low 'coooo-hoooo'. *Afrikaans.* Namakwaduifie.

Cinnamon Dove *Aplopelia larvata* (360) 26 cm
Very difficult to observe, as it keeps to the thicker tangles of bush in deep forest, and is seen most often when it virtually 'explodes' from the leaf litter to fly off at great speed. When seen feeding on the forest floor, the greyish face and throat, cinnamon-coloured breast, and dark back slightly bronzed with green will help to identify this furtive dove. *Status.* Favours forest and is thus very rare in the Park. Has been seen only in the Punda Maria/Pafuri region. *Call.* A low, somewhat raspy 'hooo-oooo' is given from dense thickets. *Afrikaans.* Kaneelduifie.

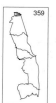

Tambourine Dove *Turtur tympanistria* (359) 22 cm
The white face and eyebrow stripe, and clear white underparts contrasting with the darker upperparts are diagnostic of this small dove. Most often seen when the bird breaks for cover, and in flight it shows the contrasting plumage and chestnut wing patches which make it easy to identify. *Status.* Associated with forest and thus restricted to forest-like riverine woodland in the Park. Common only at Pafuri, but has been recorded in similar habitats on the other larger rivers. *Call.* A series of 'du-du-du' notes similar to those of Greenspotted Dove but, instead of descending in scale, this call trails off at the end. *Afrikaans.* Witborsduifie.

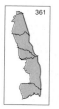

Green Pigeon *Treron calva* (361) 30 cm
The delicate green and grey coloration camouflages this pigeon in the leafy canopies it frequents and makes it very difficult to distinguish. When seen clambering around a fruiting tree, sometimes hanging upside down, it closely resembles a parrot. At close range the red and white bill, and pale eye can be seen, as well as the bright, almost sulphur-yellow trousers and underbelly, and the chestnut undertail. When a group feeding in a tree is disturbed, the birds 'explode' from the canopy with loud claps of the wings and fly off at great speed in different directions. *Status.* A common breeding resident found along all major rivers and their tributaries in the Park. A fruit-eating species (especially wild figs), and often common in trees bearing ripe fruit. Relatively tame and sometimes seen at close range in restcamps where such trees are present (such as in front of the restaurant at Skukuza). *Call.* A series of liquid whistles 'thweeeloo, tleeeoo'. *Afrikaans.* Papegaaiduif.

Rock Pigeon *Columba guinea* (349) 33 cm
The large, lozenge-shaped, bare red skin encircling the eyes is diagnostic. The back and wings are reddish-brown and finely speckled with white, and the remainder of the body is greyish with a chestnut wash across the breast. *Status.* Recorded from a few widely scattered localities, but very rare in the Park. May be resident on the cliffs and gorges of the Luvuvhu River but there are no breeding records. *Call.* A deep, booming 'hooo-hooo-hooo' and a softer 'coocoo-coocoo'. *Afrikaans.* Kransduif.

Namaqua Dove ♂

Namaqua Dove ♀

Cinnamon Dove

Tambourine Dove

Green Pigeon

Rock Pigeon

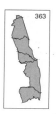

Brownheaded Parrot *Poicephalus cryptoxanthus* (363) 24 cm
Differs markedly from the Cape Parrot, being considerably smaller with a more greenish plumage and a brown head. Also, lacks any red on the shoulders and in flight shows conspicuous yellow underwings. Imm. is generally duller and has less vivid yellow underwings. *Status.* A common breeding resident found throughout the Park, and made conspicuous by its calls. *Call.* A typical parrot-like raucous shriek. *Afrikaans.* Bruinkoppapegaai.

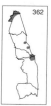

Cape Parrot *Poicephalus robustus* (362) 35 cm
Very much larger than Brownheaded Parrot and with conspicuous red shoulders. In flight shows a red leading edge to the wing and lacks the vivid yellow underwings of Brownheaded Parrot. A gregarious, noisy species sometimes occurring in large flocks which vocalize both when feeding and in flight. *Status.* A breeding resident restricted to the northern half of the Park. Occurs as far south as Bangu Mouth on the Olifants River and is reasonably common in the Pundu Maria/Pafuri area. *Call.* Various loud, harsh screeches and squawks. *Afrikaans.* Grootpapegaai.

Purplecrested Lourie *Tauraco porphyreolophus* (371) 46 cm
At a distance or in poor light may appear almost black, but when put to flight the brilliant vermilion patches towards the wing tips are conspicuous. The purple crest and iridescent purple and green on the face contrast with the bright red encircling the eyes. Will sit motionless in a tree until disturbed and then will leap from one branch to the next or take flight showing the diagnostic red wing patches. *Status.* A common breeding resident restricted mainly to the larger rivers which support better-developed riverine forests. *Call.* A loud 'kok-kok-kok-kok'. *Afrikaans.* Bloukuifloerie.

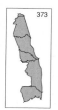

Grey Lourie *Corythaixoides concolor* (373) 48 cm
A very familiar bird of the bushveld and, with its call, one of the best-known species in the Park. Its overall grey appearance, long tail and rounded floppy wings seen in flight make it unmistakable. In silhouette and at a distance can appear very much like a giant mousebird. *Status.* A very common and conspicuous breeding resident. Occurs throughout though is less common in the mopane areas. *Call.* A harsh, nasal 'waaaay' or 'kay-waaaay' gives rise to its vernacular name of the 'go-away' bird. *Afrikaans.* Kwêvoël.

Burchell's Coucal *Centropus superciliosus* (391) 44 cm
An unmistakable large bird which has a dark glossy cap, creamy white underparts, a conspicuous chestnut back and wings, and a long floppy black tail. Imm. has a brown head, a noticeable white eyebrow stripe and white or buff flecking on the nape and hind neck. *Status.* A common breeding resident found throughout, mainly near water and watercourses. Conspicuous due to its habit of sunning itself on exposed branches. *Call.* A liquid bubbling 'doo-doo-doo-doo', descending in scale, then rising towards the end of the phrase. *Afrikaans.* Gewone Vleiloerie.

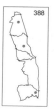

Black Coucal *Centropus bengalensis* (388) 35 cm
In breeding plumage is unmistakable with its all-black body contrasting markedly with chestnut back and wings. Non-breeding ad. and imm. might be confused with Burchell's Coucal but are noticeably smaller and lack the white eyebrow stripe. *Status.* An extremely rare and erratic vagrant to the Park, most likely to be seen in swampy or long-grass areas. *Call.* A typical bubbling coucal call and other 'poopoop' and 'cuik' notes. *Afrikaans.* Swartvleiloerie.

Brownheaded Parrot

Cape Parrot

Purplecrested Lourie

Grey Lourie

Burchell's Coucal

Black Coucal

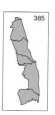

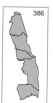

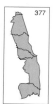

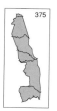

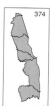

Klaas's Cuckoo *Chrysococcyx klaas* (385) 18 cm
In the Park only likely to be confused with Diederik Cuckoo but differs by being duller overall, having less white on the wings, and a dark brown eye with a less developed white eye-stripe. Female differs from female Diederik Cuckoo by the lack of white spotting on the wing and by having more extensive barring over the lower breast and flanks. Imm. differs from imm. Diederik Cuckoo by having a dark brown, not bright red bill. *Status.* Records throughout the year suggest that it may be resident in the Park but appears to be less common in winter. This may be due to the fact that it is mainly silent during this time. Breeds in the Park in summer. *Call.* A soft 'huee-jee' repeated five or six times. *Afrikaans.* Meitjie.

Diederik Cuckoo *Chrysococcyx caprius* (386) 18 cm
Distinguished from the less conspicuous Klaas's Cuckoo by having shinier bronzy-green plumage, a bright red eye and a much broader white eye-stripe extending well behind the eye. The white markings and spotting on the wings are more extensive than in Klaas's Cuckoo. Female differs from female Klaas's Cuckoo by being brighter, having a greater amount of white behind the eye and white spotting on the wings. Imm. has a bright red bill. *Status.* A common and conspicuous breeding summer visitor. Parasitizes the weavers mainly, and in particular the Lesser Masked and Spottedbacked weavers. *Call.* A clear, persistent 'dee-dee-deedereek'. *Afrikaans.* Diederikkie.

Redchested Cuckoo *Cuculus solitarius* (377) 30 cm
Differs from the similar European and African cuckoos by having very much darker upperparts and a diagnostic chestnut breast. Imm. is very different from ad., being black above and heavily barred black and white below. *Status.* A common summer visitor to the Park. A shy bird which is conspicuous only by call. Known to parasitize the wagtails, thrushes and robins. *Call.* The well-known trisyllabic 'weet-weet-weeeo'. *Afrikaans.* Piet-my-vrou.

African Cuckoo *Cuculus gularis* (375) 33 cm
Closely resembles European Cuckoo, and they are not easily distinguished. However, the African Cuckoo's call, heard during summer, is unmistakable, and at very close range it can be seen that the bill is yellow with a black tip, not mainly black as in the European Cuckoo. Female and imm. are barred with brown, rufous and black, and female is allegedly much greyer than female European Cuckoo. *Status.* Owing to the similarity of this species and the European Cuckoo, their exact status in the Park is uncertain. Appears to be a fairly common and widespread breeding summer visitor known to parasitize the Forktailed Drongo. *Call.* Similar to the Hoopoe's 'hoop-hoop' call. Female utters a fast 'kik-kik-kik'. *Afrikaans.* Afrikaanse Koekoek.

European Cuckoo *Cuculus canorus* (374) 33 cm
Not readily distinguished in the field from African Cuckoo except at very close range when the bill is seen to be black with only a trace of yellow at the base, not yellow with a black tip. Both species are common during summer but a bird seen in early summer showing a near-perfect plumage will almost certainly be the African Cuckoo as the European Cuckoo will show a very worn and heavily moulted plumage at this time after its long migration from the northern hemisphere. *Status.* As a result of the similarity of the African and European cuckoos, their status in the Park is uncertain. Appears to be a fairly common and widespread non-breeding summer visitor. *Call.* Silent in our region. *Afrikaans.* Europese Koekoek.

Klaas's Cuckoo ♂

Klaas's Cuckoo ♀

Diederik Cuckoo ♂

Diederik Cuckoo ♀

Redchested Cuckoo (ad.)

Redchested Cuckoo (imm.)

African Cuckoo

European Cuckoo

Thickbilled Cuckoo *Pachycoccyx audeberti* (383) 34 cm
Often mistaken for a small bird of prey because of its shape, grey upperparts and barred tail, but the clear, white underparts should distinguish it. Imm. might be confused with the larger Great Spotted Cuckoo because of the similar white spotting on the back, but it lacks a crest and its head and nape are flecked with white. Has a very upright stance when perched, unlike other large cuckoos which perch in a more horizontal pose, often with wings held slightly drooped. *Status.* A very rare summer visitor, recorded from only a few widely scattered localities. *Call.* A repeated 'chee-cher-cher' and a 'wee-yes-yes'. *Afrikaans.* Dikbekkoekoek.

Striped Cuckoo *Clamator levaillantii* (381) 38 cm
Very similar in most aspects to the smaller Jacobin Cuckoo but the distinct black striping on the throat and breast distinguishes it. Imm. is a browner version of ad. but also shows diagnostic striping on the throat which separates it from imm. Jacobin Cuckoo. Larger and more conspicuous than Jacobin Cuckoo, the Striped Cuckoo is also much more vocal and does not occur in a black phase in this part of Africa. *Status.* A fairly common and widespread breeding summer visitor. Parasitizes Arrowmarked Babbler. *Call.* A loud 'kleeo-kleeo-kleeo' and a faster 'che-che-che-che'. *Afrikaans.* Gestreepte Nuwejaarsvoël.

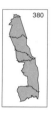

Great Spotted Cuckoo *Clamator glandarius* (380) 39 cm
A large, noisy cuckoo which is unmistakable with its long grey crest, creamy-buff throat, dark back liberally spotted with white, and long, white-tipped tail. Imm. is unlikely to be confused with any other cuckoo, showing creamy-buff underparts, a black cap and crest, conspicuous white spotting on the back, and chestnut patches in the wings. Imm. Thickbilled Cuckoo also shows a white-spotted back but has clear white underparts, a white-flecked crown and nape and lacks a black crest. *Status.* Uncommon, recorded widely but sparsely in the Park. A breeding summer visitor probably parasitizing mainly Burchell's Starling. *Call.* A loud 'keeeow-keeeow-keeeow' and a shorter, crow-like 'kark'. *Afrikaans.* Gevlekte Koekoek.

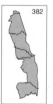

Jacobin Cuckoo *Clamator jacobinus* (382) 34 cm
Likely to be confused only with Striped Cuckoo but differs by being slightly smaller and having clear white underparts. A black form also occurs which might be mistaken for a Black Cuckoo but the noticeable crest and white patches in the wings distinguish it. Imm. is a browner version of ad. and has creamy-buff underparts. *Status.* Common and conspicuous breeding summer migrant to the Park, parasitizing a variety of species but probably mainly Blackeyed Bulbul and Goldenbreasted Bunting. *Call.* A frequently repeated 'klee-klee-kleeuu-kleeuu'. *Afrikaans.* Bontnuwejaarsvoël.

Black Cuckoo *Cuculus clamosus* (378) 30 cm
Often located by its diagnostic call, but when seen is easily identified by its all-black plumage and typical cuckoo shape. Might be mistaken for a black phase Jacobin Cuckoo but lacks the crest and white wing patches. Imm. has a brown cast to its plumage. When flushed sometimes shows a very swift and twisting flight action unlike other cuckoos. *Status.* Generally rare in the Park but more common in the south-west in the Pretoriuskop/Malelane area and in the extreme north around Punda Maria. A breeding summer migrant, probably parasitizing Boubou Shrikes. *Call.* A droning, mournful 'whoo-whee-whoo-whoo-whee' or a fast 'yow-yow-yow-yow'. *Afrikaans.* Swartkoekoek.

Thickbilled Cuckoo

Striped Cuckoo

Great Spotted Cuckoo

Jacobin Cuckoo

Black Cuckoo

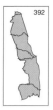

Barn Owl *Tyto alba* (392) 34 cm
In twilight hours could easily be confused with the similar Grass Owl but is paler and shows less contrast between the upper- and underparts. At close range this golden-buff and white owl with its white heart-shaped face and black eyes is unmistakable. *Status.* An uncommon breeding resident in the Park, recorded throughout the area though more often heard than seen. Nests in buildings in some of the restcamps and outstations, and also uses old Hamerkop nests. *Call.* Many and varied calls, the most usual being an eerie 'shreeee'. *Afrikaans.* Nonnetjie-uil.

Grass Owl *Tyto capensis* (393) 36 cm
Easily confused with Barn Owl which is similar in size and shape but distinguished in flight when the dark upperparts are seen to contrast more markedly with the pale underparts. At close range the heart-shaped face appears grey, not white and the underparts are darker and more heavily flecked than the Barn Owl's. *Status.* Probably resident (possibly on the grassy flats in the north-eastern parts of the Park) but there are no breeding records. *Call.* Normally silent but hisses loudly when disturbed at the nest. *Afrikaans.* Grasuil.

Pel's Fishing Owl *Scotopelia peli* (403) 63 cm
Unlikely to be confused with any other owl because of its large size and overall 'ginger' appearance. During daylight hours may be found roosting in the canopy of a tree when its round head and large, dark brown eyes are evident, as are the barring on its back and the streaking on its front. Imm. is similar to ad. in shape and also has a large rounded head and dark eyes but is very pale over the head, breast and underparts, and has a pale tawny back barred with dark brown to black. *Status.* This bird's habit of roosting in leafy tree canopies during the day makes it difficult for the regular visitor to observe. Fairly common only at Pafuri where it is a breeding resident. A few scattered records exist for the Letaba, Olifants and Sabie rivers, and the Olifants Trail offers reasonable opportunities of seeing it. *Call.* A deep, booming 'hoo-huuuum' and a jackal-like wailing. *Afrikaans.* Visuil.

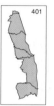

Spotted Eagle Owl *Bubo africanus* (401) 43-50 cm
Of the three large owls that occur in the Park this species is probably the most abundant and regularly seen. Two colour phases occur, one greyish and the other more rufous. Distinguished at rest by its large size, mottled black, buff and white plumage, very large yellow eyes and conspicuous 'ear' tufts. *Status.* A common and widespread breeding resident. As with other nocturnal birds, is difficult to observe in daylight but is often seen on the roads at night. *Call.* A loud, far-carrying 'huu-whooo'. *Afrikaans.* Gevlekte Ooruil.

Giant Eagle Owl *Bubo lacteus* (402) 60-65 cm
During daylight this enormous owl is unmistakable. It appears generally very grey and has dark, not yellow eyes. *Status.* A common and widespread breeding resident, though less common than the previous species. *Call.* A pig-like 'unnh-unnh-unnh' grunting. *Afrikaans.* Reuse Ooruil.

Barn Owl

Pel's Fishing Owl

Spotted Eagle Owl

Grass Owl

Giant Eagle Owl

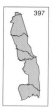

Whitefaced Owl *Otus leucotis* (397) 28 cm
A small owl identified by its white facial disc bordered by a narrow black line. Noticeably larger than Scops Owl, it has bright orange eyes and a generally grey-flecked plumage with conspicuous 'ear' tufts. *Status.* Very rare in the Park, recorded from widely scattered localities with no apparent pattern to its distribution. *Call.* A fast, hooting 'doo-doo-doo-doo-hohoo'. *Afrikaans.* Witwanguil.

Scops Owl *Otus senegalensis* (396) 20 cm
Only two small owls have conspicuous 'ear' tufts, this and the Whitefaced Owl. Confusion should not arise as Scops Owl is smaller and very much slimmer. Its plumage resembles dead bark and during the day when it presses its body against a tree trunk it is perfectly camouflaged. *Status.* A common breeding resident recorded throughout. On any night it can be heard giving its characteristic call almost anywhere in the Park. *Call.* A soft, croaking, frog-like 'prrrup-prrrup'. *Afrikaans.* Skopsuil.

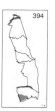

Wood Owl *Strix woodfordii* (394) 35 cm
Not likely to be confused with any other owl occurring in similar habitat. A medium-sized brown owl showing heavily barred, brown and buff underparts and a pale, finely barred facial disc with large dark brown eyes. The head is very rounded and lacks 'ear' tufts, and the plumage varies from dark to very dark brown and russet. *Status.* Rare in the Park; largely limited to riverine bush along the larger, permanent rivers. Common, however, along the Luvuvhu and Limpopo rivers at Pafuri where it is resident. *Call.* Close to the well-described 'tuwhit-towhoo' call but rendered as 'huoo-hoo-hoo', with the female's reply a higher-pitched 'weooo'. *Afrikaans.* Bosuil.

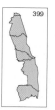

Barred Owl *Glaucidium capense* (399) 21 cm
Most likely to be confused with Pearlspotted Owl but is larger, has heavily barred upperparts with conspicuous white edging to the scapular feathers, and spotted underparts with obvious barring on the breast. Differs in shape from Pearlspotted Owl, being dumpier and having a more pronounced head. *Status.* Uncommon, occurring mainly in riverine vegetation and along well-wooded, dry watercourses. Apparently more common in the north. *Call.* A soft, frequently repeated 'kerrr-kerrr-kerrr' and a 'trru-trrre'. *Afrikaans.* Gebande Uil.

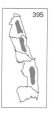

Marsh Owl *Asio capensis* (395) 36 cm
At rest appears fairly uniform dark brown with paler underparts. The small 'ear' tufts situated just above the dark brown eyes are hardly noticeable. In flight the contrast between upperparts and underparts is obvious as are the pale buff 'windows' in the primaries. *Status.* Uncommon in the Park, probably restricted to the rank grassy flats in the north-east. Breeds and is probably resident in the Park. *Call.* A harsh 'krikkk-krikkk'. *Afrikaans.* Vlei-uil.

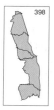

Pearlspotted Owl *Glaucidium perlatum* (398) 18 cm
This tiny owl may be seen during daylight hours, and is very easily identified by the greyish back which is heavily spotted with white, its spotted front and the considerable streaking on the flanks and breast. Differs from the Barred Owl by its smaller size, slightly longer tail, and lack of conspicuous barring on the back and throat. Shows two false 'eyes' on the back of the head. *Status.* A common and widespread breeding resident. *Call.* A series of 'tu-tu-tu-tu' whistles which rise in pitch and end in a clear 'wheeoo-wheeoo'. *Afrikaans.* Witkoluil.

Whitefaced Owl

Scops Owl

Wood Owl

Barred Owl

Marsh Owl

Pearlspotted Owl

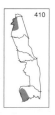

Pennantwinged Nightjar *Macrodipteryx vexillaria* (410) 28 cm
Breeding male is unmistakable having a broad white bar across the primaries and white elongated inner primaries which trail far behind the bird in display flight. The female is fairly nondescript and is distinguished from the similarly sized European Nightjar by its richer brown appearance. *Status.* Very rare throughout most of the Park but fairly common in the Punda Maria area. Also frequents the area around Pretoriuskop. *Call.* A soft piping note and bat-like squeaking. *Afrikaans.* Wimpelvlerknaguil.

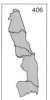

Rufouscheeked Nightjar *Caprimulgus rufigena* (406) 24 cm
Very difficult to distinguish from Fierynecked Nightjar except in that it has an orange-buff, not rufous collar, lacks rufous on the breast and is altogether more greyish. Female differs from female Fierynecked Nightjar by lacking any white tail spots. *Status.* A rare summer migrant to the Park, recorded from widely scattered localities. As with other nightjars can usually be identified only by its call. *Call.* A 'kow-kow-kow', a choking call note 'chukoo-chukoo', and a soft purring sound. *Afrikaans.* Rooiwangnaguil.

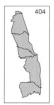

European Nightjar *Caprimulgus europaeus* (404) 25-28 cm
A large, chunky nightjar similar in size to Pennantwinged Nightjar but very much greyer overall. Females of these species are very difficult to separate unless seen resting when this species appears very much greyer. *Status.* A common non-breeding summer migrant. *Call.* Silent in our region. *Afrikaans.* Europese Naguil.

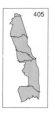

Fierynecked Nightjar *Caprimulgus pectoralis* (405) 24 cm
Almost identical to Rufouscheeked Nightjar at rest and in flight but differs by having a rich chestnut face which extends on to the nape to form a collar. Female is distinguished from female Rufouscheeked Nightjar by having off-white tips to the outer tail feathers. *Status.* The most common of the nightjars, recorded throughout the area. Also the most conspicuous nightjar because of its prolonged call, which is one of the characteristic sounds of the Park and by far the best way of identifying this species. A breeding resident. *Call.* A diagnostic whistled 'whue-whe-whe-whe-whe', the last notes faster and descending in pitch. *Afrikaans.* Afrikaanse Naguil.

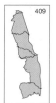

Mozambique Nightjar *Caprimulgus fossii* (409) 24 cm
In the Park probably the easiest nightjar to identify in flight, as the entire edge of its outer tail feathers is white. Female is similar to male except that the outer tail feathers are buff, not white. *Status.* A fairly common breeding resident. *Call.* A gurgling, churring sound. *Afrikaans.* Laeveldnaguil.

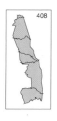

Freckled Nightjar *Caprimulgus tristigma* (408) 28 cm
The darkest nightjar of the region. At rest appears dark slate-grey with very fine barring overall and a little white showing on the throat. In flight resembles most other nightjars but the habitat from which it is flushed should identify it. *Status.* A locally common breeding resident which inhabits rocky outcrops. *Call.* A yapping 'kow-kow-kow-kow'. *Afrikaans.* Donkernaguil.

Pennantwinged Nightjar (br.♂)

Rufouscheeked Nightjar

European Nightjar

Fierynecked Nightjar

Mozambique Nightjar

Freckled Nightjar

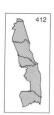

Black Swift *Apus barbatus* (412) 18 cm
This all-dark swift is extremely difficult to distinguish from the European Swift unless excellent viewing conditions prevail or, ideally, both birds are seen together in the air. Paler than European Swift, and the inner secondaries are slightly paler than the remaining wing and back and form a diagnostic pale panel in the wing. *Status.* Associated with cliffs; resident only in the cliffs at Lanner Gorge where it breeds. May occur anywhere in the Park out of its summer breeding season. *Call.* A high-pitched screaming at breeding sites. *Afrikaans.* Swartwindswael.

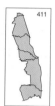

European Swift *Apus apus* (411) 17 cm
Almost impossible to distinguish from Black Swift unless seen under ideal viewing conditions. This species is a uniform dark brown, appearing black in the field, has no pale panel on the inner wings, and shows a smaller white area on the throat. Sometimes occurs in large numbers and does not often mix with flocks of the local Black Swift. *Status.* A non-breeding summer visitor from Europe with an uncertain status because of its similarity to the Black Swift. May occur anywhere in the Park. *Call.* Silent in Africa. *Afrikaans.* Europese Windswael.

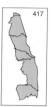

Little Swift *Apus affinis* (417) 14 cm
This is the smallest of the three black swifts that show white rumps, and it is easily identified by its large, square, white rump and square-ended tail. *Status.* A very common and highly gregarious breeding resident which occurs throughout the Park. Favours man-made constructions for nesting sites, particularly large structures such as bridges and high buildings. *Call.* Soft twittering and high-pitched screeching. *Afrikaans.* Kleinwindswael.

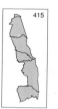

Whiterumped Swift *Apus caffer* (415) 15 cm
Resembles most closely the Horus Swift from which it differs by being more slender with a longer, more deeply forked tail and a small, U-shaped white rump. Mottled Spinetail vaguely resembles this species but shows a small area of white on the vent and, at close range, diagnostic mottling on the throat. *Status.* A very common breeding resident which occurs throughout the Park. It favours man-made constructions for nesting sites but, in contrast to Little Swift, selects smaller constructions such as culverts under tarred roads. Sometimes mixes with Little Swift at these sites. *Call.* Normally silent. *Afrikaans.* Witkruiswindswael.

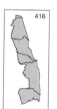

Horus Swift *Apus horus* (416) 16 cm
Very difficult to distinguish from Whiterumped Swift but is chunkier, has only a shallow fork in the tail which appears square-ended when closed, and shows a large expanse of white on the rump. More easily differentiated from Little Swift by its forked tail, although both species show a large white rump. *Status.* A locally common breeding resident. Breeds along the Luvuvhu, Olifants and Letaba rivers where it nests in holes tunnelled into sandbanks, in dongas and culverts, and, more particularly, in the rainwater ditches on the approach to the high-water bridge over the Letaba River, which is a good place to see them. *Call.* Normally silent. *Afrikaans.* Horuswindswael.

Black Swift

European Swift

Little Swift

Whiterumped Swift

Horus Swift

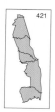

Palm Swift *Cypsiurus parvus* (421) 17 cm
A tiny swift, palest of all swifts seen in the Park and by far the most slender and streamlined. In flight the tail appears very long and pointed, but when spread is seen to be deeply forked. The wings are very long, narrow and widely swept back. Any small, very slender swift seen flying around palm trees is most certainly this species. *Status.* A very common breeding resident. It can be seen around any of the taller lala palms in the area, particularly in the Letaba and Shingwedzi restcamps. It has been recorded nesting on buildings in Skukuza. *Call.* A soft, high-pitched scream. *Afrikaans.* Palmwindswael.

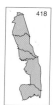

Alpine Swift *Apus melba* (418) 22 cm
This large swift might be mistaken at long range for either the smaller European or Black Swift, but the clearly visible white patch on the belly is diagnostic and distinguishes it. Frequently seen in company of other swifts. *Status.* An uncommon non-breeding vagrant, recorded throughout the Park all year round. *Call.* A loud trilling whistle. *Afrikaans.* Witpenswindswael.

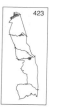

Böhm's Spinetail *Neafrapus boehmi* (423) 9 cm
A tiny swift, quite unlike any other swift in the Park and easily identified by its almost tailless appearance. The bird is very dark brown above with a white belly, vent and uppertail, and the fluttering, almost bat-like flight is diagnostic. Plumage coloration resembles that of Brownthroated Martin but the virtual lack of a tail and the peculiar flight action of Böhm's Spinetail distinguish it. *Status.* An uncommon breeding resident occurring only in the extreme north of the Park, although has been recorded a few times south of Pafuri at Shingwedzi and in the Olifants area. Careful 'skywatching' in the Pafuri area is nearly always rewarded with views of this bird. *Call.* Recorded as a high-pitched 'tri-tri-tri-peep'. *Afrikaans.* Witpensstekelstert.

Mottled Spinetail *Telacanthura ussheri* (422) 14 cm
May be confused with Little, Whiterumped or Horus swifts, all of which show white rumps but in this species the white extends on to the vent, and from below it shows a small, triangular, white patch at the base of the undertail. At close range and when the bird swoops low, the mottling and striping on the throat can be seen clearly. Any small, dark swift with a white rump seen flying in and out of baobab trees will be this species. *Status.* The northern part of the Park is the only locality where this and Böhm's Spinetail are likely to be seen in South Africa. An uncommon breeding resident using baobab trees for nesting sites. Baobabs close to the road in the Pafuri area should be scanned during summer as this species never strays far from its nest while breeding. Known to breed in the baobab to the east of the tarred road, one kilometre north of the bridge over the Luvuvhu River on the H1-9, and in the group of baobabs through which the S-64 cuts; also in a baobab in the Nyalaland Trails camp. *Call.* Recorded as a soft twittering and a 'zi-zick'. *Afrikaans.* Gevlekte Stekelstert.

Palm Swift

Alpine Swift

Böhm's Spinetail

Mottled Spinetail

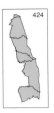

Speckled Mousebird *Colius striatus* (424) 35 cm
Darker and browner than Redfaced Mousebird, and differentiated by its blackish face and bicoloured bill which shows a white lower mandible and black upper mandible. Flight action is slow and floppy, and not sustained as in Redfaced Mousebird. Gregarious, moving in small groups which can be seen flying from bush to bush in a 'follow-my-leader' fashion. *Status.* Common breeding resident though less common and conspicuous than the Redfaced Mousebird. Tends to be confined to thick bush. *Call.* A harsh 'zhrrik-zhrrik'. *Afrikaans.* Gevlekte Muisvoël.

Redfaced Mousebird *Colius indicus* (426) 34 cm
A paler, more compact bird than Speckled Mousebird with a stronger, swifter flight. The red base to the bill and the red face, when seen, are diagnostic, and in flight the pale grey rump contrasts slightly with the browner back and tail. More common than Speckled Mousebird and conspicuous as it flies in flocks giving its characteristic call. *Status.* A common breeding resident. Utilizes open savanna as well as riverine habitats. *Call.* In flight a 'whee-whe-whe' is uttered, the first note being the highest. *Afrikaans.* Rooiwangmuisvoël.

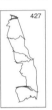

Narina Trogon *Apaloderma narina* (427) 34 cm
An unmistakable bird, very brightly coloured with crimson underparts offset by an iridescent green head, back and tail and a silvery-white undertail. Female and imm. are duller than male, having a pinkish throat and breast. A very furtive species and although brilliantly coloured can be difficult to detect in its leafy canopy. *Status.* A breeding resident at Pafuri only, and the best opportunities of seeing it are at the Pafuri picnic spot and in the Matjulu Valley in the Bushman's Trails area. A few records from the Sabie River suggest that it may be resident there in small numbers. It is extremely rare elsewhere in the Park. *Call.* A soft, owl-like 'hooo-hooo'. *Afrikaans.* Bosloerie.

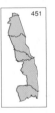

Hoopoe *Upupa epops* (451) 28 cm
The long decurved beak, black and white back, wings and tail, and cinnamon-coloured body render it unmistakable. When flushed the strikingly patterned wings and tail are noticeable, and when the bird alights it often raises its long, black-tipped crest. *Status.* A common and widespread breeding resident which has become very tame in the Park's restcamps. *Call.* A frequently uttered 'hoop-hoop-hoop'. *Afrikaans.* Hoephoep.

Scimitarbilled Woodhoopoe *Phoeniculus cyanomelas* (454) 26 cm
Smaller and more slender than Redbilled Woodhoopoe and with an all-black, not red bill which is noticeably decurved. Although imm. Redbilled Woodhoopoe also has a black bill it is almost straight, not decurved and the bird is much larger than this species. *Status.* A fairly common but unobtrusive breeding resident. Occurs throughout the Park. *Call.* A high-pitched whistling 'sweep-sweep-sweep' and harsher chattering. *Afrikaans.* Swartbekkakelaar.

Redbilled Woodhoopoe *Phoeniculus purpureus* (452) 36 cm
Likely to be confused only with the smaller Scimitarbilled Woodhoopoe but differs by having a red, not black bill which is not as decurved, and by its red legs and feet. Imm. has a black bill and may be mistaken for the Scimitarbilled Woodhoopoe but its much larger size and its short, less decurved bill distinguish it. *Status.* A common and conspicuous breeding resident which occurs throughout, favouring areas with large trees. *Call.* Harsh chattering and cackling calls, usually uttered by groups of birds. *Afrikaans.* Gewone Kakelaar.

Speckled Mousebird

Redfaced Mousebird

Narina Trogon

Hoopoe

Scimitarbilled Woodhoopoe

Redbilled Woodhoopoe

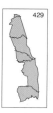

Giant Kingfisher *Ceryle maxima* (429) 46 cm

Size alone should render this kingfisher unmistakable. In the male the long powerful bill, shaggy crest, dark grey upperparts finely speckled with white, rufous breast and black and white barred belly are distinctive. The female has a blackish breast band and a dark rufous belly. *Status.* A common breeding resident found throughout the Park on all major rivers and dams. *Call.* A loud, harsh 'kahk-kah-kahk'. *Afrikaans.* Reuse Visvanger.

Halfcollared Kingfisher *Alcedo semitorquata* (430) 20 cm

The long black bill is diagnostic and this species could be mistaken only for imm. Malachite Kingfisher which also has a dark bill but which is smaller and lacks the turquoise crest of this species. *Status.* An uncommon breeding resident recorded at scattered points throughout the Park on the major water bodies. Most often seen on the Sabie River, particularly from the low-water bridge at Skukuza. *Call.* A high-pitched 'chreep' or softer 'peek-peek'. *Afrikaans.* Blouvisvanger.

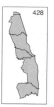

Pied Kingfisher *Ceryle rudis* (428) 28 cm

No other kingfisher in the Park shows the striking black and white plumage of this species. Male shows a double black breast band and female a single band. Imm. resembles female but shows black scaling on the underparts. Frequently hovers over open water before suddenly plunge-diving for food. *Status.* A very common breeding resident which can easily be seen on any of the Park's rivers and dams. *Call.* A rattling twitter and a sharp, high-pitched 'chik-chik'. *Afrikaans.* Bontvisvanger.

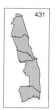

Malachite Kingfisher *Alcedo cristata* (431) 14 cm

Differs from the smaller Pygmy Kingfisher by having the blue-green on the crown extending to the eye. Imm. has a black bill and could be mistaken for the Halfcollared Kingfisher, but is smaller with paler underparts and lacks the blue half-collar of that species. *Status.* A fairly common but inconspicuous breeding resident occurring on the permanent water bodies throughout the area. Frequents fresh-water habitats and not the wooded or forest habitat of the Pygmy Kingfisher. *Call.* A high-pitched 'wheep-wheep' given in flight. *Afrikaans.* Kuifkopvisvanger.

Pygmy Kingfisher *Ispidina picta* (432) 13 cm

More often encountered away from water in forest or wooded habitat where the similar Malachite Kingfisher would not occur. Pygmy Kingfisher is also smaller than the Malachite Kingfisher, has mauve or lilac patches around the ear coverts and has the blue on the head restricted to the crown and not extending to the eye. *Status.* An uncommon and unobtrusive breeding summer migrant recorded throughout the Park. *Call.* A soft 'chip-chip' flight note. *Afrikaans.* Dwergvisvanger.

Giant Kingfisher ♀

Halfcollared Kingfisher

Pied Kingfisher ♀

Malachite Kingfisher

Pygmy Kingfisher

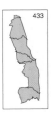

Woodland Kingfisher *Halcyon senegalensis* (433) 23 cm
A noticeably blue kingfisher with a diagnostic bi-coloured bill: red on the upper mandible, black on the lower. Often seen prominently perched on top of a tree where it delivers its song and flicks its wings, displaying the black and white underwing pattern. A small percentage of this species in the Park shows an all-red bill and might be confused with Mangrove Kingfisher. *Status.* A very common breeding summer migrant, conspicuous because of its striking colours and characteristic loud call. Occurs throughout the area, both near and far from water. *Call.* A loud, piercing 'trrp-trrrrrrrrr', the latter part descending. *Afrikaans.* Bosveldvisvanger.

Greyhooded Kingfisher *Halcyon leucocephala* (436) 20 cm
Another brightly coloured kingfisher which differs from the Woodland Kingfisher by having an all-red bill and from the Brownhooded Kingfisher by having a grey or pale grey head and a diagnostic chestnut belly. The colouring on the wings and tail is deep lilac or cobalt-blue and thus very different from the paler blue on both the Brownhooded and Woodland kingfishers. *Status.* A very uncommon breeding summer visitor recorded throughout the area. More common in some localities in some years. *Call.* A loud, whistling 'cheeo cheeo weecho-trrrr'. *Afrikaans.* Gryskopvisvanger.

Brownhooded Kingfisher *Halcyon albiventris* (435) 24 cm
The all-red bill might lead to confusion with the Greyhooded Kingfisher but the Brownhooded Kingfisher lacks the diagnostic chestnut belly of that species. The head is streaked with grey or brown and the chest has a faint chestnut wash and is lightly streaked with brown. The blue in the wings and tail is more noticeable when the bird is in flight. *Status.* A common resident found throughout the Park. *Call.* A whistled 'kee-kee-kee-kee' and a harsher alarm note 'klee-klee-klee'. *Afrikaans.* Bruinkopvisvanger.

Striped Kingfisher *Halcyon chelicuti* (437) 18 cm
A small, drab kingfisher with a lightly streaked breast and flanks. When perched shows a dark cap which is slightly streaked, a dark line running through the eye, and a pale collar. The bill has a black upper mandible and red lower mandible. The blue in the wings and tail only becomes apparent in flight or in display as the bird flicks and spreads its wings, when the black and white underwing pattern is also visible. *Status.* A generally uncommon but locally common breeding resident which can be seen anywhere in the area. An unobtrusive species except when calling which it often does communally, many others joining with the bird that began. *Call.* A high-pitched, piercing 'cheer-cherrrr', the last notes running rapidly together. *Afrikaans.* Gestreepte Visvanger.

124

Woodland Kingfisher

Greyhooded Kingfisher

Brownhooded Kingfisher

Striped Kingfisher

Little Bee-eater *Merops pusillus* (444) 17 cm
This tiny bee-eater is not likely to be confused with any other in the Park. Its overall green and yellow plumage, square-ended, dark-tipped tail and buffy yellow underparts make it easy to identify. In flight the bright russet underwings are conspicuous. *Status.* A fairly common breeding resident but a small and inconspicuous species. Found throughout the Park. *Call.* A 'zeet-zeet' or 'chip-chip'. *Afrikaans.* Kleinbyvreter.

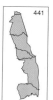

Carmine Bee-eater *Merops nubicoides* (441) 36 cm
This large bee-eater is unmistakable with its rose-red plumage, dark blue cap and undertail, and green rump. Imm. resembles ad. but is slightly paler and lacks the central tail projections. Occurs in small and sometimes large groups and is a common attendant at bush fires. *Status.* A common non-breeding summer migrant arriving in early to mid-December. Tends to be more common in the southern half of the Park than in the mopane areas. *Call.* A deep 'terk-terk'. *Afrikaans.* Rooiborsbyvreter.

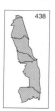

European Bee-eater *Merops apiaster* (438) 28 cm
The only bee-eater in the Park to show a chestnut back and upper wings. The underparts are bright turquoise blue and separated from the yellow throat by a black line. In flight shows almost translucent pale rufous wings and bright blue underparts. Often occurs in very large numbers, flying high in the air and calling continuously. *Status.* A common non-breeding summer migrant found throughout the Park. Arrives in early summer. *Call.* Far-carrying flight calls, 'prrrup' and 'krroop-kroop'. *Afrikaans.* Europese Byvreter.

Whitefronted Bee-eater *Merops bullockoides* (443) 24 cm
The combination of scarlet and white throat, pinkish breast, white forehead, green back and uppertail, and deep cobalt-blue undertail coverts renders this bee-eater unmistakable. *Status.* A locally common breeding resident. Occurs in small parties, almost always associated with rivers, and breeds in sandy river banks. Most common on the larger permanent rivers where alluvial soils constitute the river banks (particularly the Luvuvhu, Letaba and Olifants rivers). *Call.* A 'qrrruk, qrrruk' and twittering noises when roosting. *Afrikaans.* Rooikeelbyvreter.

Bluecheeked Bee-eater *Merops persicus* (440) 31 cm
Similar in size to European Bee-eater but differs by having long, pointed tail projections and a predominantly green plumage. At close range the reddish throat, black line though the eye, and bluish line above and below the eye are diagnostic. Imm. is dowdier than ad. and has shorter central tail projections. *Status.* An uncommon non-breeding summer visitor, usually associated with water. Recorded regularly only along the Limpopo River and thus inaccessible to most visitors. Has been recorded further south as far as Nwanetsi. *Call.* A liquid 'prrrup' and 'prrreo'. *Afrikaans.* Blouwangbyvreter.

Little Bee-eater

Carmine Bee-eater

European Bee-eater

Whitefronted Bee-eater

Bluecheeked Bee-eater

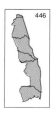

European Roller *Coracias garrulus* (446) 31 cm
More squat and bulkier than Lilacbreasted and Racket-tailed rollers but differs most notably by the lack of tail streamers. Differs from imm. Lilacbreasted and Racket-tailed rollers, which also lack noticeable tail streamers, by having a clear demarcating line between the blue head and chestnut back, and lacks the faint lilac wash across the breast seen in imm. Lilacbreasted Roller. *Status.* A very common non-breeding visitor arriving in midsummer, when it becomes the most abundant roller in the Park. *Call.* Normally silent in our region but when alarmed will give a 'krack-krack' call. *Afrikaans.* Europese Troupant.

Racket-tailed Roller *Coracias spatulata* (448) 36 cm
Often mistaken in the Park for a Lilacbreasted Roller but has a blue, not lilac breast, and tail streamers with spatulate tips. The tail streamers are lost in winter and it might then be confused with European Roller, but that species has a chestnut back and an all-blue head. Flight pattern differs from that of Lilacbreasted Roller by being more undulating, not direct or straight. *Status.* Very rare in the Park, but has been recorded throughout the year which suggests that it might be resident. Usually seen only in the Pafuri area but unconfirmed records exist from Olifants and Pretoriuskop. *Call.* Similar to that of Lilacbreasted Roller but higher pitched with more cackling. *Afrikaans.* Knopsterttroupant.

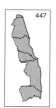

Lilacbreasted Roller *Coracias caudata* (447) 36 cm
A roller frequently seen in the Park. Its lilac breast and throat are diagnostic and are clearly visible when the bird is perched. Tail streamers lack the spatulate tips of the Racket-tailed Roller. Imm. lacks the long tail streamers of ad. and has a faint lilac wash across the breast which differentiates it from European Roller. *Status.* A very common and conspicuous breeding resident recorded throughout the Park. *Call.* Harsh squawks and screams when displaying. *Afrikaans.* Gewone Troupant.

Broadbilled Roller *Eurystomus glaucurus* (450) 27 cm
Not strikingly coloured when seen perched, appearing overall dark cinnamon with a diagnostic bright yellow bill. In flight resembles a small falcon but the blue outer tail feathers and lilac wing coverts will rule out any confusion. *Status.* A breeding summer migrant to the Park, fairly common in the Punda Maria/Pafuri area but less common further south except at Shingwedzi restcamp where it is also quite common. Recorded as far south as the Olifants River. *Call.* Harsh screams and cackles. *Afrikaans.* Geelbektroupant.

Purple Roller *Coracias naevia* (449) 38 cm
The largest of the rollers and the darkest in appearance. Diagnostic features include a pale yellow eyebrow stripe, lilac-brown underparts heavily streaked with white and, in flight, bright purple wing patches. *Status.* A fairly common breeding resident recorded throughout the area. Numbers may increase in summer due to population movements. *Call.* In display flight utters a 'karaa-karaa'. *Afrikaans.* Groottroupant.

European Roller

Racket-tailed Roller

Broadbilled Roller

Lilacbreasted Roller

Purple Roller

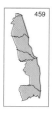

Southern Yellowbilled Hornbill *Tockus flavirostris* (459) 55 cm
Might be confused with the smaller Redbilled Hornbill but has a large, yellow, not red bill. Female Grey Hornbill has a partly yellow bill but differs by having an all-dark head and dark brown, not yellow eyes. Shows less conspicuous white spotting on primaries than Redbilled Hornbill. *Status.* A very common and widespread breeding resident. *Call.* A rapid, hollow-sounding 'tok tok tok tok tok toka toka toka'. *Afrikaans.* Geelbekneushoringvoël.

Crowned Hornbill *Tockus alboterminatus* (460) 54 cm
Considerably larger than Redbilled Hornbill and has a deeper-based, longer red bill and an all-dark head, neck and breast. Also, lacks conspicuous white spotting on the wings and back. Some birds show a variable amount of white flecking on the head which in some cases forms a distinct white eyebrow stripe. *Status.* Restricted to the larger well-wooded rivers of the Park where it is probably a breeding resident. Most common on the Luvuvhu River at Pafuri and on the Sabie River around Skukuza. *Call.* A whistling 'chleeoo chleeoo'. *Afrikaans.* Gekroonde Neushoringvoël.

Redbilled Hornbill *Tockus erythrorhynchus* (458) 46 cm
Smaller than Southern Yellowbilled Hornbill and has a shorter red, not yellow bill. Differs from the much larger Crowned Hornbill which also has a red bill by having conspicuous white spotting on the back, wings and primaries. *Status.* A locally very common breeding resident, associated with game concentrations and overgrazed conditions. Occurs throughout the Park. *Call.* A series of rapid 'wha wha wha wha wha' calls followed by a 'kukwe kukwe' note. *Afrikaans.* Rooibekneushoringvoël.

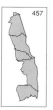

Grey Hornbill *Tockus nasutus* (457) 46 cm
A small grey and brown hornbill which has a dark bill and a conspicuous white eyebrow stripe. Male has a black and white bill and female a maroon and cream bill. Flight action is very floppy and buoyant. *Status.* A common to very common breeding resident which occurs throughout the Park. *Call.* A soft, plaintive whistling 'phee pheeoo phee pheeoo'. *Afrikaans.* Grysneushoringvoël.

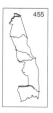

Trumpeter Hornbill *Bycanistes bucinator* (455) 58-65 cm
A noisy hornbill, its wailing cry carrying over long distances. Larger than Crowned Hornbill and has a much bigger, dark, not red, beak. Male has a conspicuous casque on the upper mandible. In flight the wings make a loud whooshing noise and the black and white wing and body pattern is distinctive. *Status.* A locally common breeding resident. Feeds mainly on wild figs and is thus restricted to the larger rivers in areas with well-developed riverine habitats. Particularly common at Pafuri where it is easily located by its call. *Call.* A wailing, infantile 'waaaaa-weeeee-waaaaa'. *Afrikaans.* Gewone Boskraai.

Southern Yellowbilled Hornbill

Crowned Hornbill

Redbilled Hornbill

Grey Hornbill ♂

Trumpeter Hornbill ♂

Goldenrumped Tinker Barbet *Pogoniulus bilineatus* (471) 10 cm
A tiny barbet, easily recognized by the diagnostic black and white head striping and the uniform, pale buff or yellow underparts. The small yellow rump is diagnostic but is not easily seen in the field. The larger Acacia Pied Barbet also shows black and white head striping but has a conspicuous red forehead. *Status.* A very rare and localized breeding resident, recorded only on the Crocodile River around Crocodile Bridge. The restcamp and Bushman painting site just to the west of this camp offer the only realistic opportunity of seeing this bird in the Park. *Call.* A ringing 'doo-doo-doo-doo', repeated in phrases of four to six, not continuously. *Afrikaans.* Swartblestinker.

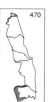

Yellowfronted Tinker Barbet *Pogoniulus chrysoconus* (470) 11 cm
May be confused with Goldenrumped Tinker Barbet but lacks the bold black and white head striping and has an inconspicuous yellow forehead and a black and white patterned, not uniform black back. *Status.* A very rare resident in the Park being only reasonably common in the higher-lying areas around Pretoriuskop where it can usually be located by its characteristic monotonous call. *Call.* A continuous ringing 'konk-konk-konk'. *Afrikaans.* Geelblestinker.

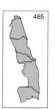

Acacia Pied Barbet *Lybius leucomelas* (465) 18 cm
Larger than the tinker barbets but smaller than the other barbets in the Park. At a distance the plumage appears mainly black and white but at closer range the bright yellow flecking on the back and wings and the distinctive red and yellow forehead are visible. The broad white eyebrow stripe and small black bib should distinguish it from the similar tinker barbets. *Status.* A generally uncommon but locally common breeding resident occurring throughout the Park. *Call.* A nasal 'nehh-nehh' and a deep 'doh-doh-doh'. *Afrikaans.* Bonthoutkapper.

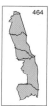

Blackcollared Barbet *Lybius torquatus* (464) 20 cm
This chunky, short-tailed barbet is quite unmistakable with its bright red face and throat, broadly bordered with black. It also shows a greenish panel in the wing. A rare variant has the red on the face replaced with bright yellow. *Status.* A common and widespread breeding resident, though rare in the areas of shrub mopane. *Call.* A far-carrying duet in which a pair sits side by side, displaying in a bobbing motion, and calls 'tooo-puudly, tooo-puudly' with the 'tooo' being higher pitched. *Afrikaans.* Rooikophoutkapper.

Crested Barbet *Trachyphonus vaillantii* (473) 23 cm
The largest of the barbets and easily recognized by its yellow and black plumage, shaggy crest and broad black breast band. Spends a lot of time on the ground feeding, but frequently sits on an exposed perch giving its trilling call. *Status.* A common and widespread breeding resident, seen in most restcamps where it has become very tame. *Call.* A sustained trilling 'trrrrrr ...'. *Afrikaans.* Kuifkophoutkapper.

Goldenrumped Tinker Barbet

Yellowfronted Tinker Barbet

Acacia Pied Barbet

Blackcollared Barbet

Crested Barbet

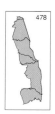

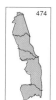

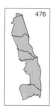

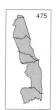

Sharpbilled Honeyguide *Prodotiscus regulus* (478) 13 cm
This small bird is more like a flycatcher in appearance than a honeyguide, and might be confused with the Dusky Flycatcher (p.178) but lacks dappling on the breast and in flight shows clear white outer tail feathers. When perched shows a clear white throat which contrasts with the grey wash across the breast and belly. From below the tail appears white. In display flight, when the birds chase each other above the woodland canopy, the white outer tail feathers and small white patch at the base of the rump are visible. *Status.* Seemingly rare but because of its nondescript appearance may be more common than suspected. *Call.* A soft, thin 'tseep' or a tinkling 'trrrrr'.
Afrikaans. Skerpbekheuningvoël.

Greater Honeyguide *Indicator indicator* (474) 20 cm
The male of this, the largest honeyguide, is easily identified by its dark crown, black throat which contrasts with the white ear coverts, and bright pink bill. Female lacks diagnostic head pattern of male and might be confused with Scalythroated Honeyguide but has a clear, not spotted breast. Imm. has a yellowish wash across the breast and, like ad., has conspicuous white outer tail feathers and a white rump. *Status.* An uncommon breeding resident occurring throughout the Park. Inconspicuous except when calling.
Call. A 'whit-purr, whit-purr' note or, when agitated, a harsh rattling chatter.
Afrikaans. Grootheuningwyser.

Lesser Honeyguide *Indicator minor* (476) 15 cm
Larger than Sharpbilled Honeyguide and has a noticeably thicker, heavier bill, black moustachial stripes and a greenish wash across the wings. Smaller than Greater Honeyguide and lacks both the diagnostic head pattern of the male of that species, and the white rump. Has a persistent call and, in display flight, one bird chases the other. *Status.* An uncommon and inconspicuous species occurring throughout the Park; probably a breeding resident. Recorded most often at Pafuri. *Call.* Emits a far-carrying 'klew klew' from a regular call-site in a leafy canopy. *Afrikaans.* Kleinheuningwyser.

Scalythroated Honeyguide *Indicator variegatus* (475) 19 cm
The most furtive of the honeyguides and more often heard than seen. If its song post is located then the bird can be viewed at virtually any time of the year. When seen, the dappled or scaled effect created by the mottling on the throat and breast are diagnostic and should rule out confusion with any other honeyguide. *Status.* A rare vagrant to the Park. Inconspicuous except when calling. *Call.* A difficult to locate, ventriloquistic 'trrrrrr' is given from a concealed call-site, usually high in a tall tree. *Afrikaans.* Gevlekte Heuningwyser.

Sharpbilled Honeyguide

Greater Honeyguide ♂

Lesser Honeyguide

Scalythroated Honeyguide

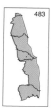

Goldentailed Woodpecker *Campethera abingoni* (483) 23 cm
The distinctive wailing call is normally the first indication of the bird's presence. Differs from the much smaller Cardinal Woodpecker by having a spotted, not barred back and by the noticeable moustachial stripes which are red in the male and black in the female. The male's crown is predominantly red but is flecked with black on the forehead. *Status.* Probably the most common woodpecker in the Park. A widespread breeding resident recorded throughout. *Call.* A loud nasal 'wheeeeeaa' shriek. *Afrikaans.* Goudstertspeg.

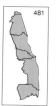

Bennett's Woodpecker *Campethera bennettii* (481) 24 cm
Most likely to be confused with Goldentailed Woodpecker in that male shows red moustachial stripes and a red crown, but has distinct spotting not streaking on the breast. Female is instantly recognizable by the dark line below the eye and the conspicuous dark brown throat. *Status.* An uncommon breeding resident. Well established in the Satara and Shingwedzi restcamps where it has become very tame and is easily located by its characteristic call. *Call.* A high-pitched, chattering 'whirrr-trrr-whrrr-itt' often uttered in duet. *Afrikaans.* Bennettse Speg.

Bearded Woodpecker *Thripias namaquus* (487) 25 cm
A large woodpecker immediately recognizable by the black and white head striping in both sexes. The male also displays a red nape. Unlike other woodpeckers, the underparts appear uniformly dark but at closer range can be seen to be finely barred grey and white. *Status.* A common breeding resident occurring throughout the Park. *Call.* Extremely loud wood tapping. A loud 'kweek-eek-eek-eek' is given. *Afrikaans.* Baardspeg.

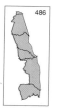

Cardinal Woodpecker *Dendropicos fuscescens* (486) 15 cm
Similar to the much larger Goldentailed Woodpecker also having yellow tail shafts but differs by having a barred, not spotted back, and lacks red moustachial stripes. Male habitually drums on dead branches in trees. *Status.* A common and widespread breeding resident occurring throughout the area. *Call.* Taps wood very rapidly and quietly. A high-pitched 'krrrek krrrek krrrek' shriek is uttered. *Afrikaans.* Kardinaalspeg.

Redthroated Wryneck *Jynx ruficollis* (489) 19 cm
The heavily patterned upperparts, mottled brown and flecked with chestnut and black, should eliminate confusion with any woodpecker. At a distance the chestnut throat and breast can appear black. It shows jerky movements, similar to those of a woodpecker, as it creeps around branches and tree trunks. *Status.* Recorded twice at Numbi Gate. *Call.* A loud, piercing 'kwik-kwik-kwik'. *Afrikaans.* Draaihals.

136

Goldentailed Woodpecker ♂

Bearded Woodpecker ♂

Cardinal Woodpecker ♂

Bennett's Woodpecker ♂

Redthroated Wryneck

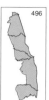

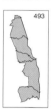

Sabota Lark *Mirafra sabota* (498) 15 cm
A small, streaked lark which regularly perches on the tops of bushes and utters its short song. Closer inspection shows it to have a fairly robust, thick-based bill, and a straight, prominent white eyebrow stripe which appears to run directly from the base of the bill to the nape. The underparts are off-white to creamy with a 'necklace' of streaking and spotting across the breast. In flight the tail appears very dark and there are no contrasting white outer tail feathers. *Status.* A very common breeding resident occurring throughout the Park. The most common and widely distributed lark in the area. *Call.* A jumbled song of rich 'chips' and twitterings. Mimics other birds. *Afrikaans.* Sabotalewerik.

Flappet Lark *Mirafra rufocinnamomea* (496) 15 cm
After the rains during summer this lark is unmistakable as it performs its display flight. Flying high over its bushveld territory, it flaps its wings creating a muffled clapping sound every few seconds. Rarely seen on the ground and generally very furtive, but when viewed shows cryptically patterned upperparts. In flight it shows rufous wing patches. *Status.* A fairly common breeding resident occurring throughout the Park, particularly in grassveld areas. *Call.* A short 'tuee' call given when perched. During display flight wings are rattled in a series of short bursts. *Afrikaans.* Laeveldklappertjie.

Monotonous Lark *Mirafra passerina* (493) 14 cm
Conspicuous only after rains, when it freely perches on the tops of small bushes or performs short aerial display flights, continuously giving its short call. This species might be confused with Sabota Lark, which has a similar habit of perching on bush tops, but shows much less streaking on the underparts, lacks the diagnostic white eyebrow stripe, and has a conspicuous white throat which contrasts with the off-white underparts. *Status.* Seasonal; locally abundant in grassveld or open bushveld habitats. *Call.* A frequently repeated 'trrp-chup-chip-choop', during the day and at night. *Afrikaans.* Bosveldlewerik.

Fawncoloured Lark *Mirafra africanoides* (497) 14 cm
Distinguished from Sabota Lark by its more buff- or fawn-coloured plumage with heavily patterned upperparts and white underparts which are only lightly streaked across the breast. In addition to the eyebrow stripe, it has a creamy-buff stripe running below the eye which Sabota Lark lacks. Differs from Monotonous Lark by having a streaked breast and by the lack of the very white throat seen in that species. *Status.* Restricted to very sandy areas and is known to be resident in the Nwambiya Sandveld which is inaccessible to the general tourist. *Call.* A jumble of harsh 'chips' and twitterings, ending in a buzzy slur, given when perched in a bush top or during the short, fluttering display flight. *Afrikaans.* Vaalbruinlewerik.

Redcapped Lark *Calandrella cinerea* (507) 16 cm
Instantly recognizable by its chestnut cap bordered by a creamy-white eyebrow stripe and by the chestnut shoulder patches. Unlike most other larks the underparts are uniform off-white and lack any streaking. In flight shows a rather longish tail with white to off-white outer tail feathers. *Status.* Prefers open or overgrazed areas and its occurrence in the Park appears to be dependent on the availability of such habitat. Localities favoured are Middelvlei Windmill north of Letaba and Roodewal on the Timbavati River. *Call.* A sparrow-like 'tchweerp' given in flight. Song is a sustained jumble of melodious phrases given during display flight. *Afrikaans.* Rooikoplewerik.

Sabota Lark

Flappet Lark

Monotonous Lark

Fawncoloured Lark

Redcapped Lark

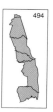

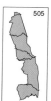

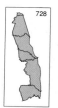

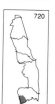

Rufousnaped Lark *Mirafra africana* (494) 18 cm
A fairly large lark which will sit on a prominent perch such as the top of a bush or termite mound and deliver its simple whistled song, occasionally flicking its wings immediately after the song. Also performs an aerial display flight, circling above its territory before parachuting down to land either on the ground or on its exposed perch. The rufous nape is not always visible unless the crest is erect. Like many other larks shows large chestnut wing patches in flight. *Status.* A fairly uncommon breeding resident which prefers open areas in grassveld, and is thus more common in the eastern half of the Park. Good localities for viewing are the Middelvlei Windmill and Kondlanjovo Plain, both to the north of Letaba. *Call.* A frequently repeated 'treelee-treelooe', given when perched. In display flight gives a jumbled mixture of imitated calls. *Afrikaans.* Rooineklewerik.

Dusky Lark *Pinarocorys nigricans* (505) 19 cm
The bold spotting on the breast and the white and black facial marks of this lark are reminiscent of the Groundscraper Thrush (p.156). It can however be distinguished by its smaller size and peculiar habit of raising its wings to slightly above body level when walking, so displaying its bold black and white underwing pattern. *Status.* A non-breeding summer visitor, usually uncommon but occasionally locally common. May occur throughout the area. *Call.* When flushed it utters a soft 'chrrp, chrrp'. *Afrikaans.* Donkerlewerik.

Chestnutbacked Finchlark *Eremopterix leucotis* (515) 12 cm
Male is unmistakable, showing a combination of a black head, white beak, white ear patches and nape, a bright chestnut back, and black underparts. Female and imm. lack the black and white patterned head of male and have dark brown to black, mottled underparts but still show the distinct chestnut back. *Status.* A fairly uncommon breeding resident which prefers open and overgrazed areas in grassveld, and thus occurs more frequently in the eastern half of the Park. More common in dry years. *Call.* Flocks in flight utter a short 'chip-chwep'. *Afrikaans.* Rooiruglewerik.

Yellowthroated Longclaw *Macronyx croceus* (728) 20 cm
The only bird in the Park to show vivid yellow underparts with a broad black breast band. It is a plump, short-tailed bird which, when viewed from behind, appears somewhat like a pipit but is much larger and when flushed shows a fanned tail with white spots on its tip. Regularly sits in the tops of bushes to sing. *Status.* A fairly common breeding resident which occurs throughout the Park in suitable habitat. Prefers long grass, particularly in low-lying areas where temporary vleis form in the rainy season. *Call.* A loud, whistled 'phooooeeet'. *Afrikaans.* Geelkeelkalkoentjie.

Striped Pipit *Anthus lineiventris* (720) 18 cm
The habitat preference of this pipit – boulder-strewn wooded hillsides – will aid identification. More boldly striped on the underparts than similar pipits and at close range a yellow wash edging the wing coverts and secondary feathers is visible. Forages on the ground but when disturbed will fly up into a tree and may be seen running along the thicker branches. *Status.* Very rare in the Park with an uncertain status. Prefers hilly areas and is thus more likely to be encountered in the south-west around Berg-en-dal. *Call.* An extremely loud, penetrating thrush-like song. *Afrikaans.* Gestreepte Koester.

Rufousnaped Lark

Dusky Lark

Chestnutbacked Finchlark ♂

Yellowthroated Longclaw

Striped Pipit

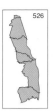

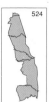

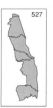

Greater Striped Swallow *Hirundo cucullata* (526) 20 cm
Far larger than the Lesser Striped Swallow and is much paler with the very fine streaking on the white breast and belly discernible only at close range. The rufous colouring on the crown and rump are paler than in Lesser Striped Swallow and there is no rufous on the vent. *Status.* A very rare summer migrant. *Call.* A twittering 'chissick'. *Afrikaans.* Grootstreepswael.

Redbreasted Swallow *Hirundo semirufa* (524) 24 cm
Might be confused with the similar but more robustly built Mosque Swallow, but differs by having rufous underparts, and a rufous throat and breast. The dark cap extends to below and behind the eye. In flight can be told from Mosque Swallow by having russet, not white wing linings. Imm. is much paler below than ad. but still can be told from Mosque Swallow by the darker headed appearance and the buffy, not white wing linings. *Status.* A fairly common breeding summer migrant found mainly in the south. Favours culverts under roads in the Park for nesting, and so the building of these may have influenced its numbers in the area. Easily observed at such culverts. *Call.* A soft warbling song. Twittering notes are uttered in flight. *Afrikaans.* Rooiborsswael.

Lesser Striped Swallow *Hirundo abyssinica* (527) 16 cm
Smaller, with a more compact body than Greater Striped Swallow's and easily distinguished by the very bold streaking on the breast which is noticeable from a distance. Further differs by having rich chestnut on the crown, nape and rump which, unlike the Greater Striped Swallow, extends on to the vent as a small rufous patch. *Status.* A common breeding resident; less common in winter which suggests that there is some movement out of the area. Breeds on buildings in the Park and is thus easily observed in the restcamps. *Call.* A descending series of squeaky, nasal 'zeh-zeh-zeh-zeh' notes. *Afrikaans.* Kleinstreepswael.

Mosque Swallow *Hirundo senegalensis* (525) 24 cm
Superficially resembles the more slightly built Redbreasted Swallow but differs in having much paler underparts and a clear white throat. Also, the dark cap does not extend below or behind the eye. In flight has a much paler appearance than Redbreasted Swallow and shows distinctive white, not rufous wing linings. *Status.* The Park offers almost the only chance of seeing this species in South Africa. A breeding resident confined mainly to the northern areas, it nests in holes in trees, favouring baobabs and large leadwoods, and may be seen around most large baobabs in summer when it breeds. One pair breeds in a large fig tree at the low-water bridge at Shingwedzi and is easily observed there. *Call.* A nasal 'harrrp', as well as a guttural chuckling. *Afrikaans.* Moskeeswael.

Greater Striped Swallow

Redbreasted Swallow

Lesser Striped Swallow

Mosque Swallow

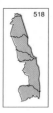

European Swallow *Hirundo rustica* (518) 18 cm
From a distance the dark head, white belly and deeply forked tail characterize
the ad. At close range the forehead and throat are seen to be brick red and
the throat is bordered by a black band. Imm. is paler red on forehead and
throat, and has much shorter tail streamers. In some birds the white breast and
belly are tinged with orange. *Status.* An abundant non-breeding summer visitor
occurring throughout the Park. *Call.* A soft, high-pitched twittering.
Afrikaans. Europese Swael.

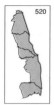

Whitethroated Swallow *Hirundo albigularis* (520) 17 cm
Unlikely to be confused with any other swallow in the Park. Has a bright white
throat, a black breast band and the remaining underparts grey, enhancing the
white throat. At close range a small, brick-red patch is noticeable on the
forehead. Although Banded Martin and Sand Martin (p.146) show a similar
breast band, both are predominantly brown, not glossy blue-black birds.
Status. A very rare summer visitor to the Park. *Call.* Soft warbles and twitters.
Afrikaans. Witkeelswael.

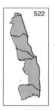

Wiretailed Swallow *Hirundo smithii* (522) 13 cm
Might be mistaken for the larger Whitethroated Swallow but differs by having
an incomplete black breast band and a bright chestnut cap. Also, the
underparts show a black line encircling the vent. The extremely thin tail
streamers are difficult to see at any distance. This tiny swallow is very rapid
in flight, performing twists and turns in its chase after aerial insects.
Status. A common breeding resident. Favours man-made structures for nest-
building sites and is therefore easily seen in restcamps and at bridges and
walls. *Call.* A sharp, metallic 'tchik'. *Afrikaans.* Draadstertswael.

Greyrumped Swallow *Hirundo griseopyga* (531) 14 cm
Often overlooked in mixed flocks of feeding swallows. If seen, the grey rump is
diagnostic although it does not contrast strongly with the blue back and tail.
The top of the head is greyish-brown but may appear black and is not a
reliable field character. In flight it may be mistaken for a House Martin (p.146)
but has a more deeply forked tail and, in reasonable viewing conditions, the
grey, not white rump can be seen. *Status.* A breeding resident seen regularly
only along the Olifants and Letaba rivers. Breeds in winter in holes in sandy
alluvial soils along the river banks. *Call.* Flight call recorded as 'chraa'.
Afrikaans. Gryskruisswael.

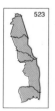

Pearlbreasted Swallow *Hirundo dimidiata* (523) 14 cm
A small, unobtrusive swallow usually seen singly or in pairs and easily
identified by the combination of pure white underparts and dark blue-black
upperparts. The only swallow to lack white spots in the tail. Might be confused
with the similar Wiretailed Swallow but lacks the chestnut cap and long tail
streamers of that species. In overhead flight differs from both the Greyrumped
Swallow and House Martin (p.146) by having white, not dark wing linings.
Status. A rare resident occurring throughout the area. *Call.* Silent.
Afrikaans. Pêrelborsswael.

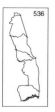

Black Saw-wing Swallow *Psalidoprocne holomelas* (536) 15 cm
An unmistakable small, all-black swallow. The tail is deeply forked and the
outer tail streamers seem to curve outwards. The flight is very erratic, with
twists and glides over woodland habitat. *Status.* Recorded only along the
Crocodile River. *Call.* A soft 'chrrp' alarm call. *Afrikaans.* Swartsaagvlerkswael.

European Swallow

Whitethroated Swallow

Wiretailed Swallow

Greyrumped Swallow

Pearlbreasted Swallow

Black Saw-wing Swallow

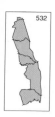

Sand Martin *Riparia riparia* (532) 12 cm
Noticeably larger than Brownthroated Martin from which it also differs by having pale underparts and a brown breast band. It might be confused with the larger Banded Martin but shows dark, not pale wing linings, a dark, not white forehead and has a more noticeably forked tail. *Status.* A very uncommon, non-breeding summer migrant recorded at scattered points throughout the Park. *Call.* Normally silent in Africa. *Afrikaans.* Europese Oewerswael.

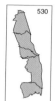

House Martin *Delichon urbica* (530) 14 cm
Easily recognized by its contrasting white rump and dark blue-black upperparts and tail. The diagnostic white feathered legs can be seen at close range when the bird is perched. Imm. has an off-white rump and might be confused with Greyrumped Swallow (p.144) but differs by having a shallow, not deeply forked tail. *Status.* A non-breeding summer migrant to the Park. Fairly uncommon but may be recorded in large flocks anywhere in the Park. *Call.* A single 'chirrp'. *Afrikaans.* Huisswael.

Banded Martin *Riparia cincta* (534) 17 cm
This large, brown and white swallow-like bird differs from the much smaller Brownthroated Martin by having white underparts with a distinct breast band and a small white spot on the forehead. Hunts insects on the wing, flying very low over the ground and regularly perching on fence wires. *Status.* A very rare migrant to the area occurring mainly in summer. *Call.* Flight call is a 'che-che-che'. Song is a jumble of harsh 'chip-choops' and more melodious warbles. *Afrikaans.* Gebande Oewerswael.

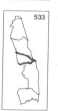

Brownthroated Martin *Riparia paludicola* (533) 12 cm
Very small in comparison to other martins and swallows, and occurs in both a pale and a dark form. The dark form is distinguished from the similar Rock Martin by its smaller size and lack of white tail spots. The pale form is uniform brown apart from a small area of white on the belly and vent.
Status. Apparently a winter visitor which breeds in holes in sandy alluvial soil along the banks of the Olifants and Letaba rivers. It can usually be seen at the sandbanks in front of the restaurant at the Letaba restcamp.
Call. Soft twittering. *Afrikaans.* Afrikaanse Oewerswael.

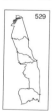

Rock Martin *Hirundo fuligula* (529) 15 cm
An all-brown swallow-like bird with a slightly forked tail which when spread shows white tail spots. Might be confused with the all-brown form of Brownthroated Martin but is much larger, has a pale throat, underparts which contrast with the slightly darker upperparts, and has white tail spots which the Brownthroated Martin lacks. *Status.* Associated with cliffs where it breeds. It is resident in the Park only at Lanner Gorge in the extreme north and possibly also in the Olifants Gorge. *Call.* Soft, indistinct twitterings. *Afrikaans.* Kransswael.

Sand Martin

House Martin

Banded Martin

Brownthroated Martin

Rock Martin

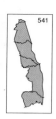

Forktailed Drongo *Dicrurus adsimilis* (541) 25 cm
An all-black bird with a deeply forked tail. In flight appears to have white on the wing tips but this is a reflection of its grey under primaries. Black Flycatcher is similar but has a very shallowly forked tail and at close range its brown, not red eye can be seen. Sits on an exposed perch from where it hawks insects and chases large birds of prey. *Status.* A common and conspicuous breeding resident occurring throughout the Park. *Call.* Mimicry and harsh 'tchwaak tchweeek' notes. *Afrikaans.* Mikstertbyvanger.

Black Flycatcher *Melaenornis pammelaina* (694) 22 cm
May be confused with a Forktailed Drongo in moult when that species' distinctly forked tail is not evident. Black Flycatcher is distinguished by its typical flycatcher shape and proportions, and by its dark brown, not red eye. Much less conspicuous than Forktailed Drongo, being quieter and preferring to feed from the mid-canopy rather than sitting high up and exposed in trees. *Status.* A fairly common breeding resident occurring throughout the Park. Appears to favour thornveld but can also be seen at many of the restcamps. *Call.* Song is a 'tzzit-terra-loora-loo'. *Afrikaans.* Swartvlieëvanger.

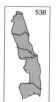

Black Cuckooshrike *Campephaga flava* (538) 22 cm
Male might be confused with Black Flycatcher but differs by having a yellow gape and, in some individuals, a yellow shoulder patch. Does not sit upright or behave as a flycatcher would but creeps through the foliage, gleaning insects from leaves and branches. Female might be confused with one of the female 'green' cuckoos but is larger, more heavily barred on the underparts and has bright yellow, not white outer tail feathers. *Status.* An uncommon breeding visitor to the Park. Favours tall trees, particularly in riverine habitats. *Call.* A high-pitched, prolonged 'trrrrrrr'. *Afrikaans.* Swartkatakoeroe.

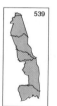

Whitebreasted Cuckooshrike *Coracina pectoralis* (539) 27 cm
The male is instantly recognizable with its all-grey head, throat and upperparts and contrasting white underparts. Female is slightly paler than male and shows a white, not grey throat. Imm. is very different from ad. and shows spotting on the white breast and barring on the upperparts. *Status.* An uncommon breeding resident which occurs mainly in the northern areas, apparently favouring tall mopane. *Call.* Male's call is a 'duid-duid' and female's is a 'tchee-ee-ee-ee'. *Afrikaans.* Witborskatakoeroe.

Grey Cuckooshrike *Coracina caesia* (540) 27 cm
This slow-moving, unobtrusive bird is easily overlooked unless the soft 'seeeeep' call-note is heard. The all-grey plumage identifies it, and at close range the white eye-ring and black patch at the bill base are visible. Female is slightly paler than male and lacks the black patch at the bill base. *Status.* Essentially a forest bird of the escarpment to the west. A very rare visitor occurring particularly at Pafuri; records in the Park are mainly for winter. *Call.* A soft, thin 'seeeeep'. *Afrikaans.* Bloukatakoeroe.

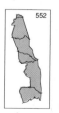

Ashy Tit *Parus cinerascens* (552) 13 cm
Extremely rare in the Park and the only grey tit found here. Differs from Southern Black Tit by having a grey body with a small amount of black and white on the wings, and a distinctive black cap and bib with contrasting white cheeks. Behaves in much the same manner as other tits and occurs either singly or in pairs. *Status.* Records of this species require confirmation. *Call.* A sharp 'klee-klee-klee-cheree-cheree' song. *Afrikaans.* Acaciagrysmees.

Forktailed Drongo

Black Flycatcher

Black Cuckooshrike ♂

Black Cuckooshrike ♀

Whitebreasted Cuckooshrike ♂

Grey Cuckooshrike ♂

Ashy Tit

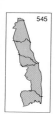

Blackheaded Oriole *Oriolus larvatus* (545) 24 cm
Male differs from other male orioles by having a diagnostic black head. Imm. is duller than ad. and has a dark brown, not black head which is flecked with buff and white. *Status.* A fairly common breeding resident in mature woodland and riverine habitats throughout the area. A noisy and conspicuous species. *Call.* A clear, liquid whistle 'pooodleeoo' and a harsher 'kweeer' note. *Afrikaans.* Swartkopwielewaal.

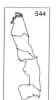

African Golden Oriole *Oriolus auratus* (544) 24 cm
The male is the brightest yellow oriole occurring in the Park and could be confused only with male European Golden Oriole from which it differs by having predominantly yellow, not black wings and a conspicuous black stripe that runs through and behind the eye. Female differs from female European Golden Oriole by being much yellower and having yellowish-green, not black wing coverts. Imm. resembles female and differs from imm. European Golden Oriole by being yellower and by having a diagnostic olive eye-stripe. *Status.* A very rare non-breeding visitor recorded mainly in the north and particularly at Pafuri. More common in summers of high rainfall. *Call.* A liquid whistle 'fee-yoo-fee-yoo'. *Afrikaans.* Afrikaanse Wielewaal.

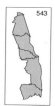

European Golden Oriole *Oriolus oriolus* (543) 24 cm
Male differs from male African Golden Oriole by having black, not yellow wings which contrast with the all-yellow body. Female is less distinct and differs from female African Golden Oriole by being a duller yellow with more green in the plumage and having much darker wing coverts. Imm. is very similar to imm. African Golden Oriole but is duller overall, has darker wings and lacks the olive eye-stripe of that species. *Status.* An uncommon non-breeding summer visitor recorded throughout the Park. *Call.* A liquid 'chleeooop'. *Afrikaans.* Europese Wielewaal.

Blackheaded Oriole ♂

African Golden Oriole ♂

African Golden Oriole ♀

European Golden Oriole ♀

European Golden Oriole ♂

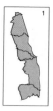

Ostrich *Struthio camelus* (1) Height 2 m
Unmistakable, being the largest bird. Male has a black and white plumage and female has the black replaced by brown. Imm. looks like a small female and a very young bird might be mistaken for a korhaan, but the extremely thick legs, broad, flattened bill and spiky, flecked plumage should rule out confusion. *Status.* Not uncommon in suitable habitat. A breeding resident on short-grass plains, mainly in the eastern parts and particularly north of the Letaba River. *Call.* Nocturnal, a booming leonine roar. *Afrikaans.* Volstruis.

Secretarybird *Sagittarius serpentarius* (118) 140 cm
This large, long-legged bird of prey may be confused only at long range – with a crane. In flight it resembles a large eagle or vulture but the very long legs project beyond the tail which, together with the elongated central tail feathers, gives the bird a diagnostic flight outline. Often seen in pairs striding across the veld. *Status.* A fairly common breeding resident occurring throughout the Park but more common on the eastern flats. *Call.* Normally silent but during display utters a deep croak. *Afrikaans.* Sekretarisvoël.

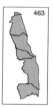

✓**Ground Hornbill** *Bucorvus leadbeateri* (463) 90 cm
An unmistakable bird, familiar in the Park. Its large size, all-black plumage, conspicuous red face and bulbous throat pouches are diagnostic. Spends most of its time on the ground in small groups and is very reluctant to fly but when it does it shows conspicuous white flight feathers. Imm. has dull yellow, not red on the face and the throat. *Status.* A common breeding resident occurring throughout the Park. *Call.* A loud, booming 'ooomph ooomph' early in the morning. *Afrikaans.* Bromvoël.

Black Crow *Corvus capensis* (547) 50 cm
Differs from Whitenecked Raven and Pied Crow by the lack of white on the iridescent black plumage and by having a much more slender beak. Flies with very shallow wing beats, not deep flapping as seen in the other two species. When perched and alarmed or agitated will continually flick its wings. *Status.* A very uncommon vagrant to the Park which will probably become more common in future as human settlements increase on the outskirts of the Park. *Call.* Normal crow-like 'kah-kah' and other deep bubbling notes. *Afrikaans.* Swartkraai.

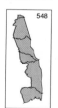

Pied Crow *Corvus albus* (548) 50 cm
A familiar black and white crow likely to be confused only with a Whitenecked Raven if seen at long range and if the white belly is not visible. Differs from that species in its more slender body shape, longer tail and thinner beak. At close range the black plumage is seen to be a mixture of iridescent deep blues, purple and black. *Status.* Fairly common in the far north where it breeds on the pylons of the Cahora Bassa powerlines. Particularly common at the Punda Maria restcamp. *Call.* Typical 'kwaaa' or 'kwooork' cawing. *Afrikaans.* Witborskraai.

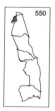

Whitenecked Raven *Corvus albicollis* (550) 54 cm
A large, powerful bird with a massive, white-tipped bill and a diagnostic white crescent on the hind neck. In flight and at long range, can be distinguished from Pied Crow by its larger, heavier head and much shorter wedge-shaped tail. *Status.* A very rare vagrant to the Park, seen only in the Punda Maria area, particularly at the restcamp. *Call.* A deep, throaty 'kwook'. *Afrikaans.* Withalskraai.

Ostrich ♂

Secretarybird

Ground Hornbill ♂

Black Crow

Pied Crow

Whitenecked Raven

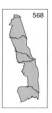

Blackeyed Bulbul *Pycnonotus barbatus* (568) 22 cm
A familiar and confiding bird, seen at all restcamps in the Park, and easily identified by its black head which has a slight crest, its greyish-brown throat and back, off-white belly, and bright lemon-yellow undertail. Imm. is duller than ad. and has a dark brown, not black head. *Status.* An abundant breeding resident occurring throughout the Park. *Call.* A harsh, sharp 'kwit, kwit, kwit' given when alarmed or when going to roost. Song is a liquid 'cheloop chreep choop'. *Afrikaans.* Swartoogtiptol.

Sombre Bulbul *Andropadus importunus* (572) 23 cm
This dull olive-green bulbul is more often heard than seen, as it tends to keep to the thicker canopy of a bush or tree. This is the only greenish-brown bulbul in the Park with a pale-coloured eye, a feature noticeable at close range. Imm. does not have such pale eyes, but the dull olive-green plumage should identify it. *Status.* A locally common breeding resident recorded throughout the Park in suitable habitat. Favours thick riverine bush and is particularly common along the Sabie, Crocodile and Luvuvhu rivers. Easily seen at the Skukuza restcamp. *Call.* A piercing 'weeewee', followed by a liquid chortle.
Afrikaans. Gewone Willie.

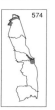

Yellowbellied Bulbul *Chlorocichla flaviventris* (574) 23 cm
Might be confused with Sombre Bulbul but is a much brighter yellow underneath. Also differs by having a dark red, not pale eye, a brown, not olive crown, and a pale, almost white, eye-ring visible at close range. Occurs in small groups and is furtive, keeping to the thicker tangles but these birds will venture out into the open when chasing one another. *Status.* A fairly common breeding resident in a few scattered localities. Can be seen at the Punda Maria, Letaba and Nwanetsi restcamps, where it has become very tame, and in the Olifants Wilderness Trails area. *Call.* A monotonous, nasal 'neh-neh-neh-neh'. *Afrikaans.* Geelborswillie.

Terrestrial Bulbul *Phyllastrephus terrestris* (569) 21 cm
As the vernacular name implies this bulbul keeps very much to the ground but also to the deeper, darker parts of the undergrowth. It is a nondescript bird with a brownish breast offset by a white throat and pale abdomen. Its behaviour is diagnostic: small parties move through the undergrowth and on the ground, scattering the leaf-litter in search of food and continually calling to each other. *Status.* A common breeding resident of thick riverine bush. Can be located near any of the larger rivers of the Park wherever such a habitat occurs, particularly along the Sabie and Luvuvhu rivers. *Call.* A soft, chattering 'trrup cherrup trrup' given by small foraging groups. *Afrikaans.* Boskrapper.

Yellowspotted Nicator *Nicator gularis* (575) 23 cm
Might be confused with either the Sombre Bulbul or, more likely, the Yellowbellied Bulbul but differs from both by having pale spotting on the wing coverts and on the tips of the secondaries. Its short song is often the only way to detect it as it keeps to the deeper parts of the canopy and is difficult to see. *Status.* An uncommon breeding resident recorded regularly only along the Luvuvhu and Limpopo rivers, and in the Bangu Gorge in the Olifants Wilderness Trails area. Visitors to the Pafuri area should listen for its characteristic call. *Call.* A short, rich, throaty chuckle.
Afrikaans. Geelvleknikator.

Blackeyed Bulbul

Sombre Bulbul

Yellowbellied Bulbul

Terrestrial Bulbul

Yellowspotted Nicator

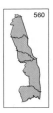

Arrowmarked Babbler *Turdoides jardineii* (560) 24 cm
A common babbler in the Park, moving in small groups which draw attention by the cackling din they produce. From a distance appears all-brown and loose-winged, but at close range the pale orange eye is evident as are the white arrow marks down the breast and belly. *Status.* A common breeding resident occurring throughout the Park; found along watercourses with thickish bush and at most restcamps. *Call.* Small parties utter a harsh churring and cackling. *Afrikaans.* Pylvlekkatlagter.

Groundscraper Thrush *Turdus litsitsirupa* (580) 22 cm
This large thrush may be seen running around open grassy areas in the Park's restcamps. Has a very upright posture and is easily recognized by the bold black and white markings on the face and by the white breast which is heavily spotted with black. Might be confused with the smaller Dusky Lark (p.140) but is distinguished by its habit of raising one wing above body level whereas Dusky Lark raises both wings at the same time. *Status.* A fairly common breeding resident of open parkland throughout the Park. Also seen in most restcamps. *Call.* This bird's specific name is derived from its characteristic song: a loud, clear, and varied whistling phrase. *Afrikaans.* Gevlekte Lyster.

Kurrichane Thrush *Turdus libonyana* (576) 22 cm
Like the Groundscraper Thrush may be seen on lawns and bare ground within the Park's restcamps. Easily recognized by its bright orange bill, black streaked moustachial stripes, greyish breast and orange flanks and belly. When disturbed will fly up into a tree where it will sit motionless until the danger has passed. *Status.* A fairly common breeding resident found along watercourses, favouring bush with a thick canopy and an open understorey; forages for food in the leaf-litter beneath. *Call.* A loud, whistling 'peet-peeoo'. *Afrikaans.* Rooibeklyster.

Familiar Chat *Cercomela familiaris* (589) 15 cm
A small, greyish-brown nondescript bird with a very upright posture and long thin legs. In flight shows a rust-coloured rump and outer tail feathers. Perches freely on rocks and outbuildings and occasionally in trees, and when alighting has a characteristic habit of flicking its wings over its rump and tail and so displaying the chestnut colour underneath. *Status.* Generally very rare but recorded regularly at Masorini Koppie near Phalaborwa where it may be resident. Otherwise recorded at a few widely scattered points throughout the Park. *Call.* A soft 'shek-shek'. *Afrikaans.* Gewone Spekvreter.

Mocking Chat *Thamnolaea cinnamomeiventris* (593) 23 cm
Male and female are very different in appearance. Male has a glossy black plumage with a diagnostic white shoulder patch, and a bright chestnut belly and undertail coverts. Female has a duller chestnut belly, lacks the white patch on the forewing, and has the breast and remaining upperparts greyish-brown. *Status.* A breeding resident inhabiting rocky outcrops and koppies and occurs throughout the Park in such habitat. Olifants restcamp is a good spot to see this species. *Call.* Song is a loud, melodious mixture of mimicked bird song. *Afrikaans.* Dassievoël.

Arrowmarked Babbler

Groundscraper Thrush

Kurrichane Thrush

Familiar Chat

Mocking Chat ♂

Mocking Chat ♀

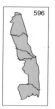

Stonechat *Saxicola torquata* (596) 14 cm
Possibly the best known of the chats in that it is often seen on an exposed
perch. Male has a pied plumage with a predominantly black head, white neck
patches, a white rump and white patches on the wings. The breast and flanks
are bright rust in colour. Female is much duller than male and has buffy to
orange underparts and a grey, not black head, but also shows the
conspicuous white wing patches and small white rump. *Status.* A non-
breeding winter visitor to the Park, uncommon but widespread throughout the
area. *Call.* A 'weet-weet' followed by a harsh 'chak'.
Afrikaans. Gewone Bontrokkie.

Mountain Chat *Oenanthe monticola* (586) 20 cm
Although occurring in an entirely different habitat, this species could be easily
confused with Arnot's Chat. Both are black with a white shoulder patch but this
species has a diagnostic white rump and white sides to the tail. The male
plumage is variable and the bird may show a grey or white cap. Female is
paler than male and lacks the white cap and shoulder but still shows the white
rump. *Status.* Recorded only in the mountainous gorges in the Pafuri area
where it probably breeds and is resident. There are no tourist roads to this area
and this species is thus unlikely to be seen by visitors. *Call.* A clear, thrush-like
whistling song interspersed with harsh chatters. *Afrikaans.* Bergwagter.

Southern Black Tit *Parus niger* (554) 16 cm
A small black bird, with white in the wings and grey barred undertail coverts.
The female is duller than the male, being less glossy on the back and having
greyish, not black underparts. Occurs in small, noisy parties, often of mixed
species, which fly through woodland. *Status.* A common and widespread
resident. *Call.* A harsh, chattering 'chrr-chrr-chrr' and a musical 'phee-cher-
phee-cher'. *Afrikaans.* Gewone Swartmees.

Arnot's Chat *Thamnolaea arnoti* (594) 18 cm
A black chat found in woodland and frequently seen perching in trees. Easily
recognized by its all-white forehead and crown, and conspicuous white
shoulder patches. Female differs from male in that it lacks the white crown and
has a white throat and breast, but still shows the conspicuous white forewings.
Status. Restricted to areas of tall mopane forest and thus found mainly in the
extreme north but occurring wherever this vegetation type is found. A locally
common breeding resident which may be seen along the roads cutting
through mopane forest: the H13-1, S59, S60 and in places along the H1-9,
north of the Luvuvhu River. Occurs in only limited areas outside the Park.
Call. A quiet, whistled 'fick' or 'feee'. *Afrikaans.* Bontpiek.

Capped Wheatear *Oenanthe pileata* (587) 18 cm
A ground-dwelling bird with a very upright posture and easily identified by its
broad black breast band, broad white eyebrow stripe, white rump, and white
outer tail feathers (best visible in flight). Imm. lacks the black breast band and
white eyebrow stripe, and is generally dowdy greyish-brown but still shows a
white rump and white sides to the base of the tail. *Status.* A very rare but
widespread bird, recorded in all seasons. Probably a non-breeding vagrant.
Call. A 'chik-chik' alarm note. Song is a loud warbling with slurred chattering.
Afrikaans. Hoëveldskaapwagter.

Stonechat ♂

Stonechat ♀

Mountain Chat ♂

Mountain Chat ♀

Southern Black Tit

Arnot's Chat ♀

Capped Wheatear

Whitethroated Robin *Cossypha humeralis* (602) 17 cm
A shy, retiring robin which might be confused with the Southern Boubou (p.186) because of its black upperparts, white wing stripe and rufous belly and flanks. Differs by having a broad white eyebrow stripe and a clear white throat and breast; also, lacks the heavy hooked bill of a shrike. Differs further by having a russet rump and outer tail feathers. *Status.* A fairly common breeding resident confined mainly to thick bush along rivers and dry watercourses. Can be located by its frequently heard sibilant call. *Call.* A repeated 'seet-cher-seet-cher' whistled phrase. *Afrikaans.* Witkeeljanfrederik.

Cape Robin *Cossypha caffra* (601) 18 cm
May be confused with Heuglin's Robin but with a good view is easily identified. Smaller than Heuglin's Robin with a less distinct white eyebrow stripe and the orange on the underparts confined to the throat and breast. Imm. is heavily spotted above and below and shows a rust rump and outer tail feathers. *Status.* Very rare in the Park and appears to be an altitudinal migrant entering the Park in winter. *Call.* Alarm call is a harsh 'chrrrr'. Song is a soft, melodious 'cherooo-weet-weet-weeeet' phrase. *Afrikaans.* Gewone Janfrederik.

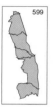

Heuglin's Robin *Cossypha heuglini* (599) 20 cm
This large, chunky robin is more often heard than seen, its explosive song emanating from deep thicket often close to water. Might be mistaken for the smaller Cape Robin but differs by having a conspicuous white eyebrow stripe which extends well behind the eye, and by the orange-red on the underparts, from the throat to the undertail coverts. *Status.* Very common in thick bush along the larger, more permanent rivers. A shy, breeding resident which is best located by its call. *Call.* A loud, explosive song with repeated, varied phrases. *Afrikaans.* Heuglinse Janfrederik.

Natal Robin *Cossypha natalensis* (600) 18 cm
Like other robins, becomes bolder and more demonstrative in twilight hours, venturing out from the thick tangles of bush where it normally lives. Easily identified by its orange face, throat and breast, slightly darker crown and nape, and contrasting powder-blue wings and back. Imm. is heavily spotted above and below and shows a rust-coloured rump and outer tail feathers. *Status.* A very secretive species which is almost certainly a breeding resident. Locally common in thick riverine bush along the major rivers, and particularly common along the Shingwedzi River in the vicinity of the Kanniedood Dam. Best located by its call. *Call.* Contact sound is a soft 'seee-saw, seee-saw'. Song is a rambling series of melodious phrases, and mimicry. *Afrikaans.* Nataljanfrederik.

160

Whitethroated Robin

Cape Robin

Heuglin's Robin

Natal Robin

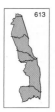

Whitebrowed Robin *Erythropygia leucophrys* (613) 15 cm
A momentary glimpse might lead to confusion with the Brown and Bearded robins but if the heavily streaked breast is seen then identification is easy. Also shows a conspicuous white eyebrow stripe, two white wing bars, a rufous rump and a white-tipped tail which is regularly cocked and often spread. *Status.* A very common and widespread breeding resident occurring in nearly all types of habitat. *Call.* A harsh 'trrrrr' alarm note and a very varied fluty song. *Afrikaans.* Gestreepte Wipstert.

Bearded Robin *Erythropygia quadrivirgata* (617) 18 cm
Easily confused with the very similar Brown Robin but differs by having bolder moustachial stripes and a cinnamon, sometimes orange, breast and flanks. Easily distinguished from the slightly smaller Whitebrowed Robin by the lack of any streaking on the throat and breast. *Status.* An uncommon breeding resident restricted mainly to riverine areas. Probably occurs along all the major rivers but appears to be more common along the Sabie and Luvuvhu rivers. *Call.* A clear, penetrating song of often-repeated mixed phrases. *Afrikaans.* Baardwipstert.

Brown Robin *Erythropygia signata* (616) 18 cm
Easily mistaken for the similar Bearded Robin. Differs by having a less boldly marked facial pattern, with brown rather than black moustachial stripes, and grey, not rich buff or orange underparts. *Status.* An extremely rare bird found mainly in the densely wooded forests of the escarpment to the west, it may occur in the Park in winter as an altitudinal migrant. Recorded only at Pafuri and Nwanetsi. *Call.* A melodious 'twee-choo-sree-sree' introduces a varied song. Alarm note is a soft 'krrrr'. *Afrikaans.* Bruinwipstert.

Whitebrowed Robin

Bearded Robin

Brown Robin

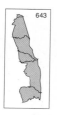

Willow Warbler *Phylloscopus trochilus* (643) 11 cm
Easily confused with the larger Icterine Warbler, both being obscure greenish-yellow birds, but differs by having a thinner, weaker bill and being much less yellow on the underparts. Some birds may appear grey with almost greyish-white underparts, and lack any suggestion of green or yellow in the plumage. *Status.* A common to abundant non-breeding summer migrant recorded throughout the area. *Call.* A soft 'hoeet hoeet' and a short melodious song, descending in scale. *Afrikaans.* Hofsanger.

Icterine Warbler *Hippolais icterina* (625) 13 cm
A larger, more robust warbler than the Willow Warbler and with a larger, heavier bill which has a bright yellow lower mandible. Generally more brightly coloured than Willow Warbler with greyish-olive upperparts and often bright lemon-yellow underparts. Moves restlessly through the bush thickets, regularly calling and singing. *Status.* A non-breeding summer migrant recorded throughout the Park but much less common than the Willow Warbler. *Call.* A jumbled song comprising harsh and melodious notes. *Afrikaans.* Spotvoël.

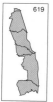

Garden Warbler *Sylvia borin* (619) 14 cm
This small, nondescript bird has no clear identification features which in itself aids identification. The overall colour is greyish-brown, the underparts paler, the bill rather thick for a warbler, and it has an indistinct pale eye-ring. Its song is sometimes the only indication of its presence. *Status.* An uncommon but widespread non-breeding summer migrant. *Call.* Song is a monotonous warbling interspersed with soft grating phrases. *Afrikaans.* Tuinsanger.

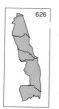

Olivetree Warbler *Hippolais olivetorum* (626) 16 cm
One of the migrant warblers which are notoriously difficult to distinguish. Large for a warbler, approaching almost the size of a small bulbul, and appears very grey, especially on the upperparts. Underparts are paler and the bill is large with a pale, yellowish lower mandible. Might be mistaken for the Fantailed Flycatcher (p.176) but its typically furtive, warbler-like habits should avoid confusion. *Status.* A very rare but widespread non-breeding summer migrant. *Call.* Most easily located by its raucous, chattering song, which it delivers from within a bush: a prolonged 'chee-chee-chaak-chaak'. *Afrikaans.* Olyfboomsanger.

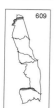

Thrush Nightingale *Luscinia luscinia* (609) 16 cm
Probably the shyest and most furtive of all the migrant warblers that occur within the Park, and the species least likely to be seen. However, its loud explosive song indicates the bird's presence and if glimpsed the following features will help identify it: dark brown upperparts, paler underparts with dappling on the throat and breast, and a long, broad tail which is warm-brown in colour. *Status.* Generally a very rare non-breeding summer migrant recorded only from the Sabie and Luvuvhu rivers, but evidence from Pafuri suggests that it may be more common in some summers than in others. *Call.* A rich warbling song interspersed with grating notes. *Afrikaans.* Lysternagtegaal.

164

Willow Warbler

Icterine Warbler

Garden Warbler

Olivetree Warbler

Thrush Nightingale

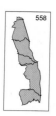

Grey Penduline Tit *Anthoscopus caroli* (558) 8 cm
The diminutive size of this bird alone should help to identify it. Occurs in small parties which flit nervously from branch to branch, often hanging upside down to glean insects. It has a tiny, short black bill, greyish upperparts and a buffish belly and flanks. *Status.* A widespread breeding resident but uncommon and inconspicuous. *Call.* A soft 'chissick' or 'tseeep'. *Afrikaans.* Gryskapokvoël.

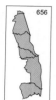

Burntnecked Eremomela *Eremomela usticollis* (656) 12 cm
If present, the chestnut throat bar is diagnostic. Otherwise this species might be confused with Greencapped Eremomela but differs by having brown, not green upperparts and the underparts more suffused with buffy-yellow. *Status.* An uncommon but widespread breeding resident. Favours acacia thickets, particularly umbrella thorn where it may occur in bird parties, though it is generally unobtrusive. *Call.* A high-pitched 'chii-cheee-cheee', followed by a sibilant 'trrrrrrrr'. *Afrikaans.* Bruinkeelbossanger.

Yellowbellied Eremomela *Eremomela icteropygialis* (653) 10 cm
The smallest of the eremomelas and easily confused with Grey Penduline Tit, but differs by its larger size, longer tail, and distinct greyish throat and breast which are finely demarcated from the buffy-yellow belly and flanks. Differs from Burntnecked and Greencapped eremomelas by its grey throat and at closer range the dark-, not pale-coloured eye. *Status.* The least common of the three eremomela species found in the Park. Favours deciduous woodland, particularly with low trees and scrub. A breeding resident. *Call.* Song is a high-pitched, frequently repeated 'tchee-tchee-tchuu'. *Afrikaans.* Geelpensbossanger.

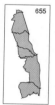

Greencapped Eremomela *Eremomela scotops* (655) 12 cm
Like other eremomelas occurs in small parties but is much more vocal than others of the same family. Differs from the similar Burntnecked Eremomela by its clear yellow breast which lacks a chestnut throat bar and by its green, not brown upperparts. *Status.* An uncommon breeding resident which favours broadleaved deciduous woodland with tall trees. Has often been recorded at the Letaba restcamp. *Call.* A repeated 'tweer-tweer-tweer'. Small groups utter a harsh 'chur-chur'. *Afrikaans.* Donkerwangbossanger.

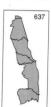

Yellow Warbler *Chloropeta natalensis* (637) 14 cm
Might be confused with the similarly coloured Icterine Warbler (p.164) but is much larger, has dark greenish-brown upperparts and much brighter yellow underparts. Its behaviour in the Park is more like that of a flycatcher: sitting on exposed perches and hawking insects either from the ground or out of the air. Has a variable plumage ranging from dark to very dark brown and russet. *Status.* Very rare in the Park, it favours long grass and reeds at the water's edge. Probably a breeding resident. *Call.* A soft 'chip-chip-cheezee-cheeze'. *Afrikaans.* Geelsanger.

166

Grey Penduline Tit

Burntnecked Eremomela

Yellowbellied Eremomela

Greencapped Eremomela

Yellow Warbler

African Marsh Warbler *Acrocephalus baeticatus* (631) 13 cm
An obscure, small warbler which frequents reedbeds and adjoining thickets.
Has warm brown upperparts, an off-white throat and a buffy belly and flanks.
Differs from Cape Reed Warbler by being smaller and much warmer buff
around the belly and flanks. Very similar to European Marsh Warbler but they
occur in different habitats: the African Marsh Warbler is almost always found
near water. *Status.* A breeding intra-Africa migrant and probably a breeding
summer visitor. Uncommon but widely recorded. *Call.* A harsher, more churring
song than that of European Marsh Warbler. *Afrikaans.* Kleinrietsanger.

Cape Reed Warbler *Acrocephalus gracilirostris* (635) 17 cm
Much larger than African Marsh Warbler which frequents the same habitat, and
has a clearer, whiter throat and breast, and a distinct white eyebrow stripe. The
bill is unusually long and robust and its legs are dark greyish-brown.
Status. A fairly common breeding resident. Occurs at most of the Park's dams
and more permanent pools where reeds and sedges are found. *Call.* A rich,
fluty 'cheerup-chee-trrrree' song. *Afrikaans.* Kaapse Rietsanger.

Broadtailed Warbler *Schoenicola brevirostris* (642) 17 cm
Most conspicuous in breeding season, when in display it flies above the grass
and calls. The very long, broad, dark tail is diagnostic. *Status.* Two records
exist for this species in the Park, both in summer. *Call.* A wheezy 'tzzzt-tzzzt'
and a high-pitched 'peee, peee'. *Afrikaans.* Breëstertsanger.

European Sedge Warbler *Acrocephalus schoenobaenus* (634) 13 cm
Differs from other reed-dwelling warblers by having a broad, buffy eyebrow
stripe and a heavily streaked crown. Almost always associated with vegetation
around fresh water. *Status.* A very rare non-breeding summer visitor.
Call. A harsh churring and chattering with sharp, melodious phrases.
Afrikaans. Europese Vleisanger.

African Sedge Warbler *Bradypterus baboecala* (638) 17 cm
Very much darker than Cape Reed Warbler, much chunkier in shape, and with
a longer and broader tail. The throat and breast are slightly dappled and the
remaining underparts are greyish-brown. Extremely furtive and skulking except
in the breeding season when it performs a short display flight over reedbeds.
Status. A fairly common breeding resident which occurs at most of the Park's
dams and permanent pools where reeds and sedges are found. *Call.* A low,
stuttered 'brrrup brrrup trrp trrp trrp' song. *Afrikaans.* Kaapse Vleisanger.

Great Reed Warbler *Acrocephalus arundinaceus* (628) 19 cm
Exceptionally difficult to see in its thicket and reedbed habitat and is normally
located by its harsh, grating song. When seen it looks like a large African
Marsh Warbler and has dark-brown upperparts and paler, buff underparts.
Status. An uncommon though widespread summer migrant. *Call.* A prolonged
'chee-chee-chaak-chaak'. *Afrikaans.* Grootrietsanger.

European Marsh Warbler *Acrocephalus palustris* (633) 13 cm
Almost indistinguishable in the field from African Marsh Warbler except that its
underparts are slightly paler and the belly and flanks are greyish, not buff. The
European Marsh Warbler is often found well away from water and not in
reedbeds or adjoining thickets. *Status.* Uncommon but recorded widely.
Call. Distinguished from the African Marsh Warbler's song by clear, melodious
phrases. *Afrikaans.* Europese Rietsanger.

African Marsh Warbler

Cape Reed Warbler

Broadtailed Warbler

European Sedge Warbler

African Sedge Warbler

Great Reed Warbler

European Marsh Warbler

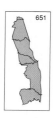

Longbilled Crombec *Sylvietta rufescens* (651) 12 cm
This small, rotund warbler which appears almost tailless, has greyish-brown upperparts with warm buff to cinnamon underparts and a distinctive, slightly decurved, long bill. A very active and restless member of bird parties, flitting to and fro and gleaning insects from the underside of leaves and twigs. *Status.* A common and widespread breeding resident. Favours thornveld habitats and can easily be located by its call. *Call.* A repeated 'trree-trriit, tree-triitt', and a harsher 'ptttt'. *Afrikaans.* Bosveldstompstert.

Yellowbreasted Apalis *Apalis flavida* (648) 13 cm
This small, long-tailed bird is very active and easily identified by the bright yellow wash across the breast. Male has a black spot in the centre of the breast, but does not show a complete black breast band. At close range the grey head with a contrasting white throat and the red, not pale eye can be seen. Differs from similarly coloured eremomelas by being very much more slender and by its long tail. *Status.* A common and widespread breeding resident. Prefers thornveld habitats and is easily located by its call. *Call.* A fast, buzzy 'chizzick-chizzick-chizzick'. *Afrikaans.* Geelborskleinjantjie.

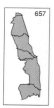

Bleating Warbler *Camaroptera brachyura* (657) 12 cm
Two forms of this small warbler occur within the Park: one has a greenish-coloured back and the other a grey back. They are similar in shape and build, both with round bodies and shortish tails which are often held cocked at a 45 degree angle. The grey-backed race, which is sometimes considered to be a different species, is easily distinguished by having definite grey upperparts which contrast slightly with the greenish wings. During the breeding season the birds bound and leap about at the bottom of a bush giving a clicking call and whirring their wings. *Status.* A very common inhabitant of tangled thickets throughout the Park, particularly along rivers and watercourses. A breeding resident easily located by its loud call. *Call.* The call is diagnostic: a nasal 'neeehhh' and a loud, snapping 'bidup-bidup-bidup'. *Afrikaans.* Kwê-kwêvoël.

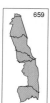

Stierling's Barred Warbler *Camaroptera stierlingi* (659) 13 cm
A bird of the mid- and upper-canopy in woodland but often seen hopping about at the base of trees. Unmistakable with its silvery-white, finely barred underparts, warm brown upperparts and bright, flesh-coloured legs and feet. *Status.* An uncommon but widespread breeding resident. Unobtrusive; usually located by its highly characteristic, almost mechanical call. *Call.* A fast, breathy 'plip-lip-lip' whistle. *Afrikaans.* Stierlingse Sanger.

Longbilled Crombec

Yellowbreasted Apalis

Bleating Warbler (green-backed form)

Stierling's Barred Warbler

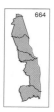

Fantailed Cisticola *Cisticola juncidis* (664) 10 cm
The four small cisticolas found in the Park are best identified by call and display flight. This is probably the most common cisticola in the Park. In display the male makes a series of erratic bounds and dips in which it intersperses a diagnostic 'zit-zit' call. *Status.* A common and widespread breeding resident. Selects open, long grass habitats – particularly those on the eastern plains – and rank conditions in wet areas throughout the remainder of the Park. More common in wet years. *Call.* A repeated 'zit-zit' or a faster 'chit-chit-chit' is given in flight. *Afrikaans.* Landeryklopkloppie.

Desert Cisticola *Cisticola aridula* (665) 10 cm
Almost identical to Fantailed Cisticola but appears paler and the tail tip is less boldly marked. In display flight male swoops down low over the ground then high into the air and gives a high-pitched tinkling call, and does not show the erratic movements of Fantailed Cisticola. *Status.* A common and widespread breeding resident. Selects open, long grass habitats, particularly those in the drier northern parts on the eastern plains. *Call.* Song is a 'zink zink zink' or 'sii sii sii'. When alarmed it utters a 'tuc tuc tuc tuc' and snaps its wings. *Afrikaans.* Woestynklopkloppie.

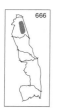

Cloud Cisticola *Cisticola textrix* (666) 10 cm
Virtually indistinguishable in plumage details from Ayres', Desert and Fantailed cisticolas but its display flight and call are diagnostic. Cruises at a high elevation, giving a soft 'see-see-see-chick-chick' and on descent will rise again sharply just before landing, without snapping its wings, and then will descend to settle in grass. *Status.* A very rare cisticola occurring in the northern grasslands. *Call.* Song, a 'see-see-see-see-chick-chick-chick', is delivered at great height. *Afrikaans.* Gevlekte Klopkloppie.

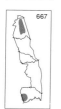

Ayres' Cisticola *Cisticola ayresii* (667) 10 cm
Almost indistinguishable from the other small cisticolas if not seen displaying or calling. Like Cloud Cisticola, display is carried out high above the ground, sometimes as high as 50 m where it utters a very soft, squeaky song which lacks any harsh notes. Just before landing it darts about snapping its wings together. *Status.*Very rare in the Park; only reported on the northern grasslands and in the south-west. *Call.* Song, a 'soo-see-see-see', is given at a great height. On descending and just before it jinks, this species loudly snaps its wings many times. *Afrikaans.* Kleinste Klopkloppie.

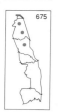

Blackbacked Cisticola *Cisticola galactotes* (675) 13 cm
Easily confused with Levaillant's Cisticola but a good sighting will show the much darker back and the mantle feathers broadly edged with buff, not grey as in Levaillant's Cisticola. *Status.* A very rare cisticola in the Park recorded a few times along the Limpopo floodplain where rank, long grass conditions occur. More recently has been recorded regularly at the Nshawu River below the dam wall. *Call.* A loud, harsh 'tzzzzzzrrp' and a louder, whistled alarm 'prrrt'. *Afrikaans.* Swartrugtinktinkie.

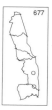

Levaillant's Cisticola *Cisticola tinniens* (677) 14 cm
Very similar to Blackbacked Cisticola, having a chestnut cap, a dark back and a long tail tipped with black and white. Differs mainly by having the mantle feathers edged with grey, not with rich buff. *Status.* Very rare but recorded from a few widely scattered localities. *Call.* A musical 'chrip-trrrup-trreee' and a wailing 'cheee-weee-weee'. *Afrikaans.* Vleitinktinkie.

172

Fantailed Cisticola

Desert Cisticola

Cloud Cisticola

Ayres' Cisticola

Blackbacked Cisticola

Levaillant's Cisticola

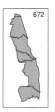

Rattling Cisticola *Cisticola chiniana* (672) 13 cm
The most prominent cisticola in the Park, often seen sitting on top of a bush, delivering its short song or harsh, scolding notes. Shows a grey-brown crown, a well-streaked brown and black back, and a long tail which is tipped with black and white on the underside. *Status.* A common breeding resident. Occurs throughout the area and is particularly conspicuous in summer when calling. *Call.* Song is a loud 'chueee-chueee-cherrrrr', with variations on this phrase. *Afrikaans.* Bosveldtinktinkie.

Redfaced Cisticola *Cisticola erythrops* (674) 13 cm
Most often detected by its loud ringing call but when seen is easily identified, being the only large cisticola in the Park with uniform, rather than streaked parts. In non-breeding plumage the side of the face is washed with a russet colour. Like the other large cisticolas, its tail is long and tipped with black and white. *Status.* A common and conspicuous breeding resident confined to reedbeds and rank waterside vegetation. *Call.* A series of piercing whistles 'weee, cheee, cheee, cheer, cheer', rising and falling in scale.
Afrikaans. Rooiwangtinktinkie.

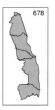

Croaking Cisticola *Cisticola natalensis* (678) 13 –17 cm
An unusually large and chunky cisticola and might at first glance be confused with a female bishop or widow bird. Differentiated from those birds by having a thinner, longer bill and a longer tail. Apart from its large size and robust shape it can be identified by its characteristic display flight and call. Female is similar to male but is noticeably smaller. *Status.* An uncommon species except in the mountains of the south-west where it is reasonably common and probably a breeding resident. Recorded from a few widely scattered localities throughout the Park. *Call.* A deep 'trrrrp' or 'chee-fro' is given during its bounding display flight or from an exposed perch. *Afrikaans.* Groottinktinkie.

Blackchested Prinia *Prinia flavicans* (685) 15 cm
Easily recognized in breeding plumage by the distinctive black breast band. Out of the breeding season when the breast band is absent, it might be confused with the Tawnyflanked Prinia but differs by being larger, having red not brown eyes, and more buffy-yellow underparts. *Status.* A very rare species with very few records, mainly from the north. Probably vagrant in the Park. *Call.* A series of drawn-out 'zzzrt-zzzzrt-zzzrt-zzzrt' notes.
Afrikaans. Swartbandlangstertjie.

Tawnyflanked Prinia *Prinia subflava* (683) 11 cm
The most frequently seen prinia in the Park and easily distinguished from the very rare Blackchested Prinia by lacking a black breast band. The very long tail which is often held cocked at a 45 degree angle should help differentiate it from any similar-looking cisticola. *Status.* A very common breeding resident throughout the Park. *Call.* A rapidly repeated 'przzt-przzt-przzt' and a harsh 'chrzzt'. *Afrikaans.* Bruinsylangstertjie.

174

Rattling Cisticola

Redfaced Cisticola

Croaking Cisticola

Blackchested Prinia

Tawnyflanked Prinia

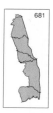

Neddicky *Cisticola fulvicapilla* (681) 11 cm
The chestnut cap, unstreaked upperparts and uniform grey underparts make
this small cisticola easy to identify. Some birds, especially those in the northern
parts of the Park, may show paler greyish underparts which contrast with the
brown upperparts. *Status.* Rare in the Park but widely recorded throughout.
Nests with eggs have been found in the Stolsnek region, thus probably a
resident species. *Call.* Song is a soft, breathy 'cheerup-cheerup-cheerup'.
Alarm call is a fast 'tictictictic'. *Afrikaans.* Neddikkie.

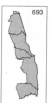

Fantailed Flycatcher *Myioparus plumbeus* (693) 14 cm
Easily confused with Bluegrey Flycatcher and best distinguished by
differences in behaviour rather than by plumage details. This species has a
habit of constantly raising its tail and at the same time spreading and turning it
from side to side thereby showing off its bright white outer tail feathers. Does
not display the same 'flycatcher' habits as Bluegrey Flycatcher but instead
creeps through the foliage gleaning insects from the underside of leaves.
Status. An uncommon but widely distributed breeding resident. Selects
savanna with tall trees. *Call.* A tremulous, whistled 'treee-trooo'.
Afrikaans. Waaierstertvlieëvanger.

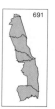

Bluegrey Flycatcher *Muscicapa caerulescens* (691) 15 cm
Easily mistaken for Fantailed Flycatcher but lacks the bright white outer tail
feathers of that species and does not display the same habit of raising and
lowering its tail. This bird is uniform ashy-grey above and white below, and
shows a pale eye-ring and a small white stripe from the base of the bill to the
front of the eye. Displays typical 'flycatcher' behaviour, darting out from a
perch to snatch insects and then returning to the same perch. *Status.* An
uncommon breeding resident which is widely distributed. Selects mature
woodland and riverine habitats. *Call.* Song is a soft 'sszzit-sszzit-sreee-sreee'.
Afrikaans. Blougrysvlieëvanger.

Titbabbler *Parisoma subcaeruleum* (621) 15 cm
This large warbler-like bird is easily recognized by its greyish plumage,
white-tipped dark tail and diagnostic chestnut undertail coverts. At close range
it shows a white eye and black streaking on the throat. Behaves very much like
a warbler, creeping through the centre and tops of bushes in search of insects.
Status. Rare in the Park, having been sighted only a few times and with no
breeding records. Its status is uncertain, but as it is a species of the drier west,
it may expand its range to the east in drier periods. *Call.* A loud, fluty
'cheruuup-chee-chee', interspersed with harsh chatters.
Afrikaans. Bosveldtjeriktik.

Neddicky

Fantailed Flycatcher

Bluegrey Flycatcher

Titbabbler

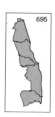

Marico Flycatcher *Melaenornis mariquensis* (695) 18 cm
Frequently mistaken for the Mousecoloured Flycatcher but is distinguished by its clear white underparts which contrast with dull brown upperparts. *Status.* A species of the drier west which occurs as a very rare vagrant to the Park. Appears to enter the area when more arid conditions prevail. The dry central areas around Bangu Windmill are good places to look for it. *Call.* Song is a soft 'tsii-cheruk-tukk'. *Afrikaans.* Maricovlieëvanger.

Mousecoloured Flycatcher *Melaenornis pallidus* (696) 17 cm
Distinguished from Marico Flycatcher by having greyish or greyish-brown, not clear white underparts. An unobtrusive, medium-sized flycatcher which occurs in small parties of three to five. *Status.* An uncommon breeding resident recorded throughout the Park. *Call.* Song is a soft, melodious warbling interspersed with harsh chitters. Alarm call is a soft 'churr'. *Afrikaans.* Muiskleurvlieëvanger.

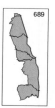

Spotted Flycatcher *Muscicapa striata* (689) 14 cm
Likely to be confused only with the smaller Dusky Flycatcher but differs by being more slender, having a distinctly streaked forehead and crown, and a streaked, not dappled breast. Displays typical flycatcher behaviour, darting after insects in flight and then returning to its perch. *Status.* A common summer migrant to the Park, occurring throughout. *Call.* An almost inaudible 'tzee'. *Afrikaans.* Europese Vlieëvanger.

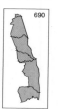

Dusky Flycatcher *Muscicapa adusta* (690) 12 cm
This small flycatcher might be mistaken for the larger Spotted Flycatcher but is greyer overall and is not as long and slender as that species. It lacks any distinct streaking on the forehead and its breast is dappled rather than streaked. A white eyebrow and a small white stripe below the eye, both absent in the Spotted Flycatcher, are visible at close range. Differs from Sharpbilled Honeyguide (p.134) by its dappled throat and breast and by the lack of white outer tail feathers. *Status.* A breeding resident restricted to the well-developed riverine habitats along major watercourses in the Park. *Call.* A soft, high-pitched 'tzzeet' and 'tsirit'. *Afrikaans.* Donkervlieëvanger.

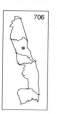

Fairy Flycatcher *Stenostira scita* (706) 12 cm
This small, delicate flycatcher is easily identified by its black face mask bordered above and below by a white stripe, by the pinkish-grey tinge across the breast, white wing stripe, and long dark tail with white outer tail feathers. It behaves much like a warbler, creeping through the foliage to glean insects, and in so doing sometimes fans its tail. *Status.* Very rare in the Park; probably a vagrant to the area. Two records exist for the Nshawu area. *Call.* A repeated, wispy 'tisee-tchee-tchee' phrase and a descending 'cher-cher-cher'. *Afrikaans.* Feevlieëvanger.

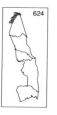

Mashona Hyliota *Hyliota australis* (624) 14 cm
This small black and white warbler is easily identified by its black upperparts, distinctive white wing patch, and buff to creamy-yellow underparts. Although resembling a small flycatcher, the bird behaves like a warbler, creeping around in the canopy of a tree to glean small insects. *Status.* A very rare breeding resident, recorded from the Punda Maria/Pafuri area only. *Call.* Trilling and chittering. *Afrikaans.* Mashonahyliota.

178

Marico Flycatcher

Mousecoloured Flycatcher

Spotted Flycatcher

Dusky Flycatcher

Fairy Flycatcher

Mashona Hyliota

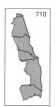

Bluemantled Flycatcher *Trochocercus cyanomelas* (708) 18 cm
A very active flycatcher, easily identified by its bluish-black head and noticeable, long, wispy crest. Female is a greyish-brown version of the male and shows only a slight crest. Flits about restlessly catching insects and spreads its tail, turning from side to side on the branch. *Status.* A flycatcher of forests and thus not entirely at home in the Park. Very rare in the area, recorded in the riverine habitats of the major rivers – probably as an altitudinal migrant from the escarpment in the west. *Call.* Harsh 'tic-tic-chaaa-chaaa' notes and a fluty, whistled song, similar to that of the Paradise Flycatcher. *Afrikaans.* Bloukuifvlieëvanger.

Wattle-eyed Flycatcher *Platysteira peltata* (705) 18 cm
Male might be mistaken for a batis because of its white underparts and black breast band but differs by having a black cap without eyebrow stripes, and a grey back and wings without any white. When seen, the red wattle above the eye is diagnostic. Female differs markedly from male in having the head and upper breast totally black and the remaining underparts white; the eye wattle is also conspicuous and diagnostic. *Status.* A breeding resident along the Limpopo and Luvuvhu rivers only, and often seen at the Pafuri picnic spot. There are a few scattered records elsewhere, namely from the Olifants River at Bangu Mouth and from the Lower Sabie restcamp. *Call.* A repeated 'wichee-wichee-wichee-wichee'. *Afrikaans.* Beloogbosbontrokkie.

Paradise Flycatcher *Terpsiphone viridis* (710) 23 cm (plus 18 cm tail)
An unmistakable flycatcher which has a blue-black head, a greyish body and a chestnut back and tail. At close range the male's cobalt-blue eye wattle and similar-coloured base to the bill can be seen. In breeding plumage the male displays an extremely long tail comprising two elongated central tail feathers. *Status.* A common breeding summer migrant through most of the Park. Resident along some of the permanent rivers such as the Sabie and Luvuvhu. Rare in winter. *Call.* Harsh 'tic-tic-chaa-chaa' notes, similar to those of the Bluemantled Flycatcher. Song is a loud 'twee-tiddly-te-te'. *Afrikaans.* Paradysvlieëvanger.

Chinspot Batis *Batis molitor* (701) 13 cm
The male of this small black and white flycatcher differs from the male Wattle-eyed Flycatcher by having a broader black breast band, a white eyebrow stripe and white in the wings. It also lacks the red eye wattle. Female has a chestnut breast band and a triangular chestnut patch on the throat (diagnostic). *Status.* A common and conspicuous breeding resident. Recorded throughout the Park and easily located by its call. *Call.* A clear 'teuu-teuu-teuu', and harsh 'chrr-chrr' notes. *Afrikaans.* Witliesbosbontrokkie.

180

Bluemantled Flycatcher ♂

Wattle-eyed Flycatcher ♂

Paradise Flycatcher ♂

Chinspot Batis ♂

Chinspot Batis ♀

African Pied Wagtail *Motacilla aguimp* (711) 20 cm
Larger and longer-tailed than Cape Wagtail and with contrasting black and
white, not grey and white plumage. Imm. is greyish-brown and white and
differs from Cape Wagtail by having large expanses of white in the wings.
Status. A very common breeding resident occurring in the vicinity of all the
Park's rivers and dams. Also often seen on the restcamp lawns. *Call.* A sharp,
high-pitched 'cheeerip' or 'chissik'. *Afrikaans.* Bontkwikkie.

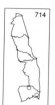

Yellow Wagtail *Motacilla flava* (714) 16 cm
Smaller than both the Cape and African Pied wagtails and differs by having
yellow or yellow-buff underparts and lacking a black breast band. The
plumage varies according to subspecies but in general the upperparts are
olive to grey, some have black caps, and most show distinct canary-yellow
underparts. *Status.* A Palearctic summer migrant, extremely rare in the Park.
Could presumably occur at any of the water bodies in the area. *Call.* A weak,
thin 'tseeep'. *Afrikaans.* Geelkwikkie.

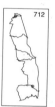

Longtailed Wagtail *Motacilla clara* (712) 20 cm
Very much slimmer and longer tailed than Cape Wagtail, this species is also
paler with grey upperparts and white, not buffy-grey underparts. In addition it
shows more extensive white in the wings and the breast band is narrower than
that of the Cape Wagtail. *Status.* Recorded on the Sabie and Luvuvhu rivers. A
bird of heavily wooded, fast-flowing streams of the escarpment, it is probably
only a very rare winter visitor to the Park, occurring as an altitudinal migrant.
Call. A sharp, high-pitched 'cheeerip' or 'chissik'. *Afrikaans.* Bergkwikkie.

Cape Wagtail *Motacilla capensis* (713) 18 cm
Very different from African Pied Wagtail, being grey and white rather than black
and white, and differs from imm. African Pied Wagtail by having a noticeable
black 'V' on the throat and by its lack of large white wing patches. Imm. has an
olive wash over the back and buffy underparts. *Status.* A very rare bird in the
Park, thought to be a casual vagrant. *Call.* A clear, ringing 'tseee-chee-chee'
call and a whistled, trilling song. *Afrikaans.* Gewone Kwikkie.

African Pied Wagtail

Yellow Wagtail

Longtailed Wagtail

Cape Wagtail

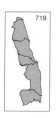

Buffy Pipit *Anthus vaalensis* (719) 18 cm
At times impossible to distinguish from Plainbacked Pipit. With experience, this species can be distinguished by its shape which is more rotund than that of Plainbacked Pipit and by the overall warmer buffy colour, especially on the flanks and belly. It also has a habit of standing very upright and continually wagging its tail. *Status.* A very rare pipit, probably nomadic to the area. Two sightings have been made at Bangu Windmill. *Call.* When flushed gives a short 'sshik'. Song, a 'tchipeep-cheree', is softer than that of the Plainbacked Pipit. *Afrikaans.* Vaalkoester.

Longbilled Pipit *Anthus similis* (717) 18 cm
Unlike the similar Grassveld, Buffy and Plainbacked pipits this bird prefers boulder-strewn grassy hillsides, and unlike Striped Pipit does not occur in thicker woodland. Despite its vernacular name, the bill is not noticeably long. It lacks the defined streaking on the breast seen in Grassveld Pipit, having a more mottled appearance, and shows distinct buffy, not white outer tail feathers. *Status.* A very rare bird, and the few existing records of it in the Park make its status uncertain. *Call.* A high-pitched, trisyllabic 'pheeet-pheeet-cher' (unlike the duosyllabic call of the Plainbacked Pipit) and a sparrow-like 'cheerup'. *Afrikaans.* Nicholsonse Koester.

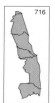

Grassveld Pipit *Anthus cinnamomeus* (716) 16 cm
Pipits are notoriously difficult to identify and this species is no exception. By far the most common pipit within the Park, it is usually found in open grassy areas and sometimes on road verges. Differs from the similar Buffy and Plainbacked pipits by having bright white, not buff outer tail feathers. *Status.* A common breeding resident occurring throughout the Park. *Call.* Song given during display flight is a 'trrit-trrit-trrit'. When flushed it utters a 'chisseet'. *Afrikaans.* Gewone Koester.

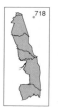

Plainbacked Pipit *Anthus leucophrys* (718) 18 cm
Virtually indistinguishable from Buffy Pipit in the field. At closer range the underparts are seen to be less buffy and the upperparts unmarked and greyer. Does not have Buffy Pipit's habit of continually wagging its tail. Differs from Grassveld Pipit by having a less distinctly marked breast and by the uniform upperparts. *Status.* Probably a breeding vagrant to the Park but very few records exist, making its status uncertain. *Call.* A loud, clear, duosyllabic 'chrrrup-chereeoo', similar in quality to the Longbilled Pipit's trisyllabic call. *Afrikaans.* Donkerkoester.

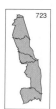

Bushveld Pipit *Anthus caffer* (723) 13,5 cm
The smallest pipit to be seen in the Park, this species has heavily but finely streaked underparts and a relatively short tail. Less demonstrative than other pipits and when feeding will creep furtively through the grass on slightly flexed legs, continually peering about. When put to flight often seeks refuge in the top of a small tree or bush. *Status.* A locally common species which may be nomadic, being fairly common in an area for a while and then disappearing. Appears to favour the broadleaved woodland areas in the western half of the Park. *Call.* A treble call note:'zrrrt-zrree-chreee'. *Afrikaans.* Bosveldkoester.

Buffy Pipit

Longbilled Pipit

Grassveld Pipit

Plainbacked Pipit

Bushveld Pipit

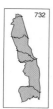

Fiscal Shrike *Lanius collaris* (732) 23 cm
Superficially resembles a boubou shrike but has a much longer tail and does not skulk and retire into thickets as those species do. Differs from the similar Fiscal Flycatcher by having a thick, heavily hooked bill, a much longer tail and the white in the wing on the scapulars, not at the base of the secondaries. Female is similar to male but has a chestnut patch on her flanks. It hunts from exposed perches in open areas. *Status.* An enigmatic species as it occurs in some numbers just outside the Park but is very rare within. Most reports are suspected misidentifications of some of the other predominantly black and white shrikes. *Call.* Harsh grating, a melodious, whistled song jumbled with harsher notes, and mimicry of other bird calls. *Afrikaans.* Fiskaallaksman.

Fiscal Flycatcher *Sigelus silens* (698) 17-20 cm
Most often confused with the Fiscal Shrike but can be distinguished by its smaller size, lighter build and much shorter tail which has white outer rectrices at the base. The white patch in the wing is located on the secondaries and base of the primaries, not on the scapulars as in Fiscal Shrike. At closer range the bill can be seen to be small, flattened and weak, not stubby and heavily hooked as in Fiscal Shrike. Female has the black plumage of male replaced with dark brown. *Status.* A very rare winter visitor to the area, and probably an altitudinal migrant from the Highveld. *Call.* A soft, weak chittering song and a 'tssisk' alarm call. *Afrikaans.* Fiskaalvlieëvanger.

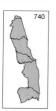

Puffback *Dryoscopus cubla* (740) 18 cm
Male is unmistakable in display or if agitated when it fluffs up its lower back into a white 'powder-puff'. When its 'powder-puff' rump is not evident it might be mistaken for Southern Boubou but lacks any rufous on the underparts, and has white scaling on the wings and a bright red eye. *Status.* A very common and conspicuous breeding resident recorded throughout the Park. *Call.* A whistled 'weeee', followed by a whip-like 'cheraak'. *Afrikaans.* Sneeubal.

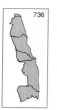

Southern Boubou *Laniarius ferrugineus* (736) 23 cm
Does not often venture into the open, preferring to skulk in the deeper tangles and thickets: more often heard than seen. When seen, resembles Fiscal Shrike but has a much shorter tail and a variable amount of buff to rufous on the underparts. Could be confused with the similar Tropical Boubou but lacks the silky white underparts of that species. *Status.* Restricted to and common in riverine habitats throughout the Park as far north as the Shingwedzi Drainage System, but possibly absent from the Luvuvhu and Limpopo rivers where it may be displaced by the Tropical Boubou: reports of the bird in this area may be misidentifications of the Tropical Boubou. *Call.* A variable duet with basic notes of 'boo-boo' followed by a 'whee-ooo'. *Afrikaans.* Suidelike Waterfiskaal.

Tropical Boubou *Laniarius aethiopicus* (737) 21 cm
Any boubou shrike seen in the northernmost parts of the Park along river courses should be carefully examined. This species might be confused with Southern Boubou but there are more striking contrasts in its plumage, the upperparts being glossy blue-black and the underparts silky white, turning to cream or pale buff on the belly and flanks. It lacks the rufous colouring on the breast, belly and flanks of Southern Boubou. *Status.* Restricted to the riverine habitats of the Limpopo/Luvuvhu River System. A common but secretive species, best located by one of its calls: a frog-like 'ghorr' is a characteristic sound of the Pafuri area. *Call.* Duet call, very similar to that of the Southern Boubou. *Afrikaans.* Tropiese Waterfiskaal.

186

Fiscal Shrike ♀

Fiscal Flycatcher ♀

Puffback ♂

Puffback ♀

Southern Boubou

Tropical Boubou

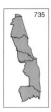

✓Longtailed Shrike *Corvinella melanoleuca* (735) 40-50 cm
An unmistakable bird with a pied plumage and an extremely long tail.
Conspicuous and easily seen, moving in small groups which inhabit an area
and keep contact with their whistled calls. *Status.* A common breeding
resident which can be seen throughout the Park in woodland and savanna
habitats. *Call.* A liquid, whistled 'peeleeo'. *Afrikaans.* Langstertlaksman.

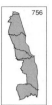

Whitecrowned Shrike *Eurocephalus anguitimens* (756) 25 cm
This large shrike is not often seen alone as it prefers to move around in small
groups. Instantly recognizable as it is the only shrike that has a white crown.
The back and wings are greyish-brown, the throat and breast are off-white
merging to buff, and the belly and flanks are buff-grey. *Status.* A widespread
species but with fairly specific habitat requirements, favouring tall acacia
woodland with an open understorey. *Call.* A shrill, whistling 'kree, kree, kree'
and harsh chattering. *Afrikaans.* Kremetartlaksman.

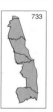

Redbacked Shrike *Lanius collurio* (733) 17 cm
A small shrike with a diagnostic plumage comprising a grey head and rump, a
contrasting chestnut back, creamy underparts and a narrow black mask. The
larger Lesser Grey Shrike lacks the chestnut on the back. Female and imm.
are reddish-brown above and have greyish-brown crescentic barring below.
Status. A very common non-breeding summer migrant occurring in almost all
habitats throughout the Park. *Call.* A harsh 'chak, chak' and a soft warbler-like
song. *Afrikaans.* Rooiruglaksman.

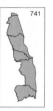

Brubru *Nilaus afer* (741) 15 cm
A small, predominantly black and white shrike, easily distinguished by the
chestnut stripe running from its shoulder to the flanks. The colour combination
of the plumage might lead to confusion with a batis, but it is a very much larger
bird and has a thick, hooked bill typical of the shrike family. Female is duller
than male and has the black in the plumage shading to brown. *Status.* A fairly
common and widespread breeding resident favouring nearly all habitats in the
Park. *Call.* The male gives a soft, trilling 'prrrr, prrrr' and the female responds
with a piercing whistle 'tioooo'. *Afrikaans.* Bontroklaksman.

✓Lesser Grey Shrike *Lanius minor* (731) 20 cm
When seen front-on might be mistaken for Redbacked Shrike but has a much
more extensive black mask and is noticeably larger. When viewed from behind
it can be seen to have a grey, not chestnut back and blackish wings with white
patches at the base of the primaries. *Status.* An uncommon non-breeding
summer migrant. Prefers the Park's open savanna areas, particularly the
eastern flats. *Call.* A soft 'chuk'. Song seldom heard in the Park.
Afrikaans. Gryslaksman.

Longtailed Shrike

Whitecrowned Shrike

Redbacked Shrike ♂

Redbacked Shrike ♀

Brubru ♂

Lesser Grey Shrike

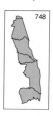

Orangebreasted Bush Shrike *Telophorus sulfureopectus* (748) 19 cm
Might be confused with the much larger Greyheaded Bush Shrike but is a
small green and yellow shrike with a diagnostic yellow forehead and a
well-marked yellow eyebrow stripe contrasting with black lores. Female is
dowdier than male and sometimes lacks the orange wash across the breast.
Status. A common and widespread breeding resident which favours areas of
thick bush, both acacia and broadleaved. *Call.* A frequently repeated
'poo-poo-poo-pooooo' and a 'titit-eeezz'. *Afrikaans.* Oranjeborsboslaksman.

Greyheaded Bush Shrike *Malaconotus blanchoti* (751) 26 cm
An extremely large and powerful shrike which, proportionately, has a very large
head and a large, thick, hooked bill. The Orangebreasted Bush Shrike is much
smaller, lacks the enormous bill and is not as brightly coloured orange on the
underparts. When viewed from behind, Greyheaded Bush Shrike might be
mistaken for a Yellowspotted Nicator as it shows spotting on the wing coverts
and tips of the secondaries but the large size and very obviously grey head
should rule out confusion. *Status.* A common and widespread resident
occurring throughout the Park. *Call.* A drawn-out 'oooooop' and a
'tic-tic-ooop'. *Afrikaans.* Spookvoël.

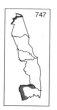

Gorgeous Bush Shrike *Telophorus quadricolor* (747) 20 cm
Hearing its ringing call is virtually the only contact one makes with this
extremely shy and furtive bird. Despite its brilliantly coloured underparts this
bird is exceptionally difficult to see in the thick tangles it inhabits because of its
habit of keeping its back to the observer and so showing its olive-green
upperparts. When viewed from the front the rich crimson throat, broad black
breast band and orange-yellow underparts are diagnostic. *Status.* Resident
only along the Limpopo and Luvuvhu rivers in the north and in the thicker bush
of the hilly south-west. Pafuri and Shabeni Kop near Pretoriuskop are good
spots to look for it while the Bukweneni Spruit in the Bushman's Trails area
offers another excellent opportunity of seeing this bird. Occurs sporadically
along the Sabie River as far east as Skukuza and occasionally elsewhere in
suitable habitat. *Call.* An often-repeated 'conk-conk-queet' and variations of
this call. *Afrikaans.* Konkoit.

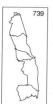

Crimsonbreasted Shrike *Laniarius atrococcineus* (739) 23 cm
Not easily seen in spite of its brilliant colouring as it prefers to remain in the
thicker parts of the bush. When glimpsed, only a flash of the crimson, black
and white are seen. Unlikely to be confused with any other shrike because of
the combination of its brilliant crimson underparts, glossy jet-black upperparts,
and the broad white stripe down the wing. *Status.* Essentially a species of the
drier west, but there is a small resident population to the north of the Luvuvhu
River. Recorded at a few other localities but is a vagrant elsewhere in the Park.
Call. A harsh 'trrrrr' and a whistled 'pheeee-tcherooo' duet.
Afrikaans. Rooiborslaksman.

Orangebreasted Bush Shrike

Greyheaded Bush Shrike

Gorgeous Bush Shrike

Crimsonbreasted Shrike

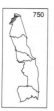

Olive Bush Shrike *Telophorus olivaceus* (750) 18 cm
Occurs in two different colour phases: an olive and a ruddy phase, the ruddy phase being the predominant one in the Park. Behaves very much like other bush shrikes, being very shy and retiring and therefore not easily seen. When observed, the bird is easily identified by its black mask, narrow white eyebrow stripe and off-white underparts washed with rufous over the throat and breast. Female is very similar to male but has a uniform grey head. *Status.* An escarpment and forest species for which there are a few records in the Park. Recorded in the Punda Maria/Pafuri region where it may be resident, but elsewhere in the Park it probably occurs as an altitudinal migrant.
Call. A whistled 'cheeoo-cheeoo-cheeoo-cheeoo' and a call similar to the Orangebreasted Bush Shrike's 'poo-poo-poo-pooooo'.
Afrikaans. Olyfboslaksman.

Threestreaked Tchagra *Tchagra australis* (743) 18 cm
Very similar to the Blackcrowned Tchagra but has a different song and a characteristic display flight which distinguish it. In plumage details it differs by having a brown, not black crown and by having a narrow black line above the white eyebrow stripe and a broad one below it. In display it performs a descending spiralling flight and utters its diagnostic song. *Status.* A common and widespread breeding resident. *Call.* Song given in aerial display is a 'wee-chee-chee-cheee'. *Afrikaans.* Rooivlerktjagra.

Blackcrowned Tchagra *Tchagra senegala* (744) 23 cm
Larger and bulkier than the Threestreaked Tchagra and most often detected by its diagnostic whistling call note. Differs from Threestreaked Tchagra by having a very broad, buffy-white eyebrow stripe and a diagnostic black stripe in the centre of the head. It also appears paler than Threestreaked Tchagra, having paler underparts which contrast strongly with the chestnut wings. *Status.* A common and widespread breeding resident. *Call.* Song is a loud, whistled 'whee-cheree, cherooo, cheree-cheroo' on a descending scale, slurring off towards the end. *Afrikaans.* Swartkroontjagra.

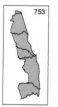

White Helmetshrike *Prionops plumatus* (753) 20 cm
Nervous and very restless, these birds move through the lower and mid-stratum of the woodland in small groups, the members following each other. The black and white patterned plumage is diagnostic as is the fluttery, almost butterfly-like flight. When seen at rest the grey head and fluffy crest, white body and black and white wings all help in identification. *Status.* A common breeding resident favouring mainly the broadleaved woodland areas throughout the Park. *Call.* A jumble of chatters and whistles. *Afrikaans.* Withelmlaksman.

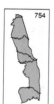

Redbilled Helmetshrike *Prionops retzii* (754) 22 cm
This bird's behaviour is very similar to that of the White Helmetshrike in that it moves around in parties of between five and ten and displays the same weak, butterfly-like flight. It shows a black head and body with paler wings, a conspicuous white undertail and white-tipped tail feathers. At close range the distinctive bright red bill, red wattle around the eye and the red legs are noticeable. *Status.* An uncommon breeding resident (far less common than White Helmetshrike) but occurring throughout. *Call.* Loud whistles and harsh chattering. *Afrikaans.* Swarthelmlaksman.

Olive Bush Shrike ♀ (ruddy form)

Threestreaked Tchagra

Blackcrowned Tchagra

White Helmetshrike

Redbilled Helmetshrike

Greater Blue-eared Starling *Lamprotornis chalybaeus* (765) 23 cm
A very common bird within the Park and one that could be easily confused with the Glossy Starling. Differs from Glossy Starling by having violet, not uniform greeny-blue flanks and belly and a broad, dark matt-blue stripe running from behind to in front of the eye. *Status.* A common and widespread breeding resident. Most common of the glossy starlings and especially abundant in the restcamps. *Call.* A nasal 'squee-aar' and a warbled song.
Afrikaans. Grootblouoorglansspreeu.

Blackbellied Starling *Lamprotornis corruscus* (768) 21 cm
Resembles Glossy Starling but is not likely to be seen with that species or even in the same habitat. Differs from Glossy Starling by being a longer, more slender bird, not quite as brilliantly glossy, and most show a paler yellow eye than Glossy Starling. Under favourable viewing conditions the matt-black belly and undercoverts may be seen. *Status.* Recorded only along the Crocodile River in the Crocodile Bridge area. May be resident there but no breeding records exist. *Call.* Harsh, chippering notes interspersed with shrill whistles.
Afrikaans. Swartpensglansspreeu.

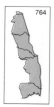

Glossy Starling *Lamprotornis nitens* (764) 25 cm
Likely to be confused only with the Blackbellied and Greater Blue-eared starlings. Differs from the former by being larger and more robust in build, and having a glossy blue, not matt-black belly. Distinguished from the Greater Blue-eared Starling by its call and by having a glossy greeny-blue rather than violet belly and flanks. *Status.* A common and widespread breeding resident, though less common than the Greater Blue-eared starling. *Call.* Song is a slurred 'trrr-chree-chrrr'. *Afrikaans.* Kleinglansspreeu.

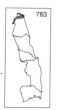

Longtailed Starling *Lamprotornis mevesii* (763) 34 cm
The extremely long, graduated and pointed tail of this starling renders it unmistakable. Burchell's Starling also shows a long tail but it is not nearly as long as in this species. At close range the plumage is seen to be glossy lilac-blue and the eye is dark, not yellow as in other glossy starlings. *Status.* Occurs only along the Limpopo and Luvuvhu rivers where it is a common breeding resident. There is no range overlap of this and the Burchell's Starling in the Park. *Call.* A harsh 'keeeaaaa' and churring notes.
Afrikaans. Langstertglansspreeu.

Burchell's Starling *Lamprotornis australis* (762) 34 cm
By far the largest of the glossy starlings, it has large, rounded wings and a longish tail. The flight is sluggish and floppy. Most often seen in pairs but sometimes may gather in small groups to feed. *Status.* A common breeding resident south of the Olifants River but less common to the north and absent from the Luvuvhu/Limpopo Drainage System where it is replaced by the Longtailed Starling. *Call.* Song is a jumble of throaty chortles and chuckles.
Afrikaans. Grootglansspreeu.

194

Greater Blue-eared Starling

Blackbellied Starling

Glossy Starling

Longtailed Starling

Burchell's Starling

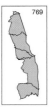

Redwinged Starling *Onychognathus morio* (769) 27 cm
This large starling with its dark plumage is immediately recognizable by its chestnut-tipped wings. Male is a dark, glossy blue which at a distance appears black. Female has a greyish head and breast. *Status.* Essentially an inhabitant of mountainous terrain and thus an uncommon and localized species in the Park. Has 'colonized' some of the restcamps where it has become very tame and breeds on buildings. *Call.* A clear, whistled 'cherleeeeoo' and a variety of other whistles. *Afrikaans.* Rooivlerkspreeu.

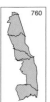

Wattled Starling *Creatophora cinerea* (760) 21 cm
Breeding male is unmistakable with black and yellow wattles on the head and a pale-grey body contrasting with the black wings and tail. Non-breeding male, female and imm. are uniform dull grey and show a contrasting black back, wings and tail and, in flight, a grey rump. *Status.* A breeding vagrant to the area; numbers extremely variable in the Park due to its highly nomadic habits. Breeds colonially in summer in knobthorn veld mainly on the eastern plains, the colonies sometimes covering many hectares. *Call.* Various hisses and cackles, and a 'ssreeeeo' note. *Afrikaans.* Lelspreeu.

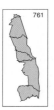

Plumcoloured Starling *Cinnyricinclus leucogaster* (761) 19 cm
The male of this small starling is unmistakable with its iridescent violet upperparts and throat contrasting with clear white underparts. Female differs markedly, lacking the male's violet colour and is heavily striped on its white underparts. *Status.* A fairly common breeding summer migrant. Occurs throughout the Park, but is less common in mopane veld. *Call.* A soft, but sharp 'tip, tip'. Song is a short series of buzzy whistles. *Afrikaans.* Witborsspreeu.

Yellowbilled Oxpecker *Buphagus africanus* (771) 22 cm
The rarer of the two oxpeckers found in the Park and easily recognized by its red-tipped yellow bill. Differs from Redbilled Oxpecker by being much paler overall and, in flight, showing a contrasting pale beige, not uniform brown rump. The bill is much larger than that of Redbilled Oxpecker and has a deeper base. *Status.* Thought for many years to have become extinct in southern Africa but has recently recolonized the Park and is now considered to be a breeding resident. Occurs mainly in the woodland habitats (north of the Letaba River) to the west but seems to avoid the eastern grasslands. It forages for ticks and flies on the larger herbivores, mainly buffalo herds; any such herd should be scanned with care to detect these birds. *Call.* A short, hissing 'kriss, kriss'. *Afrikaans.* Geelbekrenostervoël.

Redbilled Oxpecker *Buphagus erythrorhynchus* (772) 22 cm
By far the most common oxpecker found in the Park and easily distinguished from the Yellowbilled Oxpecker by its thinner and smaller, all-red bill. Differs further by having a dark, not pale rump. *Status.* A very common and conspicuous breeding resident occurring throughout the Park. Can be seen on most of the large herbivores, except elephant. *Call.* A scolding 'churrr' and a hissing 'zzzzzzzist'. *Afrikaans.* Rooibekrenostervoël.

196

Redwinged Starling ♂   Redwinged Starling ♀

Wattled Starling (br. ♂)   Wattled Starling ♀

Plumcoloured Starling ♂   Plumcoloured Starling ♀

Yellowbilled Oxpecker   Redbilled Oxpecker

Whitebellied Sunbird *Nectarinia talatala* (787) 11 cm
No other sunbird in the Park bears any resemblance to the male of this species which makes identifying it very easy. It has an iridescent blue-green head and body which contrast with the white lower breast and belly. Female is predominantly grey with much paler underparts than any other similarly sized sunbird. *Status.* A breeding resident, common throughout the area. Like the other sunbirds, it frequents the restcamp gardens. *Call.* A loud 'pichee, pichee', followed by a burst of fast, buzzy notes.
Afrikaans. Witpenssuikerbekkie.

Scarletchested Sunbird *Nectarinia senegalensis* (791) 15 cm
The male of this species is unmistakable, having an all-black body with a conspicuous scarlet patch on the lower throat and upper breast. At closer range the scarlet breast can be seen to be slightly iridescent with flecks of blue and black. Female could be confused with female Black Sunbird but has a more obviously decurved beak, and is very heavily streaked and mottled on the underparts. *Status.* A locally common breeding resident. Common in gardens of the Park but very uncommon in the woodland habitats, particularly mopane; its distribution may thus be determined by the occurrence of nectar-bearing flowers. *Call.* A loud, whistled 'cheeup, chup, toop, toop, toop' song.
Afrikaans. Rooikeelsuikerbekkie.

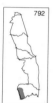

Black Sunbird *Nectarinia amethystina* (792) 15 cm
The only all-black sunbird found in the Park. The male has a uniform matt-black plumage but at close range and in good sunlight the throat can be seen to be iridescent violet and the forehead iridescent bottle-green. Only in ideal viewing conditions is the iridescent blue shoulder patch visible. Female resembles female Scarletchested Sunbird but has a less decurved bill, is paler overall with less mottling and striping on the underparts, and has more obvious buffy moustachial stripes. *Status.* A species of the Middelveld and thus recorded regularly only in the higher-lying areas around Pretoriuskop. Has been reported from a few other widely scattered localities in the area.
Call. A fast, twittering song. *Afrikaans.* Swartsuikerbekkie.

Whitebellied Sunbird ♂

Whitebellied Sunbird ♀

Scarletchested Sunbird ♂

Scarletchested Sunbird ♀

Black Sunbird ♂

Black Sunbird ♀

Marico Sunbird *Nectarinia mariquensis* (779) 14 cm
Very similar to the slightly smaller Purplebanded Sunbird but the iridescent head and back are more bronzy than green and the bill is longer and more decurved. The females are very difficult to distinguish although female Marico Sunbird has a longer, more decurved beak, is generally paler and has a yellower appearance. *Status.* The most common sunbird in the Park. A breeding resident recorded throughout. *Call.* Typical chippering sunbird calls and a fast, warbling song. *Afrikaans.* Maricosuikerbekkie.

Purplebanded Sunbird *Nectarinia bifasciata* (780) 12 cm
The male could easily be confused with the Marico Sunbird but, apart from its very different voice and song, it is smaller, has a shorter, less decurved beak and a decidedly green, not bronzy iridescent cast to the head and back. The females of both species are very similar but this species is somewhat darker and has a less decurved bill than that of female Marico Sunbird.
Status. Because of its similarity to Marico Sunbird, this bird's status in the Park is unclear and at least some of the sightings are likely to be misidentifications. Existing records suggest, however, that it is restricted mainly to the Malelane/Crocodile Bridge area. Other records exist for the extreme eastern parts of the Park as far north as the Olifants River and there is one for Punda Maria. May be a breeding resident. *Call.* A high-pitched 'teeet-teeet-tit-tit' song, accelerating at the end. *Afrikaans.* Purperbandsuikerbekkie.

Marico Sunbird ♂

Marico Sunbird ♀

Purplebanded Sunbird ♂

Purplebanded Sunbird ♀

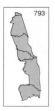

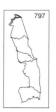

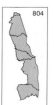

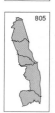

Collared Sunbird *Anthreptes collaris* (793) 10 cm
This tiny sunbird could easily be mistaken for a small warbler as it creeps among the foliage gleaning insects from the underside of leaves and twigs. Male is easily identified by its iridescent bottle-green and blue head and back, and by its bright yellow underparts. At very close range the iridescent blue breast band is noticeable. Female resembles male, also showing the short, decurved bill, but has only the top of the head and back iridescent green and blue, with the remaining underparts yellow. *Status.* A fairly common but localized breeding resident, inhabiting large trees in riverine vegetation. Particularly common along the Luvuvhu and Sabie rivers. *Call.* A soft 'tswee' and a harsher, chirpy song. *Afrikaans.* Kortbeksuikerbekkie.

Cape White-eye *Zosterops pallidus* (796) 12 cm
The most frequently seen white-eye in the Park. Differs from the much rarer Yellow White-eye by having greyish, not bright yellow underparts, green to olive-green upperparts and a green forehead and crown. Imm. lacks the white around the eye and is in general much darker than imm. Yellow White-eye. *Status.* Very localized but not uncommon where it occurs: along the Crocodile, Sabie and Luvuvhu rivers. *Call.* Small groups call a continual 'tweee-tuuu-twee-twee'. *Afrikaans.* Kaapse Glasogie.

Yellow White-eye *Zosterops senegalensis* (797) 11 cm
Could be confused only with Cape White-eye but differs by having yellower plumage: its underparts are much brighter, almost sulphury-yellow, the upperparts are yellow to dark yellow and it almost always has a yellow, not green forehead and crown. Imm. lacks the white around the eye and is darker than ad. but is still very much paler than imm. Cape White-eye. *Status.* In the Park it is restricted to the Luvuvhu and Limpopo rivers where it is not uncommon. Probably a breeding resident though there are no breeding records. *Call.* Very similar in quality to that of the Cape White-eye but this species has a faster delivery. *Afrikaans.* Geelglasogie.

Greyheaded Sparrow *Passer griseus* (804) 15 cm
Very similar to female House Sparrow but distinguished by its distinct grey head which contrasts with the chestnut mantle and white wing bar. Female is dowdier than male and has a less distinct grey head but still shows the chestnut mantle and the white wing bar. *Status.* A very common breeding resident which occurs throughout the Park. *Call.* Various chirping notes. *Afrikaans.* Gryskopmossie.

Yellowthroated Sparrow *Petronia superciliaris* (805) 15 cm
This drab, nondescript sparrow of woodland is best identified by its broad, buff-coloured eyebrow stripe, which is broader behind than in front of the eye. The yellow throat spot is diagnostic but is almost impossible to see in the field unless the bird is very close and in good sunlight. Distinguished from all other sparrows in the Park by the broad eyebrow stripe. *Status.* Fairly common and widespread throughout the Park; probably a breeding resident. Favours areas of tall, broadleaved woodland. *Call.* A three-part, whistled 'trrreep-trrreep-trrreep'. *Afrikaans.* Geelvlekmossie.

Collared Sunbird ♂

Collared Sunbird ♀

Cape White-eye

Yellow White-eye

Greyheaded Sparrow

Yellowthroated Sparrow

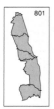

House Sparrow *Passer domesticus* (801) 14 cm
The male is easily recognized by the combination of its black throat and bib, white cheeks, and grey crown and rump. Female resembles female Greyheaded Sparrow but lacks the chestnut back and rump of that species. *Status.* This species thrives in association with man and has colonized nearly every human settlement in the Park. A breeding resident. *Call.* Various chirps, chips and a 'chissick'. *Afrikaans.* Huismossie.

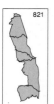

Redbilled Quelea *Quelea quelea* (821) 13 cm
Breeding male has a bright red cone-shaped bill, and a black face with variable amounts of red surrounding it. Non-breeding male and female and imm. are dull mouse-coloured birds, heavily streaked above and buff below, but still show the red bill. *Status.* Numbers fluctuate considerably in the Park, depending on rainfall. Breeds in huge colonies, usually in shrub knobthorn on the eastern flats. Typically moves in flocks which may be small or may comprise thousands of birds. When feeding close to roadsides, these flocks erupt spectacularly out of the grass at the approach of a vehicle. *Call.* Flocks make a chittering noise. Song is a jumbled mixture of harsh and melodious notes. *Afrikaans.* Rooibekkwelea.

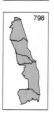

Redbilled Buffalo Weaver *Bubalornis niger* (798) 24 cm
The male is an unmistakable black weaver with a bright red bill and white patches on the primaries which become more conspicuous in flight. Female and imm. are browner versions of male and show a paler bill and white fringes to the breast and belly feathers. *Status.* A common and widespread breeding resident. Breeds and roosts in a characteristic nest of sticks and can usually be found in the vicinity of these nests at any time of the year. Favours baobab and fever trees and also windmills for nest-building. *Call.* Song is a 'chip-chip-doodley-doodley-dooo'. *Afrikaans.* Buffelwewer.

See also nest diagrams on pages 236–237

House Sparrow ♂

House Sparrow ♀

Redbilled Quelea (br. ♂)

Redbilled Quelea ♀

Redbilled Buffalo Weaver ♂

Redbilled Buffalo Weaver ♀

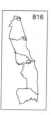

Golden Weaver *Ploceus xanthops* (816) 18 cm
Most closely resembles the Yellow Weaver and both are very rare in the Park.
Differs mainly in eye colour, this species having a pale, not red eye. The
Golden Weaver is a larger bird than the Yellow Weaver and slightly duller over
the head and back. *Status.* Very rare in the Park, having been recorded at a
few widespread localities: the Luvuvhu, Shingwedzi and Olifants rivers. Breeds
at these localities but its status in the Park is otherwise uncertain.
Call. A typical weaver-like 'chuck' and swizzling calls. *Afrikaans.* Goudwewer.

Yellow Weaver *Ploceus subaureus* (817) 15 cm
Most likely to be confused with the Golden and Cape weavers but is
distinguished from both by its smaller size, its red, not pale eye, and its
brighter yellow underparts. Differs further from the Golden Weaver by having a
smaller black bill and from the Cape Weaver by having a faint ginger wash
over the face and throat and much brighter yellow upperparts. *Status.* Only
two records exist for this species in the Park, both of breeding colonies on the
Sabie River in summer. Although it breeds in reedbeds it regularly forages in
thicker tangles of woodland. *Call.* Softer 'chuks' and swizzling than other,
larger weavers. *Afrikaans.* Geelwewer.

Spectacled Weaver *Ploceus ocularis* (810) 15 cm
Identified by the black mask running through and contrasting with the pale
yellow eye, and by the orange wash on the face and throat. The bill is longer
and much more slender than those of other similar weavers. Occurs singly or
in pairs and can be seen creeping through thickets and tangles or climbing
and clinging to the bark of trees in search of insects. *Status.* An uncommon
breeding resident and, in the Park, usually associated with the riverine
vegetation of larger rivers. *Call.* Song is a descending 'dee-dee-dee-dee-dee'.
Afrikaans. Brilwewer.

See also nest diagrams on pages 236–237

Golden Weaver ♂

Yellow Weaver (br.♂)

Yellow Weaver ♀

Golden Weaver ♀

Spectacled Weaver ♂

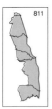

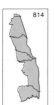

Spottedbacked Weaver *Ploceus cucullatus* (811) 17 cm
The breeding male is the largest and most robust of the three black-faced weavers that occur in the Park and the only one to have a mottled yellow and black back. Female and non-breeding male are difficult to distinguish from similarly plumaged Masked and Lesser Masked weavers. *Status.* A locally common to very common breeding resident. Breeds colonially in reedbeds and trees near water; associates in large numbers with the Lesser Masked Weaver in wild fig trees, notably the one in front of the restaurant at Skukuza. *Call.* A throaty 'chuk-chuk' and buzzy, swizzling notes.
Afrikaans. Bontrugwewer.

Masked Weaver *Ploceus velatus* (814) 15 cm
Similar to the Lesser Masked and Spottedbacked weavers. Differentiated from the Lesser Masked Weaver by having a red, not yellow eye and a yellow, not black forehead. Differentiated from Spottedbacked Weaver by its uniform olive-green rather than mottled black and yellow back. *Status.* A fairly common breeding resident recorded throughout the Park. Does not necessarily breed at sites associated with water. *Call.* A sharp 'zik, zik' and the usual swizzling weaver notes. *Afrikaans.* Swartkeelgeelvink.

Lesser Masked Weaver *Ploceus intermedius* (815) 15 cm
A smaller, more compact weaver than both the Masked and Spottedbacked weavers. Breeding male is readily distinguished from these species by having a pale, not red eye and by its grey, not brown legs. Differs further from the Masked Weaver by having a black, not yellow crown. Non-breeding male differs from non-breeding male Masked Weaver by its pale-coloured, not red eye. *Status.* A locally common breeding resident which nests colonially in reedbeds and trees near water. Often breeds in association with the Spottedbacked Weaver, one site being the wild fig tree in front of the restaurant at Skukuza. *Call.* The typical swizzling sounds of weavers.
Afrikaans. Kleingeelvink.

See also nest diagrams on pages 236–237

Spottedbacked Weaver (br. ♂)

Spottedbacked Weaver ♀

Masked Weaver (br. ♂)

Masked Weaver ♀

Lesser Masked Weaver (br. ♂)

Lesser Masked Weaver (br. ♀)

Thickbilled Weaver *Amblyospiza albifrons* (807) 18 cm
This large, dark-brown weaver with a slightly paler head is easily recognized by its massive bill, white forehead spots and white patches in the wing which are easily seen both at rest and in flight. Non-breeding male lacks the white spots on the forehead. Female and imm. are brown above, heavily streaked below and also show the diagnostic thick, heavy bill. *Status.* Rare but locally common when breeding. Breeds in *Typha* (bulrushes) and reedbeds found in the Park's rivers and dams, particularly in the southern region. Not in evidence in winter and thus probably a breeding summer visitor to the area. *Call.* A 'tweek, tweek' flight call, and chattering at the nest. *Afrikaans.* Dikbekwewer.

Redheaded Weaver *Anaplectes rubriceps* (819) 15 cm
The breeding male is unmistakable with its bright red head and upper breast, bright red bill, yellowish wings, and clear white underparts. Female and non-breeding male are also easily recognized by their lemon-yellow heads, orange-red bills and clear white underparts. *Status.* A generally uncommon breeding resident recorded throughout the Park. Seems to favour human habitations for breeding and is thus common in some of the restcamps, particularly Shingwedzi. *Call.* 'Cherrra-cherrra' and a high-pitched swizzling. *Afrikaans.* Rooikopwewer.

See also nest diagrams on pages 236–237

Thickbilled Weaver (br.♂)

Thickbilled Weaver ♀

Redheaded Weaver (br.♂)

Redheaded Weaver ♀

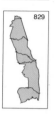

Redshouldered Widow *Euplectes axillaris* (828) 19 cm
The male is unmistakable in breeding plumage, being all-black with red shoulder patches. In non-breeding plumage may be mistaken for non-breeding Longtailed Widow but is very much smaller and the red shoulders do not show the creamy border seen in Longtailed Widow. Female might be confused with female Longtailed Widow but is much smaller and lacks the large rounded wings and laboured flight pattern. *Status.* Recorded in the southern parts of the Park only, where it seems to prefer rank, marshy areas. Breeding has been recorded in summer but its status is otherwise uncertain. *Call.* Various twittering and chirping sounds are given by the male during display. *Afrikaans.* Kortstertflap.

Redcollared Widow *Euplectes ardens* (831) 15 cm (plus 25 cm tail)
The small red crescent on the throat, noticeable at close range, is diagnostic of this bird, the male of which shows a long tail in breeding plumage. Female, non-breeding male and imm. are difficult to distinguish from the similarly coloured and sized bishop and widow birds, but they do show a bold, black-and buff-striped head pattern and have unstreaked buffy underparts.
Status. A very rare bird in the Park, recorded mainly in the higher-lying areas in the south-west where nests with eggs have been found. Also recorded in the long grass areas just north of Lower Sabie and at Orpen Dam and Punda Maria. These records were in summer and of birds in breeding plumage, suggesting that they may breed here too. Winter records are lacking but this may be because of the bird's inconspicuous non-breeding plumage.
Call. A fast, high-pitched 'tee-tee-tee-tee-tee' is given by displaying males.
Afrikaans. Rooikeelflap.

Whitewinged Widow *Euplectes albonotatus* (829) 15-19 cm
The male in breeding plumage shows a longer tail than the similar breeding Redshouldered Widow and differs further by having a combination of yellow and white, not red on the forewing. Non-breeding male is very similar to female and imm. but retains the yellow and white combination on the forewing. When breeding, male displays over its territory, showing off the white and yellow in the wings, and regularly chases females in and out of its territory. Out of the breeding season small flocks of these birds gather together and are distinguished in flight from other non-breeding widow birds by the yellow and white colouring on the forewings. *Status.* An uncommon to locally very common breeding resident. Prefers long, rank grass in damp areas.
Call. A nasal 'zeh-zeh-zeh' and a repetitive 'witz-witz-witz'.
Afrikaans. Witvlerkflap.

212

Redshouldered Widow (br.♂)

Redcollared Widow (br.♂)

Whitewinged Widow (br.♂)

Whitewinged Widow ♀

Red Bishop *Euplectes orix* (824) 14 cm
A small finch-like bird, unmistakable in breeding plumage with its bright orange and black colouring. Female, non-breeding male and imm. are almost indistinguishable from similar age and plumage groups of Golden Bishop but are generally darker and more heavily streaked on the underparts. The male performs an almost bumble bee-like display flight, puffing out its feathers and buzzing over its reedbed territory. *Status.* Generally uncommon but can be locally common in breeding localities. Breeds in *Typha* (bulrushes) beds in some of the Park's dams. Recorded throughout the area but appears to be absent in winter, although its inconspicuous non-breeding plumage may account for this. *Call.* In display male gives a buzzing, chirping song. Normal flight call is a 'cheet-cheet'. *Afrikaans.* Rooivink.

Golden Bishop *Euplectes afer* (826) 12 cm
Breeding male is easily identified by its black and yellow plumage. Female, non-breeding male and imm. are drab, nondescript, brown birds with streaking, and are distinguished from similar plumage stages of Red Bishop by being paler overall, less heavily streaked and by having a slight buffy-yellow wash on the underparts. *Status.* Very rare in the Park but recorded throughout at a few widespread localities. These records were of males in breeding plumage, however, no breeding records exist. *Call.* Buzzing and chirping notes, similar to those of Red Bishop. *Afrikaans.* Goudgeelvink.

214

Red Bishop (br. ♂)

Red Bishop ♀

Golden Bishop (br. ♂)

Golden Bishop ♀

Cuckoo Finch *Anomalospiza imberbis* (820) 13 cm

Frequently overlooked as a small non-breeding weaver but on closer inspection shows a small, conical black bill and bright yellow underparts. Plumage coloration is very variable, however, and may range from different shades of olive-green on the back to dull yellow on the underparts. *Status.* There are only a few records of this bird in the Park which may be a result of its similarity to other smallish yellow species. Recorded only in summer and thus possibly a summer migrant. Favours open grassland and vleis, and parasitizes the cisticolas, though there are no breeding records. *Call.* Described as a 'tsileu, tsileu'. A swizzling noise is uttered during display. *Afrikaans.* Koekoekvink.

Pinkthroated Twinspot *Hypargos margaritatus* (838) 12 cm

Male is difficult to distinguish from male Redthroated Twinspot, as it differs only in its pinkish-red, rather than deep red throat and breast. Female differs from female Redthroated Twinspot by being a uniform greyish-brown and showing no trace of pink or red on the throat and breast. *Status.* A very rare bird reported only from the Nyandu Sandveld in the extreme north-east and from the extreme south-east near Crocodile Bridge. *Call.* A soft, reedy trill. *Afrikaans.* Rooskeelrobbin.

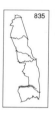

Green Twinspot *Mandingoa nitidula* (835) 10 cm

Superficially resembles the Melba Finch in that male has a red face and bill and a reddish rump and tail, but this bird is much smaller, lacks the green wash across the breast and has a black belly and flanks, heavily spotted with white. Female and imm. are very similar to male but lack the red face and are not as boldly spotted on the underparts. *Status.* Reported only from Skukuza and a few other localities further north. Essentially a species of the escarpment forests to the west, and may thus be an altitudinal migrant entering the Park sporadically. *Call.* A soft, rolling, insect-like 'zrrreet'. *Afrikaans.* Groenrobbin.

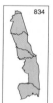

Melba Finch *Pytilia melba* (834) 12 cm

This small, brightly coloured waxbill is easily recognized by its bright red waxy bill, red face, blue-grey crown and nape, and greenish wash across its breast. The underparts are heavily barred. When seen dashing through its thicket habitat, the bright red tail and rump are conspicuous. Female is similar to male but lacks the red on the face. Because of the heavy barring on female's underparts, it might be confused with a Barred Warbler, but is distinguished by its red rump and tail, and thick, finch-like bill. *Status.* A fairly common breeding resident occurring throughout the area. Inconspicuous, but often seen in bird parties, particularly with other waxbills. *Call.* A short 'wick, wick', and a song consisting of a whistled 'trrreeee-chrrroooo'. *Afrikaans.* Gewone Melba.

216

Cuckoo Finch ♂

Pinkthroated Twinspot ♂

Pinkthroated Twinspot ♀

Green Twinspot ♂

Green Twinspot ♀

Melba Finch ♂

Melba Finch ♀

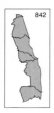

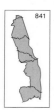

Redbilled Firefinch *Lagonosticta senegala* (842) 10 cm
Differs from both the Bluebilled and Jameson's firefinches by having a diagnostic red bill. Most closely resembles Jameson's Firefinch, having a very bright red body but is distinguished by its distinct olive to brown, not pinkish-red crown and back. Female differs from male by having the pink coloration replaced by olive and buff, and has a smattering of small white spots across the breast and flanks, but still shows the diagnostic red bill.
Status. Probably the most common of the three firefinches in the Park and a breeding resident. Favours thornveld, particularly near watercourses and where ground-cover is sparse. *Call.* A sharp, fast 'vut-vut-vut-chit-chit' and a 'sweeep'. *Afrikaans.* Rooibekrobbin.

Bluebilled Firefinch *Lagonosticta rubricata* (840) 10 cm
Resembles Jameson's Firefinch in that both have bluish-coloured bills, but is not as bright pink as Jameson's Firefinch and has grey and brown, not pink upperparts. Female is much duller than male and differs from female Jameson's Firefinch by lacking the pinkish colour of that species.
Status. A fairly common breeding resident which favours the tangled vegetation of permanent watercourses and dams, particularly where tall grass is plentiful. *Call.* A fast, clicking 'trrt-trrt-trrt-trrt', sounding like a fishing reel as the line is played out, and a 'wink-wink-wink'. *Afrikaans.* Kaapse Robbin.

Jameson's Firefinch *Lagonosticta rhodopareia* (841) 10 cm
This is the brightest and most intensely reddish-pink of all the firefinches, and differs from both the Redbilled and Bluebilled firefinches by having pinkish-red on the crown, nape and mantle. Female is not as brightly coloured as male but is much brighter than female Bluebilled and Redbilled firefinches.
Status. A common breeding resident occurring throughout the Park. Generally a savanna species, favouring areas of bush and seeding grasses.
Call. A clicking trill similar to that of the Bluebilled Firefinch, but higher pitched and interspersed with a sharp 'vit-vit-vit'. *Afrikaans.* Jamesonse Robbin.

Redbilled Firefinch ♂

Redbilled Firefinch ♀

Bluebilled Firefinch ♂

Bluebilled Firefinch ♀

Jameson's Firefinch ♂

Jameson's Firefinch ♀

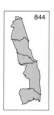

Blue Waxbill *Uraeginthus angolensis* (844) 13 cm
The male has a delicate powder-blue face and underparts and a dull brown crown, nape and back. Female is very similar to male but has a less intensely blue face and underparts. When flushed shows a blue upper tail and rump which contrast with the back. This is the most common waxbill found in the Park and is frequently seen in pairs and small parties feeding at the bottom of thickets and along roadsides. *Status.* A very common breeding resident occurring throughout the Park. *Call.* A soft 'kway-kway-sree-seee-seee-seee'. *Afrikaans.* Gewone Blousysie.

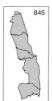

Violeteared Waxbill *Uraeginthus granatinus* (845) 15 cm
The male is unmistakable with its chestnut body, iridescent, almost waxy violet ears and deep blue rump. Female is a much paler version of male with a buff-coloured body and brown wings, but still shows the diagnostic violet ears and blue rump and, like the male, has a very long, pointed tail. Normally a shy species, keeping to the thicker tangles of bush where it forages on the ground, but regularly comes to waterholes to drink. *Status.* Uncommon, but possibly more common than suspected on account of its retiring nature. Occurs throughout the area and is probably resident, although there are no breeding records. *Call.* A soft, whistled 'tiu-woowee'. *Afrikaans.* Koningblousysie.

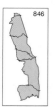

Common Waxbill *Estrilda astrild* (846) 13 cm
The delicately marked plumage of this small bird can only be appreciated at close range. Normally appears as a drab brown bird with a long, pointed tail but at close range shows very fine barring on the underparts and on the mantle and rump, and a contrasting crimson patch on the belly and vent. The small bill is bright red and a red stripe runs from the base of the bill to behind the eye. Normally seen in small groups in grassy areas or in reedbeds. *Status.* A common and widespread breeding resident favouring rank waterside vegetation alongside rivers and dams throughout the Park. *Call.* A nasal 'cher-cher-cher' and a 'ping, ping' flight note. *Afrikaans.* Rooibeksysie.

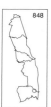

Grey Waxbill *Estrilda perreini* (848) 11 cm
This small waxbill is unmistakable with its plain grey plumage contrasting with a conspicuous red rump and upper tail coverts, and a black tail. When seen at close range it shows a dark-tipped blue beak, a black stripe through the eye, and a small area of black on the chin. Imm. is duller overall than ad. and lacks the black stripe through the eye. *Status.* There is only one record for this species, this being near Lower Sabie in March 1978. *Call.* The waxbill's typical, soft 'pseu, pseeu'. *Afrikaans.* Gryssysie.

220

Blue Waxbill

Violeteared Waxbill ♂

Violeteared Waxbill ♀

Common Waxbill

Grey Waxbill

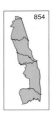

Orangebreasted Waxbill *Sporaeginthus subflavus* (854) 10 cm
Like many other small finches, this species displays a bright crimson rump in flight, but is distinguished by its bright yellow underparts and orange wash across the breast. At close range the red bill, bright red eyebrow stripe, and yellow and brown barring down the sides of the breast and flanks are visible. Female is a duller version of male, showing much less yellow on the belly and lacking the bright red eyebrow stripe. *Status.* Very rare in the Park and difficult to see as it has been recorded in long grass in damp situations only. Occurs throughout the area and is probably a breeding resident. *Call.* A soft, clinking 'zink zink zink' flight call. *Afrikaans.* Rooiassie.

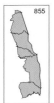

Cut-throat Finch *Amadina fasciata* (855) 12 cm
This small dappled finch is distinguished by the diagnostic red crescent on its throat. Female closely resembles male but lacks the red crescent. *Status.* An uncommon breeding resident occurring mainly in the central and northern areas. Favours weavers' nests for breeding, particularly those of Redheaded Weavers, and may be seen at these sites in late summer or, out of the breeding season, at dusk when it uses the nests for roosting. A good place to see these birds is at the Shingwedzi restcamp where many Redheaded Weaver nests are found. *Call.* An 'eee-eee-eee' flight call. *Afrikaans.* Bandkeelvink.

Redbacked Mannikin *Spermestes bicolor* (858) 9 cm
Resembles the Bronze Mannikin in that it has a black head, barred flanks and barring on the folded wing, but is distinguished by its diagnostic chestnut mantle and wing coverts. Imm. is much duller than ad. and shows a chestnut wash on the mantle and also slight barring on the fold of the wings. *Status.* Very uncommon and recorded mainly in the central and southern areas. Breeding has been recorded at Skukuza, thus probably a breeding resident. *Call.* A thin, soft 'seeet-seeet' uttered when flushed from the grass. *Afrikaans.* Rooirugfret.

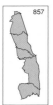

Bronze Mannikin *Spermestes cucullatus* (857) 9 cm
By far the most frequently seen mannikin in the Park, it is distinguished by its black head and bib, heavy, bicoloured bill, white breast, heavily barred flanks, and dull brown upperparts. In direct sunlight the bronzy-green shoulder can be seen. Imm. is very different from ad., being a uniform dull brown all over. *Status.* An uncommon breeding resident. Appears to be absent from the mopane areas but otherwise occurs throughout. *Call.* A soft, buzzy 'chizza, chizza'. *Afrikaans.* Gewone Fret.

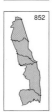

Quail Finch *Ortygospiza atricollis* (852) 9 cm
Very rarely seen on the ground unless observed drinking at a water source, and more often seen and heard flying overhead. The red bill, black face, and eye encircled by white are diagnostic as are the barred black and white breast and flanks. Female is slightly duller than male. *Status.* Restricted mainly to the grassland areas in the eastern half of the Park where it is common but inconspicuous. Nshawu Dam and the Malopenyane and Middelvlei windmills north of Letaba probably offer the best opportunities of seeing this bird. Probably a breeding resident. *Call.* In flight, gives a continual, tinny 'chillink, chillink' call. *Afrikaans.* Gewone Kwartelvinkie.

Orangebreasted Waxbill ♂

Cut-throat Finch (♂ left, ♀ right)

Redbacked Mannikin

Bronze Mannikin

Quail Finch ♀

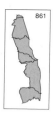

Shaft-tailed Whydah *Vidua regia* (861) 12 cm (plus 22 cm tail)
Breeding male has rich buff and black plumage with elongated central tail feathers which are extremely thin and have spatulate tips. Female, non-breeding male and imm. are virtually indistinguishable from similarly aged and plumaged Pintailed Whydah but in general have less distinct head markings and are slightly paler. *Status.* Generally uncommon though appears to be more common in the northern areas. *Call.* Similar to, but harsher than that of the Pintailed Whydah. *Afrikaans.* Pylstertrooibekkie.

Paradise Whydah *Vidua paradisaea* (862) 15 cm (plus 23 cm tail)
Breeding male is easily recognized by its very long, broad tail which tapers to a point. The plumage is also distinctive, the bird showing a black face and head, a bright golden nape, and a rich chestnut breast with white underparts. Female, non-breeding male, and imm. are nondescript brown birds and show broad, dark brown to black stripes over the head, a broad chestnut breast band, clear underparts and a mottled back. *Status.* A fairly common and conspicuous breeding resident. *Call.* A sharp 'chip-chip' and a short 'cheroop-cherrup' song. *Afrikaans.* Gewone Paradysvink.

Pintailed Whydah *Vidua macroura* (860) 12 cm (plus 22 cm tail)
The male in breeding plumage is unmistakable, having a black and white plumage, very long black central tail feathers, and a bright red bill. Shaft-tailed Whydah is similar but is buff, not white below. Female, non-breeding male and imm. are virtually indistinguishable from the similar plumage stages of Shaft-tailed Whydah but have more distinct black and white head markings. *Status.* A common breeding resident. *Call.* Displaying male gives a 'tseet-tseet-tseet' call. *Afrikaans.* Koningrooibekkie.

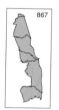

Steelblue Widowfinch *Vidua chalybeata* (867) 11 cm
The all-black male is distinguished by the combination of a bright red bill and red legs. In some areas, the red bill may appear very pale, almost white, and the bird might then resemble the Black and Purple widowfinches. Distinguished from the Black Widowfinch by having a pale panel in the folded wing and from the Purple Widowfinch by its bright red, not white or pinkish legs, and by having a blue sheen to the upperparts. Female and non-breeding male are indistinguishable from similarly plumaged widowfinches. *Status.* An uncommon resident species. *Call.* A canary-like song which includes whistled 'wheeet-wheeet-wheetoo' notes. *Afrikaans.* Staalblouvinkie.

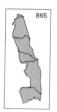

Purple Widowfinch *Vidua purpurascens* (865) 11 cm
The diagnostic white bill and whitish or pale pink legs and feet distinguish this bird from the other widowfinches in the Park. Like Steelblue Widowfinch, shows a pale panel in the folded wing. Female and non-breeding male are virtually indistinguishable from similarly plumaged widowfinches. *Status.* Very few records exist for the Park and its status is uncertain. *Call.* Described as mimicking Jameson's Firefinch. *Afrikaans.* Witpootblouvinkie.

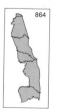

Black Widowfinch *Vidua funerea* (864) 11 cm
Breeding male has a combination of a white bill and red legs and feet. Differs from both the Purple and Steelblue widowfinches by lacking a pale panel in the folded wing and by having a matt-black plumage. Female and non-breeding male are indistinguishable from similarly plumaged widowfinches. *Status.* An uncommon resident species. *Call.* A short, canary-like jingle, and a 'chit-chit-chit'. *Afrikaans.* Gewone Blouvinkie.

Shaft-tailed Whydah (br. ♂)

Paradise Whydah (br. ♂)

Pintailed Whydah (br. ♂)

Shaft-tailed Whydah ♀

Steelblue Widowfinch (br. ♂)

Purple Widowfinch (br. ♂)

Black Widowfinch (br. ♂)

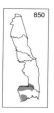

Swee Waxbill *Estrilda melanotis* (850) 10 cm
A tiny, unobtrusive waxbill with a diagnostic black patch on the throat and lower face, a grey head, olive back, and a bright red rump which contrasts with the short black tail. Female is very similar to male but lacks the black patch on the throat and face. *Status.* A very rare visitor to the Park, recorded in winter. Mainly a species of the escarpment forests, and therefore probably an altitudinal migrant. *Call.* A soft 'swee-swee' call is uttered in flight. *Afrikaans.* Suidelike Swie.

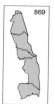

Yelloweyed Canary *Serinus mozambicus* (869) 12 cm
Probably the most familiar canary in the Park and a regular sight at most of the restcamps. The bird has a yellow face with a dark line through the eye and an obvious black moustachial stripe. The underparts are bright yellow fading to yellowish-buff on the flanks. In flight it shows a white tip to the tail. The sexes are similar, but imm. is duller overall. The Bully Canary, which might be confused with this species, is a much larger bird and has a much heavier bill. *Status.* A very common breeding resident occurring throughout the Park. *Call.* A 'zeeee-zereee-chereeo'. *Afrikaans.* Geeloogkanarie.

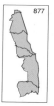

Bully Canary *Serinus sulphuratus* (877) 15 cm
Likely to be confused only with the Yelloweyed Canary but is very much larger and more robustly built, and has a noticeably large, thick bill. Differs further by having duller, more olive-coloured upperparts and by lacking the distinctive facial markings of the Yelloweyed Canary. *Status.* Only a few sightings of this bird exist for the Park, from widely scattered localities. *Call.* Deeper pitched and slower than that of other canaries. *Afrikaans.* Dikbekkanarie.

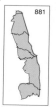

Streakyheaded Canary *Serinus gularis* (881) 15 cm
A nondescript canary, distinguished by its broad white eyebrow stripe and finely streaked forehead and crown. The underparts are uniform brown in colour and the upperparts are a darker greyish-brown. Imm. is very similar to ad. but the underparts are mottled grey and brown. *Status.* Rare in the Park and although no breeding records exist, probably a resident. Recorded from localities throughout the area, but the Olifants Trails area and Punda Maria restcamp are the best localities for seeing this bird. *Call.* A soft, weak 'trrreet', and a short song. *Afrikaans.* Streepkopkanarie.

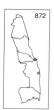

Cape Canary *Serinus canicollis* (872) 13 cm
The tinkling, trilling call of this small canary is often the first indication of its presence. The male is olive-green to yellow in colour and has a diagnostic yellow forehead and crown which contrast with the blue-grey nape and sides of the neck. Female is duller, has a more heavily streaked back and has the grey on the head extending further around the breast. Imm. has a mainly grey body which is streaked with dark brown, and a contrasting yellow tail. *Status.* There have been only a few sightings of this bird in the Park from scattered localities in the central parts (Letaba and Nwanetsi). *Call.* A clear 'sklereee' and, in flight, a twittering tinkle. *Afrikaans.* Kaapse Kanarie.

Swee Waxbill ♂

Swee Waxbill ♀

Yelloweyed Canary

Bully Canary

Streakyheaded Canary

Cape Canary ♂

Cape Canary ♀

Lemonbreasted Canary *Serinus citrinipectus* (871) 10 cm
Most likely to be confused with Yelloweyed Canary but differs by having the
yellow colouring confined to the throat and breast, not extending to the belly
and vent. It has a distinct grey and white facial pattern and lacks the yellow
head stripes of the Yelloweyed Canary. In flight shows a bright yellow rump.
Female has a similar head pattern but lacks yellow on the underparts, these
being more buff in colour. *Status.* This species appears to have a very strong
association with lala palms, particularly as sites for breeding. Has been seen
attending nests in these palms in November in the extreme north-east at
Crooks Corner. *Call.* Similar to that of the Blackthroated Canary, but higher
pitched and shorter. *Afrikaans.* Geelborskanarie.

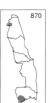

Blackthroated Canary *Serinus atrogularis* (870) 11 cm
Probably the drabbest canary of the family, its diagnostic bright yellow rump
contrasting vividly with the rest of its plumage. Only at close range is the
grizzled black and buff throat visible. *Status.* Recorded only in the far north
and south-west; possibly a very rare vagrant to the Park. *Call.* A prolonged
series of wheezy whistles and chirrups. *Afrikaans.* Bergkanarie.

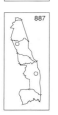

Larklike Bunting *Emberiza impetuani* (887) 14 cm
The lack of any diagnostic or marked field characters on this very drab and
dowdy bird is in itself an aid to identification. It is overall dull brown and buff
and has a slight reddish tinge on the folded wing. Behaves in typical bunting
fashion, hopping over stones and grubbing for food on bare ground. *Status.* A
species of the drier western areas, not resident in the Park. Appears to erupt
into the Park in large numbers during extremely dry periods. *Call.* A soft, nasal
'tuc-tuc' and a short, snappy song. *Afrikaans.* Vaalstreepkoppie.

Rock Bunting *Emberiza tahapisi* (886) 14 cm
The black and white head pattern, cinnamon underparts and black throat
distinguish this bird. It differs from Cape Bunting by lacking the chestnut patch
on the wings. Female and imm. do not show the marked head pattern of the
male but still show the diagnostic cinnamon underparts. *Status.* A locally
common breeding resident associated with rocky outcrops or stony regions.
Call. A grating, rattled song and a soft 'pee-wee'. *Afrikaans.* Klipstreepkoppie.

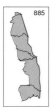

Cape Bunting *Emberiza capensis* (885) 16 cm
The greyest of all the buntings seen in the Park, this species has chestnut
forewings which contrast with the greyish body. Like other buntings, it has a
black and white striped head. Imm. has less definite head markings and
shows a duller chestnut patch on the forewing. *Status.* Very rare in the Park;
some sightings may have been misidentifications. *Call.* A buzzy, ascending
'zzoo-zeh-zee-zee', and a short chirping song.
Afrikaans. Rooivlerkstreepkoppie.

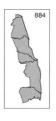

Goldenbreasted Bunting *Emberiza flaviventris* (884) 16 cm
The noticeable black and white striped head pattern combined with the golden
wash across the breast and belly help to identify this bird. When flushed, it will
fly up to settle in a tree, thus displaying its conspicuous white outer tail
feathers. Female and imm. have a less distinct head pattern than the male.
Often encountered singly or in pairs, foraging on the ground. *Status.* A
common and widespread breeding resident. *Call* A nasal, buzzy 'zzhrrr'. Song
is a varied 'weechee-weechee-weechee'. *Afrikaans.* Rooirugstreepkoppie.

228

Lemonbreasted Canary (♀ left, ♂ right)

Blackthroated Canary

Larklike Bunting

Rock Bunting ♂

Cape Bunting

Goldenbreasted Bunting

GLOSSARY

Accidental. A vagrant or stray species not normally found within the Park.

Adult. A bird with a plumage that does not change in subsequent moults.

Altitudinal migrant. Migrates from high to low altitudes at the onset of cold weather.

Carpal. The bend of the wing at the base of the primaries.

Cere. Bare, coloured skin at the base of a raptor's bill.

Colonial. Associating in close proximity, while roosting, feeding or breeding.

Coverts. Groups of feathers covering the bases of the major flight feathers or an area or structure such as an ear.

Crest. Elongated feathers on the forehead, crown or nape.

Cryptic. Having protective colouring or camouflage.

Decurved. Curving downwards.

Diagnostic. Pertaining to a feature or character which is pertinent to identifying a particular species.

Diurnal. Active during daylight hours.

Eclipse plumage. Dull plumage attained by male ducks and sunbirds during a transitional moult.

Endemic. Restricted to a certain region.

Eyebrow. Usually referring to a stripe above the eye.

Eye-stripe. A stripe running from the base of the bill directly through the eye.

Facial disc. A bird's face, disc-like in form, being well defined and typically flat in owls and harriers.

Field mark. A distinctive plumage mark which aids identification.

Flush. To rouse or put to flight.

Frontal shield. A bare patch of skin at the base of the bill and forehead which is often brightly coloured.

Gape. Basal opening of the bill.

Immature. A bird that has moulted from juvenile plumage but has not yet attained adult plumage. Can also encompass juvenile plumage.

Juvenile. The first full feathered plumage of a young bird.

Leading edge. The front edge of a wing.

Lore. The area between the bill and the eye.

Malar stripe. A stripe running downwards from the side of the lower mandible.

Mandible. A bird's bill or beak.

Mantle. The combined area of the back, upperwings and scapulars.

Mask. A black or dark area which encloses the eyes and part of the face.

Migrant. A species which undertakes (usually long-distance) flights from its wintering to breeding areas.

Montane. Pertaining to mountains.

Moustachial stripe. A stripe running from the base of the bill down the side of the throat.

Nape. The upper hind neck.

Nocturnal. Active at night.

Overwintering. Pertaining to a bird which remains in an area instead of migrating.

Palearctic. North Africa, Greenland, Europe and Asia north of the Himalayas, southern China and South East Asia.

Parasitize. When a bird lays its eggs in the nest of another species for the purposes of incubation.

Phase. A plumage colour stage.

Primaries. The outermost major flight feathers of the wing.

Race. A geographical population of a species; a subspecies.

Range. A bird's distribution.

Raptor. A bird of prey.

Riparian. Riverine vegetation or habitat.

Resident. A species not prone to migration, remaining in the same area all year round.

Rufous. Reddish-brown.

Scapulars. The group of feathers on the back, at the base of the upperwing.

Secondaries. The longest wing feathers on the back, from the mid-wing to the wing base.

Shoulder. The area immediately in front of the carpals on a folded wing.

Speculum. A patch of distinctive colour on the secondaries of ducks.

Territory. An area that a bird establishes and then defends from other birds.

Tertials. The inner secondary feathers which lie close to the body.

Vagrant. Rare and accidental to the region.

Vent. The undertail region of a bird, extending to the legs.

BIRD TOPOGRAPHY

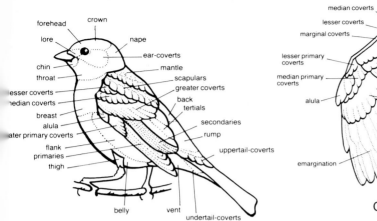

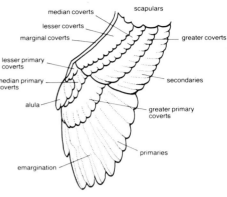

Chart of upperwing

median coverts
scapulars
lesser coverts
marginal coverts
greater coverts
lesser primary coverts
median primary coverts
secondaries
alula
greater primary coverts
emargination
primaries

Chart of underwing

notch
inner web
outer web
shaft
primaries
median under primary coverts
lesser under primary coverts
greater under primary coverts
marginal underwing coverts
lesser underwing coverts
median underwing coverts
greater underwing coverts
secondaries
axillaries

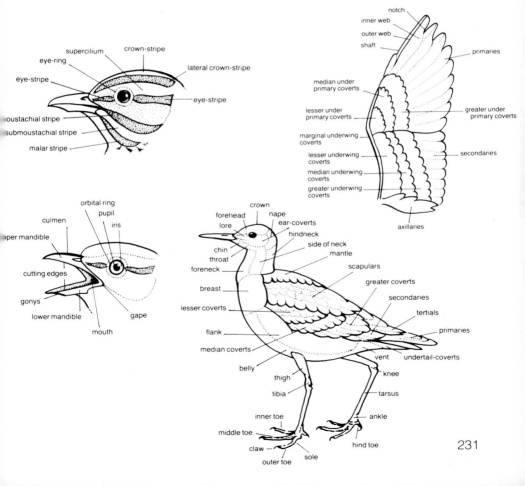

BIRDS OF PREY UNDERWING PATTERNS

Birds of prey are notoriously difficult to identify. The wide range of sex- and age-related plumages lead to much confusion when it comes to the identification of these birds, whether at rest or in flight. the most obvious features to look for on a bird of prey in flight are the diagnostic markings on the underparts (for example, a contrasting black and white underwing pattern as in the Bateleur, black carpal patches as in the Osprey, or a rufous tail as in the Jackal Buzzard).

While field characters undoubtedly assist with in-flight identification, because of the considerable plumage variation that exists in birds of prey it is often better to learn to distinguish the overall size and shape of the various birds.

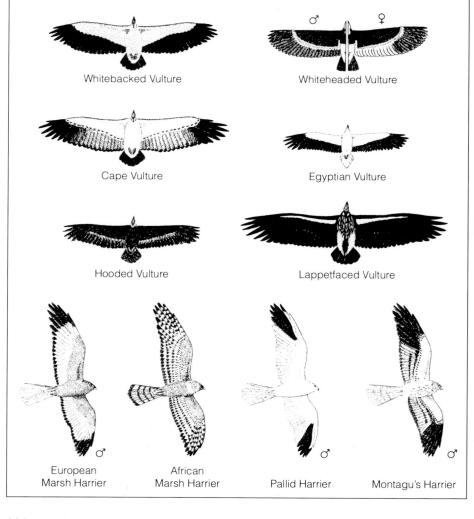

Whitebacked Vulture

Whiteheaded Vulture

Cape Vulture

Egyptian Vulture

Hooded Vulture

Lappetfaced Vulture

European Marsh Harrier

African Marsh Harrier

Pallid Harrier

Montagu's Harrier

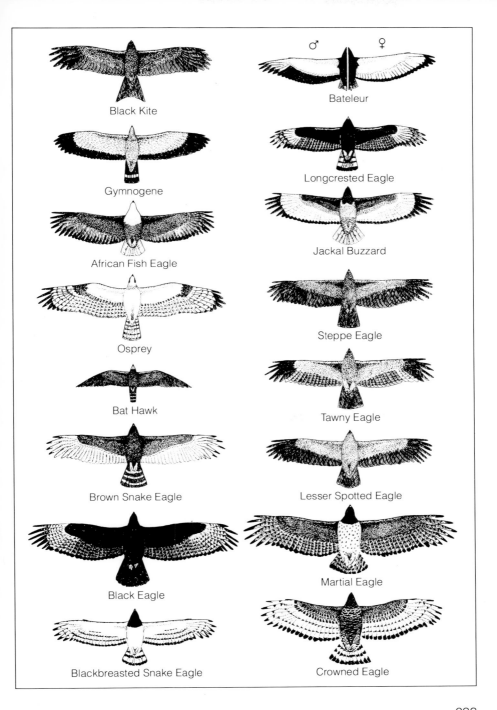

Black Kite

Bateleur
♂ ♀

Gymnogene

Longcrested Eagle

African Fish Eagle

Jackal Buzzard

Osprey

Steppe Eagle

Bat Hawk

Tawny Eagle

Brown Snake Eagle

Lesser Spotted Eagle

Black Eagle

Martial Eagle

Blackbreasted Snake Eagle

Crowned Eagle

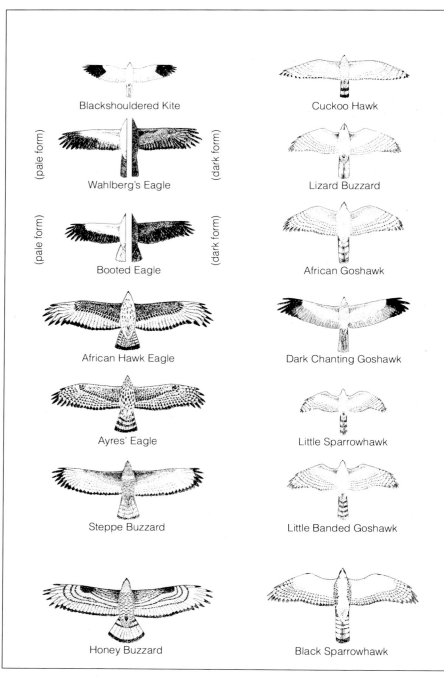

Blackshouldered Kite

Cuckoo Hawk

(pale form) Wahlberg's Eagle (dark form)

Lizard Buzzard

(pale form) Booted Eagle (dark form)

African Goshawk

African Hawk Eagle

Dark Chanting Goshawk

Ayres' Eagle

Little Sparrowhawk

Steppe Buzzard

Little Banded Goshawk

Honey Buzzard

Black Sparrowhawk

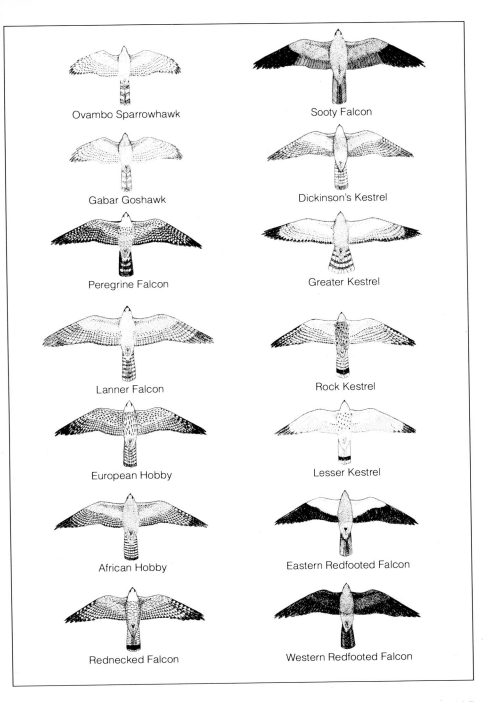

Ovambo Sparrowhawk

Sooty Falcon

Gabar Goshawk

Dickinson's Kestrel

Peregrine Falcon

Greater Kestrel

Lanner Falcon

Rock Kestrel

European Hobby

Lesser Kestrel

African Hobby

Eastern Redfooted Falcon

Rednecked Falcon

Western Redfooted Falcon

NESTS SEEN IN THE KRUGER NATIONAL PARK

Redheaded Weaver
A very untidy nest, made from thin twigs rather than grass. Sometimes has dead leaves and bits of paper woven into it. Solitary; loosely strung from thin branches

Lesser Masked Weaver
The only small weaver nest to have a noticeable tunnel. Tunnel is not as untidy as Redheaded Weaver's. Colonial, sometimes with Spottedbacked Weaver; often suspended inside tree canopy, usually over water

Spectacled Weaver
The very long tunnel leading to the nest is diagnostic of this species. Solitary; suspended from tips of branches, often overhanging a gulley or stream

Thickbilled Weaver
The tidiest and most neatly woven of all the weavers' nests. Colonial; always situated in reed beds

Golden Weaver
The nest is larger and untidier than the similar Yellow Weaver's nest. Solitary; attached to drooping branch or upright reeds over water

Yellow Weaver
Nest has smoother finish than Masked, Spottedbacked and Golden Weavers' nests. Colonial; suspended between reeds, or from drooping branches over water

Masked Weaver
The Masked Weaver's nest is generally more compact and slightly smaller than that of the Spottedbacked Weaver. Colonial; in outer twigs of trees and bushes, usually in small clusters away from water

Spottedbacked Weaver
Nest is larger and more loosely constructed than the similar Masked Weaver's nest. Colonial; in trees and bushes, often suspended over water

Wattled Starling
Variable in shape, sometimes appearing oval. May be confused with that of Redbilled Buffalo Weaver, but nests are invariably in large colonies; situated in tree or bush

Redbilled Buffalo Weaver
Usually a large, untidy and bulky nest made from thorny twigs. Communal; situated on branch of large tree

Hamerkop
An untidy mess of grass, twigs and a host of other bits and pieces comprise this huge, conspicuous nest

Termite nest
Resembles a bird's nest but the even mud surface and lack of grass and twigs indicate that it is a termite nest

Raptor nest on top of tree
Large eagles and vultures often have very large nests in the top of a tree

Raptor nest within a tree
Smaller birds of prey usually nest within a tree canopy

SUGGESTED FURTHER READING

Berruti, A. and Sinclair, J.C. 1983. *Where to Watch Birds in Southern Africa.* Cape Town: C. Struik.

Ginn, P.J., McIlleron, W.G., and Milstein, P. 1989. *The Complete Book of Southern African Birds.* Cape Town: Struik Winchester.

Maclean, G.L. 1984. *Roberts' Birds of Southern Africa.* 5th ed. Cape Town: The Trustees of the John Voelcker Bird Book Fund.

Newman, K.B. 1983. *Newman's Birds of Southern Africa.* Johannesburg: Macmillan South Africa.

Newman, K.B. 1987. *Birds of the Kruger National Park.* Johannesburg: Southern Book Publishers.

Pickford, P. and B., and Tarboton, W. 1989. *Southern African Birds of Prey.* Cape Town: Struik.

Sinclair, I. 1987. *Field Guide to the Birds of Southern Africa.* 2nd ed. Cape Town: Struik.

Sinclair, I. 1990. *Southern African Birds: A Photographic Guide.* Cape Town: Struik.

Sinclair, I., Meakin, P. and Goode, D. 1990. *Common Birds.* Struik Pocket Guide Series. Cape Town: Struik.

Sinclair, J.C., Mendelsohn, J.M., and Johnson, P. 1981. *Everyone's Guide to South African Birds.* Johannesburg: CNA.

PHOTOGRAPHIC CREDITS

page 67: **Gabar Goshawk** (ad.) P. Pickford, (imm.) T. Carew/Photo Access, (melanistic) P. Pickford; **Ovambo Sparrowhawk** (ad.) P. Pickford, (imm.) M. Goetz
page 69: **Peregrine Falcon** (ad.) P. Pickford, (imm.) N. Myburgh; **Lanner Falcon** (ad. & imm.) J.F. Carlyon
page 71: **European Hobby** P. Pickford; **African Hobby** Peter Steyn; **Rednecked Falcon** R. Rogoff; **Sooty Falcon** P. Pickford; **Dickinson's Kestrel** P. Pickford; **Greater Kestrel** A. Weaving
page 73: **Rock Kestrel** (m) Roy Johannesson, (f) J. Sobey; **Lesser Kestrel** (m) A. Weaving, (f) N. Myburgh; **Eastern Redfooted Kestrel** (m) P. Pickford, (f) J. van Jaarsveld; **Western Redfooted Kestrel** (m & f) P. Pickford
page 75: **Coqui Francolin** (f) B.C. Harmse, (m) J. Sobey; **Crested Francolin** L. Hes/Photo Access; **Shelley's Francolin** S.C. Hendriks; **Natal Francolin** M. Craig-Cooper; **Swainson's Francolin** B.C. Harmse; **Rednecked Francolin** W. Nicol
page 77: **Doublebanded Sandgrouse** (m) P. Pickford, (f) G.D.M. Craig-Cooper; **Kurrichane Buttonquail** S.C. Hendriks; **Harlequin Quail** S.C. Hendriks; **Common Quail** N. Brickell
page 79: **Black Crake** (ad.) P. Craig-Cooper, (imm.) J&B Photographers/Photo Access; **African Rail** J.J. Brooks; **Baillon's Crake** N. Myburgh; **African Crake** P.J. Ginn; **Corncrake** P. Sterry/Nature Photographers; **Buffspotted Flufftail** I. Sinclair; **Redchested Flufftail** J.J. Brooks
page 81: **Lesser Moorhen** Peter Steyn; **Moorhen** (ad.) W. Nichol, (imm.) G. Allan; **Redknobbed Coot** (ad. & imm.) J.F. Carlyon; **Purple Gallinule** J. Laurie/Photo Access; **Lesser Gallinule** W.R. Tarboton
page 83: **Blackbellied Korhaan** L. Hes/Photo Access; **Redcrested Korhaan** A. Weaving; **Kori Bustard** J.F. Carlyon; **Stanley's Bustard** Peter Steyn; **Helmeted Guineafowl** A. Weaving; **Crested Guineafowl** W. Nicol
page 85: **Caspian Plover** J. Sobey; **Chestnutbanded Plover** N. Myburgh; **Ringed Plover** P. Pickford; **Kittlitz's Plover** J.F. Carlyon; **Threebanded Plover** S.C. Hendriks; **Whitefronted Plover** P. Pickford
page 87: **Lesser Blackwinged Plover** L. Hes; **Crowned Plover** A. Weaving; **Whitecrowned Plover** A. Weaving; **Blacksmith Plover** S.C. Hendriks; **Wattled Plover** K. Delport/Photo Access
page 89: **Marsh Sandpiper** J.F. Carlyon; **Greenshank** J.J. Brooks; **Wood Sandpiper** G.D.M. Craig-Cooper; **Green Sandpiper** P. Sterry/Nature Photographers; **Ruff** J.J. Brooks
page 91: **Turnstone** P. Pickford; **Sanderling** L. Hes/Photo Access; **Dunlin** R. Tidman/Nature Photographers; **Curlew Sandpiper** L. Hes; **Little Stint** Peter Steyn; **Common Sandpiper** A. Weaving
page 93: **Painted Snipe** B.C. Harmse; **Ethiopian Snipe** J. Sobey; **Water Dikkop** L. Hes; **Spotted Dikkop** L. Hes
page 95: **Redwinged Pratincole** Roy Johannesson; **Bronzewinged Courser** L. Hes; **Burchell's Courser** M. Goetz; **Threebanded Courser** R.S. Daniell; **Temminck's Courser** T. Carew/Photo Access
page 97: **Greyheaded Gull** (ad.) A. Weaving, (imm.) I. Sinclair; **Whitewinged Tern** (br.) I. Sinclair, (non-br.) M.D. England/Ardea; **Whiskered Tern** (br.) J.J. Brooks
page 99: **Avocet** J.F. Carlyon; **Blackwinged Stilt** Peter Steyn; **Sooty Tern** G.K. Brown/Ardea; **Arctic Skua** W.R. Tarboton
page 101: **Mourning Dove** S.C. Hendriks; **Redeyed Dove** Geoff McIlleron; **Cape Turtle Dove** P. Pickford; **Laughing Dove** N. Myburgh; **Greenspotted Dove** J. Sobey; **Bluespotted Dove** N. Brickell
page 103: **Namaqua Dove** (m) P. Craig-Cooper, (f) J.J. Brooks; **Cinnamon Dove** W. Nicol; **Tambourine Dove** P. Craig-Cooper; **Green Pigeon** P. Craig-Cooper; **Rock Pigeon** Roy Johannesson

page 105: **Brownheaded Parrot** S.C. Hendriks; **Cape Parrot** N. Brickell; **Purplecrested Lourie** S.C. Hendriks; **Grey Lourie** L. Hes; **Burchell's Coucal** M. Craig-Cooper; **Black Coucal** A. Weaving
page 107: **Klaas's Cuckoo** (m & f) Geoff McIlleron; **Diederik Cuckoo** (m & f) Geoff McIlleron; **Redchested Cuckoo** (ad.) S.C. Hendriks, (imm.) N. Myburgh; **African Cuckoo** Geoff McIlleron; **European Cuckoo** K. Carlson/Nature Photographers
page 109: **Thickbilled Cuckoo** (illustr.) G. Arnott; **Striped Cuckoo** J. Sobey; **Great Spotted Cuckoo** J. van Jaarsveld; **Jacobin Cuckoo** E. Helm; **Black Cuckoo** I. Sinclair
page 111: **Barn Owl** L. Hes; **Pel's Fishing Owl** P. Pickford; **Spotted Eagle Owl** P. Pickford; **Grass Owl** J. van Jaarsveld; **Giant Eagle Owl** L. Hes
page 113: **Whitefaced Owl** L. Hes; **Scop's Owl** J.F. Carlyon; **Wood Owl** P. Pickford; **Barred Owl** P.J. Ginn; **Marsh Owl** J. Sobey; **Pearlspotted Owl** P. Craig-Cooper
page 115: **Pennantwinged Nightjar** A. Weaving; **Rufoushcheeked Nightjar** W. Tarboton; **European Nightjar** L. Hes; **Fierynecked Nightjar** J.F. Carlyon; **Mozambique Nightjar** P.J. Ginn; **Freckled Nightjar** J.F. Carlyon
page 117: **Black Swift** Geoff McIlleron; **European Swift** K. Wothe/Bruce Coleman Ltd; **Little Swift** J. Sobey; **Whiterumped Swift** N. Myburgh; **Horus Swift** Geoff McIlleron
page 119: **Palm Swift** Geoff McIleron; **Alpine Swift** Geoff McIlleron; **Böhm's Spinetail** (illustr.) G. Arnott; **Mottled Spinetail** Geoff McIlleron
page 121: **Speckled Mousebird** P. Craig-Cooper; **Redfaced Mousebird** J.J. Brooks; **Narina Trogon** J.J. Brooks; **Hoopoe** A. Weaving; **Scimitarbilled Woodhoopoe** P.J. Ginn; **Redbilled Woodhoopoe** P.J. Ginn
page 123: **Giant Kingfisher** J.J. Brooks; **Halfcollared Kingfisher** Geoff McIlleron; **Pied Kingfisher** J. Sobey; **Malachite Kingfisher** L. Hes; **Pygmy Kingfisher** P. Pickford
page 125: **Woodland Kingfisher** P. Craig-Cooper; **Greyhooded Kingfisher** P. Craig-Cooper; **Brownhooded Kingfisher** P. Pickford; **Striped Kingfisher** L. Hes
page 127: **Little Bee-eater** N. Myburgh; **Carmine Bee-eater** J. Sobey; **European Bee-eater** A. Weaving; **Whitefronted Bee-eater** B.C. Harmse; **Bluecheeked Bee-eater** P. Pickford
page 129: **European Roller** S.C. Hendriks; **Broadbilled Roller** P.J. Ginn; **Racquettailed Roller** W. Nicol; **Lilacbreasted Roller** S.C. Hendriks; **Purple Roller** Peter Steyn
page 131: **Southern Yellowbilled Hornbill** P. Craig-Cooper; **Crowned Hornbill** Peter Steyn; **Redbilled Hornbill** P.J. Ginn; **Grey Hornbill** S.C. Hendriks; **Trumpeter Hornbill** A. Weaving
page 133: **Goldenrumped Tinker Barbet** P. Pickford; **Yellowfronted Tinker Barbet** P.J. Ginn; **Acacia Pied Barbet** B.C. Harmse; **Blackcollared Barbet** Geoff McIlleron; **Crested Barbet** S.C. Hendriks
page 135: **Sharpbilled Honeyguide** (illustr.) G. Arnott; **Greater Honeyguide** M. Goetz; **Lesser Honeyguide** N. Myburgh; **Scalythroated Honeyguide** Geoff McIlleron
page 137: **Goldentailed Woodpecker** Geoff McIlleron; **Bearded Woodpecker** W. Tarboton; **Cardinal Woodpecker** Peter Steyn; **Bennett's Woodpecker** J.F. Carlyon; **Redthroated Wryneck** J.F. Carlyon
page 139: **Sabota Lark** J.J. Brooks; **Flappet Lark** (illustr.) G. Arnott; **Monotonous Lark** J.F. Carlyon; **Fawncoloured Lark** B. Ryan; **Redcapped Lark** N. Myburgh
page 141: **Rufousnaped Lark** Geoff McIlleron; **Dusky Lark** I. Sinclair; **Chestnutbacked Finchlark** S.C. Hendriks; **Yellowthroated Longclaw** P.J. Ginn; **Striped Pipit** Peter Steyn
page 143: **Greater Striped Swallow** Geoff McIlleron;

Redbreasted Swallow A. Weaving; Lesser Striped Swallow
Geoff McIlleron; Mosque Swallow A. Weaving
page 145: European Swallow J. Sobey; Whitethroated Swallow
J. Sobey; Wiretailed Swallow J.F. Carlyon; Greyrumped
Swallow P.J. Ginn; Pearlbreasted Swallow J.J. Brooks; Black
Saw-wing Swallow L. Hes
page 147: Sand Martin E. Duscher/Bruce Coleman Ltd; House
Martin W. Tarboton; Banded Martin J.J. Brooks; Brownthroated
Martin Geoff McIlleron; Rock Martin G.D.M. Craig-Cooper
page 149: Forktailed Drongo B.C. Harmse; Black Flycatcher
J.F. Carlyon; Black Cuckooshrike (m & f) Geoff McIlleron;
Whitebreasted Cuckooshrike Geoff McIlleron; Grey
Cuckooshrike (R.S. Daniell); Ashy Tit Geoff McIlleron
page 151: Blackheaded Oriole J.F. Carlyon; African Golden
Oriole (m & f) P.J. Ginn; European Golden Oriole (m) M.D.
England/Ardea, (f) D. Avon/Ardea
page 153: Ostrich Raymonde Johannesson; Secretarybird A.
Weaving; Ground Hornbill Roy Johannesson; Black Crow P.
Craig-Cooper; Pied Crow A. Weaving; Whitenecked Raven P.
Pickford
page 155: Blackeyed Bulbul P.J. Ginn; Sombre Bulbul Geoff
McIlleron; Yellowbellied Bulbul B.C. Harmse; Terrestrial Bulbul
L. Hes; Yellowspotted Nicator G.R. Nichols
page 157: Arrowmarked Babbler S.C. Hendriks;
Groundscraper Thrush P.J. Ginn; Kurrichane Thrush Geoff
McIlleron; Familiar Chat G.D.M. Craig-Cooper; Mocking Chat
(m) P. Craig-Cooper, (f) J. Sobey
page 159: Mountain Chat (m) S.C. Hendriks, (f) Geoff
McIlleron; Southern Black Tit B.C. Harmse; Arnot's Chat J.F.
Carlyon; Capped Wheatear J.J. Brooks; Stonechat (m) W.
Nichol, (f) B.C. Harmse
page 161: Whitethroated Robin L. Hes; Cape Robin J.J.
Brooks; Heuglin's Robin P.J. Ginn; Natal Robin N. Brickell
page 163: Whitebrowed Robin B.C. Harmse; Bearded Robin L.
Hes; Brown Robin N. Dalton
page 165: Willow Warbler A.P. Barnes/Natural Science Photos;
Icterine Warbler H. Reinhard/Bruce Coleman Ltd; Garden
Warbler R. Richter/Ardea; Olivetree Warbler (illustr.) G. Arnott;
Thrush Nightingale R. Richter/Ardea
page 167: Grey Penduline Tit P.J. Ginn; Burntnecked
Eremomela W. Tarboton; Yellowbellied Eremomela W. Nichol;
Greencapped Eremomela P.J. Ginn; Yellow Warbler P.J. Ginn
page 169: African Marsh Warbler B. Ryan; Cape Reed Warbler
Peter Steyn; Broadtailed Warbler T. Harris/Tvl. Museum;
European Sedge Warbler D. Avon/Ardea; African Sedge
Warbler N. Myburgh; Great Reed Warbler D. Avon/Ardea;
European Marsh Warbler F. Blackburn/Nature Photographers
page 171: Longbilled Crombec N. Nichol; Yellowbreasted
Apalis Peter Steyn; Bleating Warbler P.J. Ginn; Stierling's
Barred Warbler (illustr.) G. Arnott
page 173: Fantailed Cisticola Geoff McIlleron; Desert Cisticola
W. Tarboton; Cloud Cisticola Geoff McIlleron; Ayres' Cisticola S.
W. Kirk; Blackbacked Cisticola G.R. Nichols; Levaillant's
Cisticola Roy Johannesson
page 175: Rattling Cisticola B.C. Harmse; Redfaced Cisticola
O. Hildebrand; Croaking Cisticola G.R. Nichols; Tawnyflanked
Prinia Peter Steyn; Blackchested Prinia Geoff McIlleron
page 177: Neddicky N. Myburgh; Bluegrey Flycatcher L. Hes;
Titbabbler Geoff McIlleron
page 179: Marico Flycatcher B.C. Harmse; Mousecoloured
Flycatcher J.F. Carlyon; Spotted Flycatcher W. Tarboton; Dusky
Flycatcher Geoff McIlleron; Fairy Flycatcher J.J. Brooks;
Mashona Hyliota P.J. Ginn
page 181: Bluemantled Flycatcher Geoff McIlleron;

Wattle-eyed Flycatcher Peter Steyn; Paradise Flycatcher J.J.
Brooks; Chinspot Batis (m) Geoff McIlleron, (f) J.F. Carlyon
page 183: African Pied Wagtail P.J. Ginn; Yellow Wagtail N.
Myburgh; Longtailed Wagtail Peter Steyn; Cape Wagtail S.C.
Hendriks
page 185: Buffy Pipit P.J. Ginn; Longbilled Pipit Peter Steyn;
Grassveld Pipit L. Hes; Plainbacked Pipit P.J. Ginn; Bushveld
Pipit W. Tarboton
page 187: Fiscal Shrike Geoff McIlleron; Fiscal Flycatcher J.
Carlyon; Puffback Shrike (m & f) Geoff McIlleron; Southern
Boubou L. Hes; Tropical Boubou P.J. Ginn
page 189: Longtailed Shrike A. Weaving; Whitecrowned Shrike
L. Hes; Redbacked Shrike (m) J. Sobey, (f) L. Hes; Brubru P.J.
Ginn; Lesser Grey Shrike M. Goetz/ Tvl. Museum
page 191: Orangebreasted Bush Shrike P.J. Ginn; Greyheaded
Bush Shrike P. Craig-Cooper; Gorgeous Bush Shrike M. Goetz;
Crimsonbreasted Shrike W. Tarboton
page 193: Olive Bush Shrike Geoff McIlleron; Threestreaked
Tchagra Geoff McIlleron; Blackcrowned Tchagra Geoff
McIlleron; White Helmetshrike P. Craig-Cooper; Redbilled
Helmetshrike P.J. Ginn
page 195: Greater Blue-eared Starling J.F. Carlyon;
Blackbellied Starling Geoff McIlleron; Glossy Starling Roy
Johannesson; Longtailed Starling J. Sobey; Burchell's Starling
S.C. Hendriks
page 197: Redwinged Starling (m) Geoff McIlleron, (f) S.C.
Hendriks; Wattled Starling (m) D. Sobey, (f) P. McPherson;
Plumcoloured Starling (m) S.C. Hendriks, (f) A. Weaving;
Yellowbilled Oxpecker Peter Steyn; Redbilled Oxpecker L. Hes
page 199: Whitebellied Sunbird (m) N. Myburgh, (f) B.C.
Harmse; Scarletchested Sunbird (m & f) N. Myburgh; Black
Sunbird (m) Geoff McIlleron, (f) S.C. Hendriks
page 201: Marico Sunbird (m) W. Nichol, (f) B.C. Harmse;
Purplebanded Sunbird (m & f) M. Goetz
page 203: Collared Sunbird (m) J.F. Carlyon, (f) P.J. Ginn;
Cape White-eye J.J. Brooks; Yellow White-eye J. van
Jaarsveld; Greyheaded Sparrow J. Sobey; Yellowthroated
Sparrow Geoff McIlleron
page 205: House Sparrow (m & f) P.J. Ginn; Redbilled Quelea
(m) S.C. Hendriks, (f) B.C. Harmse; Redbilled Buffalo Weaver
(m & f) P.J. Ginn
page 207: Golden Weaver (m) L. & T. Bomford/Ardea, (f) S.C.
Hendriks; Yellow Weaver (m) Geoff McIlleron, (f) P. Pickford;
Spectacled Weaver N. Myburgh
page 209: Spottedbacked Weaver (m) S.C. Hendriks, (f) B.C.
Harmse; Masked Weaver (m) S.C. Hendriks, (f) P.J. Ginn;
Lesser Masked Weaver (m) M. Craig-Cooper, (f) J.F. Carlyon
page 211: Thickbilled Weaver (m & f) S.C. Hendriks;
Redheaded Weaver (m) P. Craig-Cooper, (f) P.J. Ginn
page 213: Redshouldered Widow S.C. Hendriks; Redcollared
Widow Geoff McIlleron; Whitewinged Widow (m & f) S.C.
Hendriks
page 215: Red Bishop (m & f) S.C. Hendriks; Golden Bishop
(m & f) S.C. Hendriks
page 217: Cuckoo Finch P.J. Ginn; Pinkthroated Twinspot
(m & f) N. Brickell; Green Twinspot (m & f) N. Brickell; Melba
Finch (m) B.C. Harmse, (f) J.J. Brooks
page 219: Redbilled Firefinch (m) S.C. Hendriks, (f) N. Brickell;
Bluebilled Firefinch (m) N. Brickell, (f) B.C. Harmse; Jameson's
Firefinch (m) P.J. Ginn, (f) J. van Jaarsveld
page 221: Blue Waxbill P. Craig-Cooper; Violeteared Waxbill
(m & f) S.C. Hendriks; Common Waxbill J.J. Brooks; Grey
Waxbill P. Craig-Cooper
page 223: Orangebreasted Waxbill S.C. Hendriks; Cutthroat

240

INDEX TO COMMON NAMES

Numbers in **bold** refer to the main species' entry.

242

INDEX TO SCIENTIFIC NAMES

INDEX TO AFRIKAANS NAMES

249

NOTES